MORE WEIGHTS AND MEASURES

½ cup butter = ¼ pound or 1 stick

2½ cups granulated sugar = 1 pound

2⅓ cups firmly packed brown sugar = 1 pound

4 to 4½ cups sifted powdered sugar = 1 pound

2 large eggs = 3 small eggs

1 lemon = 3 to 4 tablespoons juice

Grated peel of 1 lemon = 1½ teaspoons

1 orange = 6 to 8 tablespoons juice

Grated peel of 1 orange = 1 tablespoon

½ pound Cheddar cheese = 2 cups grated cheese

1 pound ground coffee = 80 tablespoons

OVEN TEMPERATURES

	Degrees F.
Very slow	250 to 275
Slow	300 to 325
Moderate	350 to 375
Hot	400 to 425
Very hot	450 to 475
Extremely hot	500 to 525

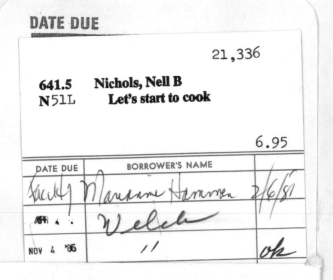

Let's start to cook

Let's start to cook

NEVER-FAIL RECIPES FOR BEGINNERS

By Nell B. Nichols

B.S., FOODS AND NUTRITION, KANSAS STATE UNIVERSITY

M.S., FOODS AND NUTRITION/JOURNALISM, UNIVERSITY OF WISCONSIN

FIELD FOOD EDITOR · FARM JOURNAL

ILLUSTRATED BY KAY LOVELACE SMITH

DOUBLEDAY & COMPANY, INC., GARDEN CITY, NEW YORK

ISBN: 0-385-05975-2 TRADE
0-385-06471-3 PREBOUND

Library of Congress Catalog Card Number AC 66–10369

Copyright © 1966 by Farm Journal, Inc.

All Rights Reserved

Printed in the United States of America

15   14   13   12   11

CONTENTS

CONTENTS

Specially for you

THIS Cookbook is different—it's the beginning cook's very own. We wrote it for you cooks who want to learn how to fix really good food, without a lot of trial and error. Stick to the recipes and you can be successful right from the start. You might call it a how-and-why Cookbook because it tells you exactly how to handle food in the recipes so you'll have good luck and be proud of what you make. And it tells you why you do what the recipe suggests.

It's just as easy—and much smarter—to learn to cook the right way and by up-to-date methods from the start. That's what we show you how to do.

Many famous men and women boast that cooking is their favorite hobby. They say it is fun to make wonderful dishes and then to share them with their friends. Good food really makes new friends, too— whether the cook is an opera star or a girl who bakes a marvelous chocolate cake for the picnic, or a boy who grills extra-good hamburgers over coals for the gang.

Cooking is a science as well. Every good cook is something of a chemist even though she works with mixing bowls and measuring cups instead of test tubes, and with good-to-eat foods instead of acids and powders. So we give you the scientific behind-the-recipe facts: Our recipes tell not only how much baking powder to add in making the coffee cake, but what baking powder is made of and why it causes the coffee cake to double in height while it bakes. And we tell about the million explosions that take place in the kettle when you pop corn—also what's wrong when the corn doesn't pop and what you can do about it.

Cooking also is an art. You don't use brushes and paints as a rule (although you do when you frost sugar cookies with egg-yolk paint). Just think of the pretty pictures you make with salads and the arrangements on platters of foods you've cooked. If you follow the recipes in this book, you'll understand why the foods you fix will make people who see them really eat first with their eyes. It's the look of food that often gives it appetite appeal and makes everybody want to taste.

Smell is important, too. We mention often with recipes how tempting the aroma of a dish is—Pecan Cookies à la mode, for instance. The fragrance of the cookies while they bake on a waffle iron, with the crowd gathered round, is heavenly.

You can give your family and friends a good time with the food you fix from recipes in this Cookbook. Soon the people who taste and enjoy what you make will pass word around that you're the best young cook in the county. Then you are on your way—your talent is both recognized and appreciated. If you belong to a 4-H Club or Girl Scouts, you may win prizes and badges!

Please follow the recipes in this book closely—at least when you start to cook. It's a good idea for all cooks, no matter how experienced, not to tamper with recipes. The ingredients are balanced like a chemical formula and when you disturb this balance, you may be disappointed in what you make. You can add your own touches by changing the seasonings or by serving the food a different way or in a different dish. Later on, when you've learned about the chemistry or science of cooking, you can branch out a little more and experiment on your own.

Do get the habit of looking in the Index to find the recipe or information you want—the Index is one of the most useful sections of any cookbook. The clever cook doesn't attempt to remember all her recipes—especially when she's new at cooking. Your Index will help you find recipes and to build meals with them.

THE WAY GOOD COOKS DO IT

Play safe when you cook

Make good use of pot holders to avoid burns. When you stir food while it cooks, steady the saucepan or skillet by holding onto the handle with a pot holder. Stir with the other hand, using a wooden spoon or a spoon with a wooden or plastic handle. Metal spoon handles get hot. When you take hot food from the oven, use a pot holder in each hand. First pull out the oven shelf or rack a little to make the removal easier.

Dry your hands after washing them. Wet hands are slippery—they're what some people call butter hands. Slips mean spills and often burns.

Turn saucepan and skillet handles in (over the range) so no one will bump into them and cause spills.

Plug in and disconnect electric appliances with dry hands. To disconnect the appliances, pull the plug straight out. If you pull on the cord, you may loosen the wires.

Peel vegetables and fruits with a vegetable peeler—it peels them thinly and avoids waste—and cut away from you. This will save your fingers from cuts.

Slice, chop and dice foods on a cutting board instead of holding them in your hands. This is one way to treat your thumb kindly.

How to use the recipes

1. Read all of the recipe—that means every word. If there's anything you don't understand, ask someone who has cooked a lot about it. If the recipe you are using refers to a second recipe (such as Chocolate Sauce for Brownies à la mode), look in the margin for the page number. Turn to this page, read the second recipe and be sure that you understand every step in it. Decide which of the two recipes to make first. Sometimes you will want to make the second recipe first to have it ready.

2. Bring out all the tools and utensils you'll need. Check sizes and content with those given in the recipe.

3. Get out all the ingredients you'll need.

4. Start the oven heating if you're baking.

5. Measure the ingredients carefully.

Always use pot holders

Turn handles in

Cut away from you

Use a cutting board

6. Mix the ingredients by recipe directions.

7. Cook and test for doneness as suggested in the recipe.

8. Remember that in recipes, servings do not mean people. A recipe that makes 6 servings may not serve 6 people if somebody is especially hungry and wants two helpings.

Measuring tools you will need

When you start to cook, you will avoid disappointing failures if you measure the ingredients carefully. In fact, no matter how much you have cooked, it always pays to measure the ingredients called for in a recipe. Recipes are made for accurate—level, not heaping—measurements.

Measuring tools

For liquids, you need: a 1-cup measuring cup with a lip for pouring and a rim above the 1-cup line—a safety rim above the cup that prevents spills. The 2-cup and 1-quart measuring cups also are handy. It is especially easy to read the measurement marks on *glass* measuring cups because you can see the level (top) of the liquid through the glass.

For dry foods, you need: a set of metal, nested measuring cups that hold ¼ cup, ⅓ cup, ½ cup and 1 cup.

A set of measuring spoons with spoons that hold 1 tablespoon, 1 teaspoon, ½ teaspoon and ¼ teaspoon. The sets that also have spoons that hold ½ tablespoon and ⅛ teaspoon are excellent.

How to measure

For liquids: Pour a thin liquid such as vanilla into a measuring spoon until full. Pour thick liquids, such as honey and molasses, into a measuring spoon until full and then level off the top with the straight edge of a knife. Or pour them into a measuring cup. Scrape the liquid out of the spoon or cup with a rubber spatula. By pouring the liquid instead of dipping the measuring spoon or cup into it, you will avoid dripping liquid in the mixing bowl that may give you an overmeasurement or that you will have to clean from the working surface. To measure milk and other liquids, use a cup with a rim above the 1-cup line to avoid spills, instead of the nested metal cup used in dry ingredients. Always place the cup on a flat surface and read the measurement at eye level.

Read at eye level

For baking powder, baking soda and salt: Dip the spoon of the right size into the dry ingredients until it is full. Then level off the top with the straight edge of a knife or metal spatula.

For white and powdered sugars: If the sugar is lumpy, sift it before measuring or put it through a sieve. Then spoon it lightly into the measuring cup and level off the top with the straight edge of a knife.

For brown sugar: If it is lumpy, roll it with a rolling pin or put it into a slow oven (300° F.), and let it warm for a few minutes and then roll it. Spoon it into the cup and pack it down with the spoon so that when you turn it out, it holds its shape.

For flour: If the recipe calls for sifted flour (all-purpose), sift it onto a square of waxed paper and then measure it. You need not sift instant-type flour. Spoon the flour lightly into the measuring cup until the cup is full. Then level off the top with the straight edge of a knife without packing it down.

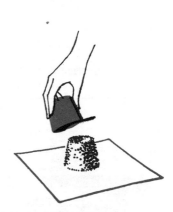

Brown sugar holds its shape

For shortening: Scoop the shortening out of the can or package with a spoon and pack it firmly into a 1-cup, ½-cup, ⅓-cup or ¼-cup measuring cup up to the top. Or pack it firmly in a measuring spoon (usually 1 tablespoon). Then level the top off with the straight edge of a knife and remove the shortening from the cup or spoon.

For butter or margarine: Measure like shortening. Many wrappers have a printed measuring guide. If you have a pound of butter or margarine, each ¼-pound stick will measure ½ cup or 8 tablespoons. Half of a ¼-pound stick will measure ¼ cup or 4 tablespoons. Half of a ¼-cup is 2 tablespoons.

For melted shortening, butter or margarine: Measure it either before or after melting. The measure will be the same. When the fat is hard, it's easier to measure it if you melt it first. Salad oil is easy to measure in a measuring cup or spoon.

For other foods: Pack shredded or grated cheese lightly into the measuring cup until it's level with the top. Pack dried fruits, such as raisins and dates, into the cup and press gently to level off the top. Pack chopped nuts and shredded or flaked coconut lightly into the measuring cup and level off the top. Pack soft bread crumbs lightly into the cup and press gently to level off the top. Spoon fine dry bread crumbs into the cup and level off the top with the straight edge of a knife.

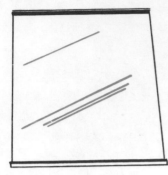

Large baking sheet

Mixing bowls

Utensils you'll need

Here are the utensils most frequently called for in this Cookbook's recipes. You probably have most of them in your kitchen.

Large baking sheet: Baking sheets come in three sizes, 14×10, 15½×12 and 17×14 inches. The size to use depends on the size of your oven. Use one that is at least 2 to 4 inches narrower and shorter than your oven so the heat can move around the food and bake it evenly. Shiny baking sheets are better than dull, dark ones because they give the undercrust of foods like cookies, biscuits and rolls a delicate brown crust.

Mixing bowls in four different sizes, from one holding 2 cups up to 16 cups (½ to 4 quarts)

Casseroles: one 6-cup and one 8-cup (1½ to 2 quarts)

Double boiler with a bottom kettle that holds 2 to 3 quarts. To use, fill the bottom kettle with 2 inches of water. Bring the water to a boil, put the food in the top of the double boiler and cook over boiling or hot (below boiling) water, as the recipe directs.

Round layer cake pans: two 8×1½ inches and two 9×1½ inches

Square cake pans: one 9×9×2 inches and one 8×8×2 inches

Casserole

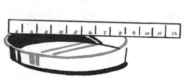

Round cake pans

Square cake pan

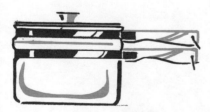

Double boiler

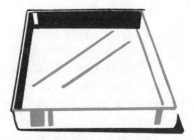

Oblong cake pan

Oblong cake or baking pan: 13×9×2 inches

Loaf pan: 9×5×3 inches or an 8½ ×4½ ×2½ -inch oven-proof glass pan

Muffin pan: medium size, 2½ inches across top and 1¼ inches deep. You can use the pan for gelatin molds as well as muffins and cupcakes.

Loaf pan

Large covered pan that holds from 6 to 10 quarts. Can be a saucepan, kettle, or the Dutch oven type

Piepans: at least one 9-inch and one 8-inch

Jelly roll pan: 15½ ×10½ ×1 inches

Roasting pan without cover and with rack—12 to 15 inches long, 10 to 12 inches wide, and 2 or 3 inches deep

Saucepans in 4-cup and 8-cup sizes (1-quart and 2-quart)

Skillets: one 10-inch with a cover and one 7-inch

Muffin pan

Teflon-lined pans: The big advantage of Teflon is that the cleanup is easier. We recommend that you always read and follow the manufacturer's instructions that come with your pans. In our Test Kitchens we grease the pans lightly just as you do other pans, except tube pans for angel, sponge or chiffon cakes. The light greasing makes the cakes and muffins come out of the pan more easily. You can use fry pans without fat, however. When you use Teflon, whether fry pans or baking pans, though, don't use sharp spoons or knives or you'll scratch the Teflon lining.

Dutch oven

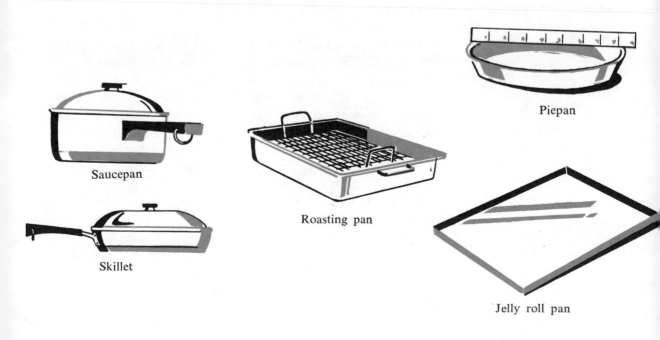

Saucepan

Skillet

Roasting pan

Piepan

Jelly roll pan

How to measure utensils

Keep a ruler and a measuring cup handy in the kitchen to measure the size of your pans and how much your utensils hold. You will find the size and content stamped on the bottom of many utensils, but here's how to find out for yourself if they're not stamped.

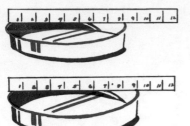

Measure your pans

Pan sizes: With a ruler, measure across the top of the pan from the inside of the rim on one side to the inside of the rim on the .opposite side. Measure cake, pie, loaf and roasting pans, muffin-pan cups and skillets this way. It's easy to measure how deep the pans are—how high the sides are.

Casserole sizes: With a measuring cup, fill the casserole to the brim with water, keeping track of how many cups of water it takes. Measure saucepans, mixing bowls, both parts of the double boiler, kettles, Dutch ovens the same way.

Electric appliances

One of the important advantages of electric cooking appliances is their controlled heat. Here are some of the favorites of good cooks:
Skillet or fry pan
Waffle iron or baker
Griddle for pancakes and sandwiches

Before you cook foods, you have to get them ready. Some of the electric appliances most used in mixing foods are these:
Mixer, considered by most good cooks as something they couldn't do without. They save "elbow grease" and do an excellent job of beating, creaming, mixing and whipping.
Portable beater for beating and whipping foods
Blender for mixing, chopping, whipping and liquefying foods
Food chopper (grinder) for cutting foods into small pieces, as for sandwich fillings
Follow the manufacturer's directions for using all electric appliances. These usually come on the label or in a booklet. Look for this or ask for it when you are helping to shop for a new piece of equipment. That's all it takes to have good luck with them—and from the start.

Tools you'll find helpful

Baster

Rotary hand beater

Pastry brush for greasing pans and brushing dough with melted fat

Pastry blender

Can opener, hand or electric

Food chopper for grinding foods properly and quickly

Cookie cutters of different sizes and shapes to use with cookies and biscuits

Kitchen fork with two tines

Set of graters, fine to coarse

Fruit juicer, a reamer for lemon, orange and grapefruit juices

Knives: long blade and saw-tooth edge for slicing breads; long, narrow blade to slice meats; paring knife; French chef's knife for dicing, cubing, chopping and shredding foods placed on a cutting board

Potato masher

Baster   Rotary beater

Pastry brush

Pastry blender

Cookie cutters

Grater

Can openers

Fruit juicer

Kitchen fork

Set of knives

Potato masher

Food chopper

Molds

Vegetable parer

Molds of different shapes and sizes, for gelatin salads

Vegetable parer with floating blade for peeling thinly potatoes, carrots and other vegetables

Pastry cloth

Rolling pin with stockinet cover

Sturdy kitchen scissors

Slicer for hard-cooked eggs

Angel cake slicer for cutting cake and hard ice cream from home freezer

Rubber spatulas

Spatulas with metal blades: at least two, one with long, narrow blade; the other shorter with broad blade

Long-handled wooden spoon

Large slotted spoon to remove cooked foods from liquid

Strainers or Sieves: one tea-size or small and one large enough to do the work of a colander. (A colander, a metal pan with large holes, is nice to have, too.)

Angel cake slicer

Pastry cloth and rolling pin

Egg slicer

Kitchen scissors

Rubber spatula

Metal spatulas

Wooden spoon

Slotted spoon

Strainers

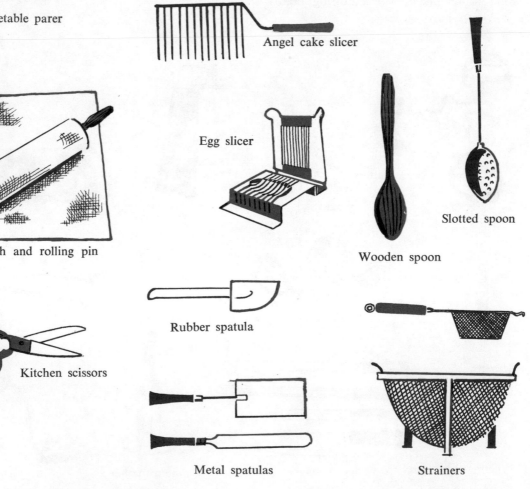

Flour sifter
Cake tester
Candy thermometer
Meat thermometer, shield or dial type
Timer with an alarm to tell you when the food has cooked long enough
Tongs for use in handling hot foods
Wire beater for mixing egg yolks and whites and stirring gravy

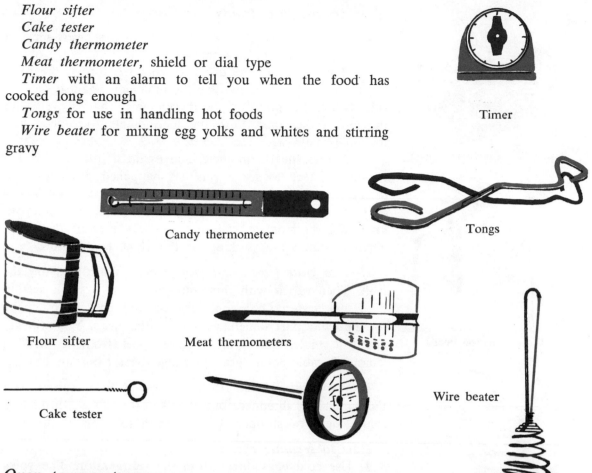

Timer

Candy thermometer

Tongs

Flour sifter

Meat thermometers

Cake tester

Wire beater

Oven temperatures

You have an easier time being a good cook than your grandmothers had because most ovens have temperature controls. (If your oven doesn't have a heat control, use a tested oven thermometer.) You don't have to guess how hot the oven is. Many of the failures in cooking are caused by using the wrong oven heat. It's really important to follow the recipe directions for heating your oven.

Although the recipes in this Cookbook give the exact oven temperatures to use, here's what the different temperatures mean.

	Degrees Fahrenheit
Very Slow	250 to 275
Slow	300 to 325
Moderate	350 to 375
Hot	400 to 425
Very Hot	450 to 475
Extremely Hot	500 to 525

Using a meat thermometer

Grating lemon peel

How to prepare foods

How to use a meat thermometer: With a skewer, make a hole in the meat through the fat side to the center of the roast. Then measure the distance from the top of the roast to its center by holding the thermometer against the cut side. Notice the point on the thermometer that is even with the top of the roast. Push the thermometer this deep into the hole made with the skewer.

Sometimes the thermometer moves up a little during the roasting. Check to see if this has happened. Press the top of the thermometer down with your hand (use a pot holder to protect your hand). If the temperature drops, you will know the thermometer was not in the center of the roast. Then continue the cooking to the right temperature.

How to grate lemon and orange peel: Wash and dry the fruit. Then rub it with short strokes across a small section of a fine grater. Grate only the colored part of the peel, for the white part sometimes has a bitter taste. You will get about 1 tablespoon grated lemon peel from a medium lemon, 2 tablespoons grated orange peel from an orange.

How to grate cheese: If the cheese is firm, rub it over the grater or shredder, but if it's soft, rub it through a coarse sieve or strainer. Use a spoon to press it through.

How to separate eggs

1. Use cold eggs direct from the refrigerator. The yolks are one third fat, which is firm when chilled, so the yolk breaks less easily when cold.

2. Tap the shell at the center of the egg with a knife blade to crack it. Use care not to cut into the yolk. Hold each egg over a bowl.

3. With the crack facing upward, press your thumbs into the crack made with the knife and pull the shell apart. Keep the yolk in one half, the white in the other. Let the white pour out of the shell into the bowl.

4. Move the yolk back and forth from shell half to shell half until all the white has poured off.

5. Try not to get even a tiny fleck of the yolk in the white. Even a dot of the yolk prevents the white from beating up well. If any yolk does get in, scoop it out with one of the eggshell halves or with paper toweling or a spoon. Or use an egg separator.

6. Let the separated eggs stand at room temperature to

warm before beating them. They will beat faster and better if you do.

How to beat egg whites: Egg whites, beaten until stiff, will stand in peaks when the beater is lifted just above them. The points will bend over. They have a moist shiny look. Egg whites, beaten *very* stiff, have peaks that stand without bending over when the beater is lifted out of them. They look dry. Your recipe tells you whether to beat the whites stiff or very stiff.

How to make croutons: Trim crusts from bread slices and then butter the bread. Place the bread on a cutting board and cut it in ½-inch cubes. Spread the cubes in a shallow pan and toast them in a slow oven (300° F.) until lightly browned. You can spread bread with garlic butter.

How to fix dry bread crumbs: Put slices of bread in a very slow oven (250° F.) to dry out, but do not let them brown. Or let them sit out to dry overnight or several hours at room temperature. Put the bread in a plastic or heavy paper bag and crush it into crumbs by rolling the bag with a rolling pin.

You can make bread crumbs in your electric blender, too—flip it on and off until the crumbs are made.

Or put the bread through the food chopper, using the fine blade.

Cover and store any unused bread crumbs in the refrigerator or freezer for quick use later on.

And you also can buy the crumbs ready-to-use in convenient packages.

How to whip cream: Chill the small bowl of the electric mixer and the beaters if the weather is warm. Or chill a hand beater and mixing bowl. Beat the *chilled* heavy cream until it starts to thicken. Continue beating until the cream stiffens and holds its shape. Test by dropping a little of the cream off the beaters into the bowl—if it mounds and holds its shape, it is whipped enough. If you beat it too long, the cream will curdle and it may turn to butter. Chill. One cup of heavy cream makes 2 cups whipped cream.

Sweetened Whipped Cream: When the cream you are whipping starts to thicken, gradually add the sugar and vanilla. If you are whipping 1 cup of heavy cream, you will want to add from 2 to 4 tablespoons sugar (the

Stiff: the points bend over

Very stiff: peaks don't bend

Make bread crumbs in bag

Does it mound? It's ready

Cutting fat into flour

Flouring a pastry cloth

Chopping a green pepper

Chopping nuts

amount depends on how sweet you like it) and beat in ¼ teaspoon vanilla. Usually sweetened whipped cream is the kind served on top of desserts.

How to freeze whipped cream:

1. Spread a sheet of waxed paper on a baking sheet.

2. Whip the cream as directed and drop it, 2 tablespoons at a time, in mounds on the waxed paper. You will have 16 mounds.

3. Place whipped cream in the freezer for about 2 hours or until firm. If you do not want to use it within a few hours, put the frozen mounds in a plastic bag, seal and put back in the freezer. To use, place a mound of frozen whipped cream on each serving of dessert and let it thaw 10 to 20 minutes (while main part of meal is eaten).

How to cut fat into flour: Use a pastry blender. If you do not have a blender, use two knives. Cut through the fat and flour or flour mixture, moving the knives like the blades of scissors. Continue until the flour-coated pieces of fat, such as vegetable shortening, lard, butter or margarine, are the size your recipe suggests. For piecrust, they should be the size of small peas and for biscuits, smaller—like coarse crumbs or coarse cornmeal.

How to flour a pastry cloth and stockinet-covered rolling pin: Rub a little flour into the pastry cloth with your hand. It will disappear into the meshes in the cloth. Brush off any loose flour on the pastry cloth. Then roll the stockinet-covered rolling pin around on the pastry cloth. When you roll pastry and cookie, biscuit and other doughs, they will not stick either to the pastry cloth or rolling pin. And what's more important, the pastry and doughs will not take up extra flour which would make them tough.

How to chop a green pepper: Wash the pepper and with a small knife, cut through the pepper around the stem end. Lift out the stem and seeds. Cut as much of the pepper as you think you will need into narrow strips. Place three or four strips close together on a cutting board and with a long-bladed knife, cut through all of the strips at the same time to make small pieces.

How to chop nuts: You can use broken nuts in many recipes. Just break the nuts with your fingers or cut them with scissors, letting them fall into a measuring cup. To chop nuts coarsely, spread them on a cutting board. Chop them with a long, straight knife this way: Hold the point of the knife on the cutting board with one hand, the handle of the knife with the other hand. The blade should be just above the nuts. Cut down through the nuts, moving the handle of the knife in a semicircle over the nuts. Or use a nut chopper.

How to chop and mince onion: Cut a slice from the end of a peeled onion and discard it. Then divide the cut end of the onion in little squares with a small knife. Cut the squares as deep into the onion as you like. Then slice the onion. Presto! the squares fall off and you have chopped onion. For minced onion, make very tiny squares and slice the onion very thin.

How to make onion juice: Cut one slice off the end of the onion. Then scrape the onion's cut surface with a knife or teaspoon—juice collects in spoon. Or cut the onion in halves and remove the juice with the lemon reamer—just the way you extract juice from a lemon.

How to dice celery: Clean the celery, lay four stalks close together on a cutting board, and cut through all the stalks at the same time. You can cut it in as small or large pieces as you like, but ½-inch slices are a good size. To dice *finely,* cut stalks through lengthwise several times first. You can cut asparagus and rhubarb this way.

How to chop raisins and dates: Cut raisins and dates in small pieces with the kitchen scissors. To keep the fruit from sticking to the scissors, dip the blades in water.

How to melt chocolate: Melt chocolate pieces and squares in a small saucepan over low heat or in the top of the double boiler over hot, not boiling, water. Watch out that the chocolate doesn't burn. Chocolate contains fat—no doubt you've heard it called cocoa butter—that scorches at a low temperature and gives the chocolate an unpleasant taste. You can buy *unsweetened* chocolate which you do not have to melt, in small plastic bags. Each bag holds the same amount of chocolate as 1 square of unsweetened chocolate.

How to peel tomatoes: Hold the tomato on a spoon and dip it into a saucepan of simmering water for half a minute. (If you leave it in the water longer, heat will soften the tomato.) Take it out and the skin will slip off easily.

If you're peeling 6 or more tomatoes, save time by putting them in a colander or other metal strainer or sieve. Plunge them into the simmering water for half a minute. Then take them out and slip off the skins.

Chopping an onion

Scrape onion surface

Use a fruit juicer

Chopping raisins and dates

Peeling a tomato

How to make the Drugstore Wrap: Place food to be wrapped in the center of a large sheet of heavy-duty aluminum foil (or other wrapping material). Bring the two longest ends together over the food and fold these ends down in 1-inch folds until the wrap is tight against the food. Then fold the two open sides over toward each other and press down to seal. (If you did not use foil, seal with tape.)

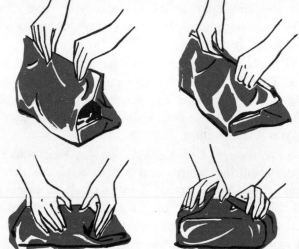

Garnishes give food appeal

Good cooks rely on garnishes to help make food inviting. It may be only a radish rose, a carrot or bacon curl or a frill of lettuce that gives the salad appeal. Or slices of oranges topped with jellied cranberry sauce or a few spiced crab apples or peaches that make the platter of chicken especially tempting. But whatever your garnish is, be sure it *tastes as good as it looks*. And keep it simple.

Often the garnish adds a color note that gives eye appeal —a scoop of red raspberry sherbet or a cluster of grapes on a fruit salad, wedges of lemon sprinkled with a little paprika with fish, shreds of yellow cheese on green vegetables and a whole strawberry speared on a drinking straw in the glass of an icy fruit drink.

Use your imagination in garnishing the food you fix. You'll find suggestions with many of our recipes and you'll dream up many more ways to trim foods attractively. Even the serving plate or dish can dress up a food with its color, shape and size.

When scientists get together, they speak a scientific language. Doctors talk to one another in medical terms. Cooks also have many words of their own. Here are some of the words they use the most and what they mean. You'll find them in many recipes you want to use. And you'll want to understand what good cooks are talking about when you are "swapping" recipes and discussing with them how you fixed a dish.

Bake: To cook in the oven. But when you're cooking meats in the oven, it's called roasting, except for ham. You *bake* bread, cookies and pies; you *roast* beef, pork, lamb and veal.

Baste: To moisten food while it is cooking. You either spoon the liquid, such as broth or melted fat, over the food or use a baster. Basting keeps food from drying out.

Beat: To work a mixture hard and fast with regular movements to make it smooth and to introduce air. You'll beat foods both with a spoon, a beater or electric mixer.

Blend: To mix two or more foods or ingredients thoroughly.

Boil: To cook food in water or other liquid, such as broth at boiling temperature—when small bubbles rise to the top of the liquid and break. Slow boiling cooks as fast as boiling hard. It's smart to get the habit of lowering the heat when a food boils—that makes it boil gently and slowly. The foods won't boil over so easily and leave burned food on the range and pan that have to be scoured off later. And gentle boiling helps keep the food from boiling dry and scorching.

Broil: To cook food with dry heat directly under the flame or electric unit or over coals. You often call broiling over coals "grilling."

Chop: To cut food in small pieces, usually with a knife, scissors, electric blender or a food chopper. There are onion, nut and other special choppers as well.

Coat: To roll food in flour, sugar, nuts, or whatever the recipe calls for—in order to coat the food evenly all over. Sometimes you dip the food in egg, milk or cream before rolling it in the flour or other coating.

Combine: To mix ingredients thoroughly.

Cream: To beat shortening with a spoon or an electric

mixer to make it smooth and fluffy. When you make cakes, you often cream the shortening with the sugar. If you use a spoon, rub the shortening against the side of the bowl to soften it and then beat it until fluffy.

Cube: To cut food in small pieces usually about ½ to 1 inch in size. Generally, you put the food on a cutting board and cut it with a knife. See *Dice.*

Cut in: To mix shortening with dry ingredients, such as flour when you make piecrust. You work the shortening and flour together to make crumbs either with a pastry blender or two table knives, moved like scissors.

Dice: To cut in very small pieces, about ¼ inch, the same way you cube foods.

Dissolve: To mix a dry food, such as flour or sugar, with a liquid, such as milk, broth or fruit juices, until the dry food goes into solution.

Flake: To pull food apart in flakes with 1 or 2 forks. You flake fish to tell when it's cooked enough.

Fold: An over-and-under motion used to add a new ingredient to what you are making—for example, adding beaten egg whites to the cake batter. With a spoon or rubber spatula, cut down through the batter at one side of the bowl until you reach the bottom. Then move the spoon or spatula across the bottom to the other side of the bowl, bring it up almost to the top of the batter and then across to the other side. Keep on doing this until the egg whites are mixed into the batter.

Grate: To shred food by rubbing it on a grater. Some foods usually need to be grated rather coarsely—cheese is one. Other foods need to be grated fine—lemon and orange peel.

Grease: To rub *lightly* with shortening, butter, margarine or salad oil. You can use either a pastry brush or a piece of waxed paper or paper toweling to apply shortening.

Grind: To chop food by putting it through a food chopper. Food choppers have at least 2 blades. You use the blade with little holes to chop foods fine, the blade with big holes to chop foods coarse.

Knead: To work and press dough with the heels of your hands. This is usually done with bread and other yeast doughs.

Mince: To chop very fine.

Roast: To cook meats and poultry, uncovered and without adding water, in oven heat. It's really cooking in dry heat.

Scald: To heat a liquid just to the simmering point—never let it boil. You often scald milk when making yeast breads.

Scramble: To stir and mix foods while they cook. This is what you do when you scramble eggs.

Shred: To tear or divide food into long, narrow pieces with a grater or a sharp knife. You can shred cabbage for a salad on the coarse grater or with a knife.

Simmer: To cook slowly over *low heat.*

Sliver: To split in long, thin pieces, usually with a knife. Almonds often are split.

Snip: To cut in small pieces with scissors. This is an easy way to mince parsley.

Soften shortening: To let it stand at room temperature until soft enough to cream easily.

Stir: To move the spoon round and round—in circles—to mix foods.

Toss: To mix lightly with a tumbling motion by lifting the food up without crushing or mashing it. Usually you toss foods, like green salads, with two forks or a spoon and a fork.

Whip: To beat rapidly with a hand beater or electric mixer to trap air in the food, such as heavy cream or egg whites. The air increases the quantity and makes the food light and fluffy.

Cookies you'll love to bake

WHEN you want to go into the kitchen and cook something really good, bake a batch of cookies. If you're hungry, eat a few fresh from the oven—the best cooks taste as they work. That's part of the cooking game. Share your cookies and a drink with your friends who come over to see you, and with your family. Serve them with ice cream or fruit for a special dessert. Take them to picnics, 4-H Club meetings and other parties—they'll make a hit. Tuck them in lunch boxes.

There are so many kinds of cookies and so many ways to dress them up. But all baked cookies belong to one of two big families—the soft doughs and the stiff doughs. Then there is a newer family of cookies that never see the oven. They are the no-bake cookies—some are almost like candy.

Soft dough cookies contain a higher proportion of liquid, which includes eggs, and of flour—they are really little cakes. Bar and drop cookies belong to this family, and are the easiest baked cookies to make, so try your luck with them first.

Stiff dough cookies contain a higher proportion of sugar and shortening. They are thinner than drop and bar cookies and are crisp. The three most important kinds are molded, refrigerator and rolled cookies.

We give you recipes for all types of cookies in this book. We used all-purpose flour in testing the recipes. Take your pick and make some of the best cookies anybody ever tasted.

How to mix cookies

With an electric mixer or beater: Use medium speed for mixing the sugar and shortening and low speed for mixing in the flour and other dry ingredients. Stop the beater a few times and scrape the sides and bottom of the mixing bowl and beaters with a rubber spatula.

With a spoon: A wooden spoon with a long handle is an excellent choice. To mix soft shortening and sugar, rub them against the sides of the mixing bowl until creamy. Beat and stir in the other ingredients as the recipe suggests.

Where to bake cookies

Baking sheet: Use a baking sheet for drop, molded, refrigerator and rolled cookies. The recipes in this Cookbook tell when you use a greased or ungreased baking sheet. If a greased sheet is needed to prevent sticking, rub the surface *lightly* with salad oil or shortening. An ungreased baking sheet is easier to wash, so leave off the salad oil or shortening unless the recipe calls for it.

With one baking sheet: Place the cookies on the rack in the center of the oven. When baked, take them from the oven and spread them on a wire cooling rack as directed in the recipe. Let the baking sheet cool before placing the dough for the second batch on it. If you fail to do this, the heat of the baking sheet will melt the shortening in the dough and the cookies may spread while baking. Or skip the cooling this way: Place the dough for the second batch of cookies on a sheet of aluminum foil, cut to fit your baking sheet, while the first batch bakes. When the baked cookies are spread on the cooling rack, carefully lift the foil to the warm baking sheet and put the cookies in the oven at once.

With two baking sheets: Bake two batches of cookies at a time. Place the two racks in the oven so that they divide it into three equal parts. (Or you can turn a baking pan upside down and bake the cookies on the bottom. This makes the cookies brown evenly.)

Pan: Use a baking pan for bar cookies. Spread the dough in greased pans and bake as directed.

Tests for doneness

For bar, drop and molded cookies: Use the Fingerprint Test. Make it when the cookies are lightly browned and a few minutes before the baking time is up. Lightly press the top of the cookie with a finger tip. If your finger makes a slight dent or imprint that remains, the cookie is done.

For refrigerator and rolled cookies: Judge their doneness by color. The cookies are done when they are a light or delicate brown.

How to cool cookies

Bar cookies: Set the pan on a wire cooling rack and let the cookies partly or completely cool in the pan before cutting them. Some bar cookies are best removed from the pan while they are hot, so follow the recipe directions.

Drop, molded, refrigerator and rolled cookies: With a wide spatula, lift them from the baking sheet as soon as you take them from the oven unless the recipe tells you differently. If you leave the cookies on the hot baking sheet, they will continue baking and may become overdone and dry. Spread them on a wire cooling rack so the air can move around each cookie and cool it. This keeps steam from forming and making the cookies soft. It's also easier to get most cookies off the baking sheet without breaking while they're hot.

How to store cookies

Bar cookies: You can leave them in the pan in which you baked them. If the pan does not have a cover, make a snug-fitting one with a sheet of aluminum foil.

Soft cookies: Place them in a can with a tight lid or in a covered jar. If the cookies get a little dry, you can moisten them by putting a piece of an apple or orange in the cookie jar. Really! The cookies absorb some of the fruit's moisture. Change the fruit every day or two.

Crisp cookies: Place them in a can with a loose fitting lid. If they lose their crispness, heat the oven to 300° F. Spread the cookies in a pan or on a baking sheet, and heat them in the oven 5 minutes shortly before you serve them. (In wet weather, almost all cookies are best reheated this way.)

How to freeze cookies

Before baking: Place the dough for bar, drop, molded and rolled cookies in freezer containers. Wrap the roll of refrigerator cookie dough in aluminum foil, saran or other sheet wrapping material.

Baked cookies: Carefully arrange baked and cooled cookies on a piece of cardboard covered with waxed paper. Freeze them uncovered and then place the frozen cookies in plastic bags. Or pack them gently in a freezer container. You can protect them by using crumpled waxed paper between the layers.

How to use frozen cookies

Unbaked cookies: Thaw the dough for bar, drop, molded and rolled cookies at room temperature until you can handle it easily. Then fix and bake the cookies the same as with dough that has not been frozen. Let the dough for refrigerator cookies thaw 1 hour in the refrigerator before slicing and baking.

Baked cookies: Thaw baked cookies at room temperature without unwrapping them. It will take about 15 minutes.

BAR COOKIES

These are the cookies we said are easiest to bake. You spread the dough in a greased pan and bake it the way you bake cakes. Then you cut the cookie into squares or bars.

You might like to start with a package of good brownie, date bar and other bar cookie mixes from the supermarket. Make them as directed on the label.

Here are some recipes for made-from-scratch bar cookies almost everybody loves. So get out your measuring cup, mixing bowl and get going.

Do's for bar cookies

1. Do use the pan size the recipe recommends. If your pan is too large, the dough spreads thinner in the pan and it overbakes; the cookies will be tough and dry. If the pan is too small, the dough spreads too thick in it and the cookies may not bake through.

2. Do mix the dough the way the recipe directs. Overmixing gives bar cookies hard, crusty tops.

3. Do spread the dough evenly in the pan with a spatula or spoon so that all of it will bake in the same number of minutes.

4. Do watch the clock. When the time for baking is almost up, make the Fingerprint Test we've already described. Overbaking makes cookies dry and crumbly.

5. Do cool the cookies in the pan at least 10 minutes before cutting. Cutting the bars while they are hot makes the cookies crumble.

FUDGE BROWNIES

For a surprise, frost these brownies with chocolate and white frostings and arrange like a checkerboard

2 (1-ounce) squares unsweetened chocolate
⅓ cup soft shortening
¾ cup sifted flour
½ teaspoon baking powder
½ teaspoon salt
1 cup sugar
2 eggs
1 teaspoon vanilla
½ cup chopped or broken nuts

Brownie checkerboard

1. Start heating the oven to 350° F. Lightly grease an 8×8×2-inch pan with unsalted shortening or salad oil.

2. Put the chocolate and shortening in the top of the double boiler and melt them over hot, not boiling, water. Or melt them in a small saucepan over low heat, watching all the time so chocolate won't burn. Cool until lukewarm.

3. Sift the flour onto a square of waxed paper or into a bowl and then measure. Sift the measured flour with the baking powder and salt. Set aside.

4. Beat the sugar and eggs together in a large bowl with a spoon, or with an electric mixer on medium speed, until light. If you use an electric mixer, stop the mixer two or three times and scrape sides of bowl with a rubber spatula.

5. Beat the cooled chocolate-shortening mixture and vanilla into the egg-sugar mixture. Stir in the flour mixture or beat it in with the electric mixer on low speed. Stir in the nuts and mix well. (If you like, you can divide the nuts in half. Stir ¼ cup into the cookie dough and sprinkle the other ¼ cup on top of dough in pan just before baking.)

6. Spread evenly in the greased pan with the back of a spoon or a spatula. Bake on the rack in the center of the oven 20 to 25 minutes. The crust on top will have a dull look when the cookie is done.

Cool first . . . then cut

7. Remove the pan from the oven and set it on a wire rack to cool about 10 minutes, or until completely cooled, before cutting. Cut into 16 (2-inch) bars.

For a change

· Before cutting the baked Brownies into squares or bars, sprinkle the top lightly with powdered sugar.

BROWNIES À LA MODE

See recipe for Chocolate
Sauce, page 118

Brownie "pie" à la mode

Here's a dessert that you won't go wrong on if your friends or family are chocolate fans. (That means most Americans!) Bake the Fudge Brownie dough in a greased 9-inch round layer cake pan. Set the pan on a wire rack to cool. To serve, cut the cookie in pie-shaped pieces and top each triangle with vanilla ice cream. Pass a pitcher of Chocolate Sauce to pour over it. You can buy the sauce in a jar or can, or make it.

MAGIC PARTY SQUARES

The magic of these cookies is the way you frost them with milk chocolate candy bars. And their wonderful taste!

½ cup soft margarine or butter (¼ pound)
1 cup brown sugar, packed firmly
¾ cup sifted flour
¾ cup raw quick-cooking rolled oats
1 egg
2 tablespoons water
1 teaspoon vanilla
3 (1-ounce) milk chocolate candy bars
¼ cup chopped nuts

Magic frosting (candy bars)

1. Start heating the oven to 375° F.

2. Put the margarine, brown sugar, flour and rolled oats in a medium bowl and mix well with a pastry blender. Be sure the margarine is evenly distributed. Add the egg, water and vanilla and beat with a spoon to mix thoroughly.

3. Spread evenly in an ungreased 9×9×2-inch pan with the back of a spoon or a spatula. Bake on the rack in the center of the oven about 22 to 25 minutes. The crust on top will have a dull look when the cookie is done.

4. Remove the pan from the oven and top at once with the chocolate candy bars. Let stand about 2 minutes or until the heat softens the candy. Spread the melted chocolate over the top of the cookie to make a frosting. Sprinkle the frosting with chopped nuts. Cool cookie and cut into about 20 bars, or any number you like. (*Double Magic:* You can double this recipe and bake the cookie in a 13×9×2-inch pan. You'll need to bake it longer, about 35 to 40 minutes in all.)

CANDY BAR COOKIES

The 4-H Club girl who shares this recipe with us says the cookies taste like candy bars. Her friends agree

1 cup brown sugar
½ cup soft butter
½ cup light corn syrup
3 teaspoons vanilla
1 teaspoon salt
4 cups raw quick-cooking rolled oats
½ cup peanut butter
1 cup semisweet chocolate pieces

1. Start heating the oven to 350° F. Grease a 13×9×2-inch pan with unsalted shortening or salad oil.

2. With a spoon or electric mixer on medium speed, mix the brown sugar and butter in a large bowl until light and fluffy. Add the corn syrup, vanilla, salt and rolled oats and beat on low speed to mix ingredients well.

3. Spread the mixture evenly in the greased pan with the back of a spoon or spatula. Bake on the rack in the center of the oven 15 minutes.

4. While the mixture bakes, mix the peanut butter and chocolate in a small bowl.

5. Remove the pan from the oven and at once spread the peanut butter-chocolate mixture evenly over the top to cover until the heat melts the chocolate. When cool, cut into 27 bars and remove from the pan with a spatula.

*Great Discovery—
Chocolate*
Give credit to the ancient Aztec Indians in Mexico for discovering chocolate. They liked the flavor of the seeds from the football-shaped pods on their cacao evergreen trees so much that they used them for money as well as for cooking. The Spanish explorers carried chocolate to Europe and it became the rage almost at once. From Europe it was brought back across the Atlantic to our own eastern shores. It's been popular here ever since.

RICH BUTTERSCOTCH BARS

If you have a 1-pound box of brown sugar in the cupboard, use it. Then you don't have to measure or roll out lumps

1 pound brown sugar (2¼ to 2⅓ cups), packed firmly
1 cup soft butter
2 eggs
2 cups flour
1 teaspoon baking powder
½ teaspoon salt
1 cup walnuts, coarsely chopped or broken

1. Cook the sugar and butter in the top of the double boiler over hot, not boiling, water until the sugar dissolves.

Butterscotch Formula
Brown sugar+butter=
the delicious butterscotch taste.

Or cook them in a medium saucepan over low heat. Cool until lukewarm.

2. Start heating the oven to 350° F.

3. Add the eggs, one at a time, to the butter-sugar mixture and beat thoroughly after adding each egg.

4. Stir together the flour, baking powder and salt to mix well. Add to the butter-sugar mixture and stir in the nuts.

5. Spread evenly in an ungreased 15½×10½×1-inch pan (jelly roll pan). Bake on the rack in the center of the oven 25 minutes or until the cookie is a delicate brown; a slight dent is left when you touch the top lightly with a finger tip.

6. Remove the pan from the oven and set it on a wire rack. Cut while hot into 40 bars, or as many as you like.

DATE LOGS

Chop and measure at the same time—cut the dates fine with scissors and let them drop into the measuring cup

¾ cup sifted flour
1 cup sugar
1 teaspoon baking powder
¼ teaspoon salt
1 cup pitted cut-up dates
1 cup chopped walnuts
3 eggs, well beaten
Powdered sugar

1. Start heating the oven to 325° F. Grease a 9×9×2-inch pan with unsalted shortening or salad oil.

2. Sift the flour onto a square of waxed paper or into a bowl and then measure. Sift the measured flour with the sugar, baking powder and salt into a medium bowl. Stir the finely cut dates, walnuts and the well-beaten eggs into the flour mixture.

3. Spread evenly in the greased pan with the back of a spoon or a spatula. Bake on the rack in the center of the oven 35 to 40 minutes or until the cookie is a delicate brown; a slight dent is left when you touch the top lightly with a finger tip.

4. Remove the pan from the oven and set it on a wire rack until completely cool. Then, cut cookie into 48 strips or logs, or any number you like, and roll them in powdered sugar.

Christmas Tree
Arrange bar cookies on a tray in the shape of a triangular tree. Top it with a red star. To make the star, roll a red candy gumdrop flat and cut out a star with a small cookie cutter.

You don't have to use your imagination to figure out how drop cookies got their name—you drop the soft dough from a spoon onto a baking sheet. They're really push-and-drop cookies because you have to push the dough off the spoon with a teaspoon or a rubber spatula. If you heap the drops of cookie dough up in the center to make little peaks, the cookies will be especially attractive.

To give drop cookies a fancy look in a jiffy, press bits of nuts or candied cherries on the center of each cookie before baking. Or spread the baked and cooled cookies with cake frosting, either a quick-to-fix powdered-sugar frosting or a packaged frosting mix.

CHOCOLATE-NUT DROPS

Use a little showmanship and dress up these cookies— lightly press a nut on each one before baking

```
½ cup soft butter or margarine
6 tablespoons brown sugar
6 tablespoons honey
1 egg
1¼ cups sifted flour
½ teaspoon baking soda
½ teaspoon salt
Few drops hot water
½ teaspoon vanilla
1 (6-ounce) package semisweet chocolate pieces
½ cup chopped walnuts
```

1. Start heating the oven to 375° F. Grease a baking sheet with unsalted shortening or salad oil.

2. Beat the butter, brown sugar and honey together until

How to Store Honey
If you have used some honey out of a jar, keep the rest covered in the freezer. It will not turn dark or become sugary. Keep the jar of honey you are using every day or two in the cupboard, not in the refrigerator. It will turn sugary in the refrigerator. If honey does get sugary, set the jar in a pan of warm water and heat it.

Make Cookies the Same Size

To measure the dough dropped onto the baking sheet, use a teaspoon or tablespoon—it's easier to push the dough from a teaspoon than from a measuring spoon with its rounded bowl. Push the dough from the spoon with a rubber spatula.

If all the cookies are the same size, they will be ready to take from the oven at the same time. It takes longer for large, thick cookies to bake than small, thin ones.

Funny-face cookies

light and fluffy. Add the unbeaten egg and beat well to mix.

3. Sift the flour onto a square of waxed paper or into a bowl and then measure. Sift the measured flour with the baking soda and salt. Stir into the creamed mixture. Add the hot water and beat to mix. Stir in the vanilla, chocolate pieces and nuts.

4. Drop 2 inches apart from a teaspoon onto a baking sheet. Bake on the rack in the center of the oven 10 to 12 —minutes or until the cookies are a delicate brown; a slight dent shows when you touch the top lightly with a finger tip.

5. Remove the pan from the oven and set it on a wire rack to cool slightly. Then remove the cookies from the baking sheet with a wide spatula and spread them on a wire rack to finish cooling. Makes about 36 cookies.

MOLASSES LOLLIPOP COOKIES

Wonderful party favors and Christmas gifts for the young fry. You can get skewers at dime stores and meat counters

½ cup soft butter or margarine
½ cup sugar
1 egg
½ cup light molasses
2½ cups sifted flour
¼ teaspoon salt
1 teaspoon baking soda
1 teaspoon ginger
½ teaspoon cinnamon
½ teaspoon cloves
½ teaspoon nutmeg
2 tablespoons water
Wooden skewers, about 24, 4½ inches long

1. Start heating the oven to 375° F.

2. Beat the butter and sugar with an electric mixer on medium speed or with a spoon until light and fluffy. Add the egg and molasses and beat to mix well.

3. Sift the flour onto a square of waxed paper or into a bowl and then measure. Sift the measured flour with the salt, baking soda and spices. Add half of it to the molasses mixture and beat with the electric mixer on low speed to mix. Add the water and stir until smooth. Then mix in the second half of the flour mixture. Stir until smooth.

4. Drop rounded tablespoonfuls of the dough 4 inches

apart onto an ungreased baking sheet. Insert the pointed end of a wooden skewer (popsicle stick) into each cookie with a twisting motion.

5. Bake on the rack in the center of the oven 10 to 12 minutes or until the cookies are a delicate brown; a slight dent shows when you touch the cookie lightly with a finger tip.

6. Remove the pan from the oven and let it stand 1 minute. Then, with a wide spatula, carefully remove the lollipops to a wire rack to cool.

7. When the cookies are cool, decorate them as you like. One good way is to spread them with powdered sugar mixed with a little milk until smooth and just thick enough to spread on the cookies. Use candies, raisins, tiny candy red hots, small gumdrops and chocolate pieces to make faces and flaked or shredded coconut for hair. Wonderful for a children's party or gifts to your friends. Makes about 24 large cookies.

ORANGE-COCONUT CRISPS

Use the orange juice as it comes from the can—just thaw

   2 eggs
   ⅔ cup salad oil
   1 cup sugar
   ¼ cup frozen orange juice concentrate, thawed
   2½ cups sifted flour
   2 teaspoons baking powder
   ½ tcaspoon salt
   1 cup packaged grated coconut

1. Start heating the oven to 400° F.

2. Beat the eggs with a fork or a wire whisk in a medium bowl. Stir in the salad oil and sugar and beat until the mixture thickens. Stir in the orange juice (do not dilute).

3. Sift the flour onto a square of waxed paper or into a bowl and then measure. Sift the measured flour with the baking powder and salt. Add with the coconut to the egg mixture. Stir to mix well.

4. Drop teaspoons of dough about 2 inches apart onto an ungreased baking sheet. Press each cookie flat with the bottom of a drinking glass, oiled lightly with salad oil and dipped in sugar. Dip the glass in the sugar before flattening each cookie. Bake on the rack in the center of the

Ready to Bake
Freeze balls of this cookie dough on a tray or baking sheet. Put the frozen balls in airtight freezer containers and return them to the freezer. To bake, take out as many balls of dough as you want cookies and place them on a baking sheet. Let them stand at room temperature 30 minutes. Then flatten and bake them like the unfrozen cookie balls.

Flatten with a glass

oven 8 to 10 minutes or until the cookies are a delicate brown; a slight dent shows when you touch the top lightly with a finger tip.

5. Remove the pan from the oven and take the cookies from the baking sheet with a wide spatula. Spread them on a wire rack to cool. Makes about 36 (3-inch) cookies.

TWICE-AS-GOOD COOKIES

Melted chocolate makes these chip cookies different

  1 (6-ounce) package semisweet chocolate pieces
  1 cup sifted flour
  ½ teaspoon baking soda
  ½ teaspoon salt
  ½ cup soft butter or margarine
  ½ cup sugar
  1 egg
  ¼ cup warm water
  ½ cup chopped or broken walnuts

1. Melt ½ cup of the chocolate pieces in the top of the double boiler over hot, not boiling, water or in a small saucepan over low heat. Cool until lukewarm.

2. Sift the flour onto a square of waxed paper or into a bowl and then measure. Sift the measured flour with the baking soda and salt. Set aside.

3. Beat the butter, sugar and egg in the large bowl of the electric mixer, on medium speed, until the mixture is light and fluffy, or beat with a spoon.

4. Beat in the melted chocolate and warm water. Then beat in flour mixture on low speed just enough to mix, or mix in with a spoon.

5. Stir in the walnuts and the rest of the chocolate pieces with a spoon. Chill in the refrigerator at least 30 minutes.

6. Start heating the oven to 375° F. Lightly grease a baking sheet with unsalted shortening or salad oil.

7. Drop rounded teaspoons of the dough onto the greased baking sheet about 3 inches apart. Bake on the rack in the center of the oven 10 to 12 minutes or until a slight dent shows when you touch the top lightly with a finger tip.

8. Remove the pan from the oven and take the cookies from the baking sheet with a wide spatula. Spread them on a wire rack to cool. Makes 36 cookies.

Watch That Spread
There are four things to do to help keep drop cookies from spreading too flat when baking. 1) Chill the dough before you drop it onto the baking sheet. 2) Use a cool baking sheet. 3) Peak the drops of dough up a little. 4) And use the right oven temperature, the one given in the recipe.

If you have ever enjoyed modeling with clay, you'll love to make molded cookies. You shape the stiff dough with your hands, often into balls. To keep the dough from sticking to your hands, chill it thoroughly in the refrigerator. Then rub your hands lightly with flour or a little powdered sugar before making the balls. You may have to flour or sugar your hands several times while shaping a batch of cookies.

Often recipes direct that you flatten the balls of dough after they are on the baking sheet. Sometimes you use a fork, sometimes the bottom of a glass, dipped in sugar. Then there are thumbprint cookies— you press a hollow in each cookie with your thumb, which you fill with goodies before or after baking. Some of the cookie balls flatten while they bake; some keep their shape. You'll find all kinds among our recipes.

SNACK TIME PEANUT COOKIES

For a snack that satisfies, serve these cookies with glasses of cold milk, cups of hot cocoa or fruit juice

½ cup soft butter or margarine
½ cup peanut butter
½ cup white sugar
½ cup brown sugar, packed firmly
1 egg
1¼ cups flour
½ teaspoon baking powder
¾ teaspoon baking soda
¼ teaspoon salt

1. In a medium bowl, beat the butter, peanut butter, white and brown sugars and the egg together until the mixture is light and fluffy.

2. Stir the flour, baking powder, baking soda and salt together in another medium bowl and then stir it into the peanut-butter mixture. Chill the dough 1 hour, or until you can handle it easily.

3. Start heating the oven to 375° F. Lightly grease a baking sheet with unsalted shortening or salad oil.

Quick fork crisscross

4. Shape the chilled dough into balls the size of large walnuts. Arrange them on the greased baking sheet about 3 inches apart. Dip a fork into flour and press it first one

way and then the other to flatten each cookie and make a crisscross design.

5. Bake on the rack in the center of the oven until set, but not hard, or about 10 to 12 minutes. Remove from oven and spread cookies on rack to cool. Makes 36 (2½-inch) cookies.

SURPRISE CRACKLES

What Makes Surprise Crackles?
During the baking, the baking powder makes the chocolate cookies grow bigger. The coating of powdered sugar on them cannot expand with the cookies so it cracks. That's what makes the interesting designs on Surprise Crackles.

Cookies make their own lacy decorations while baking

2 (1-ounce) squares unsweetened chocolate
¼ cup soft butter or margarine
1 cup sifted flour
¼ teaspoon salt
1 teaspoon baking powder
1 cup sugar
2 eggs
1 teaspoon vanilla
Powdered sugar

1. Melt the chocolate and butter together in a saucepan over very low heat or in a double boiler over hot, not boiling, water. Let cool until lukewarm.

2. Sift the flour onto a square of waxed paper or into a bowl and then measure. Sift the measured flour with the salt and baking powder. Set aside.

3. Add the sugar, eggs and vanilla to the chocolate-butter mixture. Beat well. Stir in the flour mixture. The dough will be very soft. Cover it and chill overnight or until you can handle it. If you have some nuts—black walnuts, English walnuts, almonds or other nuts—add ¼ cup of them, chopped, to the dough before chilling.

4. Start heating the oven to 350° F. Grease a baking sheet with unsalted shortening or salad oil.

5. Shape the dough into small balls.

6. Put powdered sugar in a medium bowl and roll the cookie balls in it to coat completely. Place them on the greased baking sheet about 2 to 3 inches apart.

7. Bake on rack in center of oven about 8 minutes.

8. Remove the pan from the oven and take the cookies from the baking sheet with a wide spatula. Spread them on a wire rack to cool. Makes about 90 cookies.

THUMBPRINT COOKIES

You make a hollow in the cookie balls with your thumb before baking to fill with treats when the cookies are cool

½ cup sifted powdered sugar
1 cup soft butter or margarine
½ teaspoon salt
1 tablespoon vanilla
2 cups sifted flour
1 cup finely chopped or broken pecans

Make a place for treats

Thumbprint Treats
Fill the hollows in Thumbprint Cookies with Pink Icing (recipe on page 47) or the same icing tinted in other colors, or with jelly.

1. Sift the powdered sugar and measure. Beat it, the butter, salt and vanilla together until fluffy.

2. Sift the flour onto a square of waxed paper or into a bowl and then measure. Stir the sifted flour and pecans into the powdered-sugar mixture. Mix well. Chill in the refrigerator at least an hour so dough will shape easily.

3. When you are ready to bake the cookies, start heating the oven to 350° F.

4. Shape the chilled dough into small balls. Place them 3 inches apart on an ungreased baking sheet. Press a small hole in the center of each ball with your thumb tip.

5. Bake on the rack in the center of the oven about 15 minutes, or until lightly browned and set. Remove from oven and spread cookies on rack to cool. Makes 60 small cookies.

REFRIGERATOR COOKIES

Among cookies that were invented in American kitchens are the refrigerator cookies. They contain so much shortening that you have to chill them several hours before baking, which is how they got their name. The shortening makes refrigerator cookies especially crisp.

You shape the cookie dough into long rolls, wrap them in waxed paper, saran or aluminum foil and chill them in the refrigerator several hours or overnight. Then the shortening hardens and they're easy to slice and bake. If carefully wrapped so they won't dry out, you can keep the rolls of dough in the refrigerator a week or more. Then you can slice off and bake the cookies when you wish. Serve them warm from the oven—they're so good when freshly baked.

Or you can freeze the wrapped rolls of dough in the freezer and bake them any time within 6 months. When you're ready for some cookies, take the wrapped frozen dough from the freezer and leave it in the refrigerator for an hour, or on the kitchen counter 30 minutes. They'll be just right for slicing. You will find many excellent refrigerator cookie dough rolls in the supermarket. All you have to do is slice and bake them.

Refrigerator cookies are thin and crisp. Remember that the thinner you slice them, the crisper they will be.

REFRIGERATOR SCOTCHIES

Shape the roll of refrigerator dough as big around as you want your cookies—2½ inches is a good size

Refrigerator Cookie Do's
Do shape the rolls of dough with your hands until they are smooth. If it is hard to do this, chill the dough an hour before shaping.
Do wrap them tightly in waxed paper, saran or aluminum foil. If you use waxed paper, twist the ends tightly so the roll will stay wrapped. When ready to bake the cookies, remove the wrap and slice straight down with a knife that has a sharp, thin blade.
Do cut in thin slices— about ⅛ inch.
Do wrap any unused dough carefully and put it back in the refrigerator for more cookies later.

1 cup soft butter or margarine
½ cup white sugar
½ cup brown sugar, packed firmly
2 eggs
1½ teaspoons vanilla
2¾ cups sifted flour
½ teaspoon baking soda
1 teaspoon salt

1. Beat the butter, white and brown sugars, eggs and vanilla until fluffy and well mixed.

2. Sift the flour onto a square of waxed paper or into a bowl and then measure. Sift the measured flour with the baking soda and salt. Add about half of it to the shortening-sugar mixture and stir to mix well. Gradually add the rest of the flour mixture, working it into the dough with the hands. Mix thoroughly.

3. Press and shape the dough into a long smooth roll about 2½ inches in diameter. Wrap it tightly in waxed paper or aluminum foil and chill several hours or overnight.

4. When you are ready to bake some of the cookies, start heating the oven to 400° F.

5. Remove the dough from the refrigerator, unwrap it and cut off thin (⅛-inch) slices—8 slices from an inch of dough! Use a knife with a thin, sharp blade for slicing so the cookie edges will be neat. Rewrap the unused dough and put it back in the refrigerator. The dough will keep a week or longer.

6. Place the slices a little distance apart on an ungreased baking sheet and bake on the rack in the center of the oven 6 to 8 minutes, or until cookies are lightly browned.

7. Remove the pan from the oven, lift the cookies from the baking sheet with a wide spatula and spread them on

a wire rack to cool. This recipe will make about 75 (2½-inch) cookies.

CHOCOLATE REFRIGERATOR COOKIES

Slices of chocolate and nuts—pretty, too, when you give them fancy edges

1½ (1-ounce) squares unsweetened chocolate
½ cup soft butter or margarine
1 cup light brown sugar
1 egg
½ teaspoon vanilla
2 cups sifted flour
½ teaspoon baking powder
¼ teaspoon baking soda
¼ teaspoon salt
3 tablespoons milk
½ cup finely chopped nuts

1. Put the chocolate in the top of the double boiler and melt over hot, not boiling, water or melt it in a small saucepan over low heat. Cool until lukewarm.

2. Beat the butter and brown sugar with the electric mixer on medium speed or with a spoon until light and fluffy. Add the egg, chocolate and vanilla. Beat to mix thoroughly.

3. Sift the flour onto a sheet of waxed paper and then measure. Sift the flour with the baking powder, baking soda and salt into a medium bowl. Add some of it to the chocolate mixture, then add a little of the milk. Beat on mixer's low speed or with a spoon after each addition. Keep on adding the flour mixture and milk, first one and then the other, until all of these ingredients are used.

4. Stir in the nuts. They must be chopped very fine so the chilled dough can be sliced easily.

5. Shape the dough in 2 smooth rolls with your hands—make them about 2½ inches in diameter. Wrap them tightly in aluminum foil or waxed paper, twisting the ends of the paper so they will stay in place. Chill several hours or overnight.

6. When ready to bake the cookies, start heating the oven to 400° F. Unwrap the rolls of dough and cut each into thin slices with a sharp knife. Place the slices a little distance apart on an ungreased baking sheet.

Slick Trick
Pack the dough for refrigerator cookies in frozen juice cans instead of shaping it in rolls. Cover can tops with aluminum foil or waxed paper, fastened on with a rubber band, and chill. When ready to bake the cookies, cut off the bottom of the cans with a can opener that makes a smooth edge. Use the cutout lid to press against the bottom of the dough and push out just enough dough for one cookie at a time. Slice the dough, holding the knife against the can.

Why Butter Makes Refrigerator Cookies Slice More Easily
Butter gets very hard when it is cold. You will notice that it is harder when you take it from the refrigerator than lard and many margarines. This is because of the kind of fatty acids it contains. So refrigerator cookies made with butter are easier to slice than a softer dough.

Rolling in candy

7. Bake on the rack in the center of the oven 6 to 10 minutes.

8. Remove the pan from the oven, lift the cookies from the baking sheet with a wide spatula and spread them on a wire rack to cool. Makes 46 to 48 cookies.

For a change
· *Fancy edge cookies:* When you take the roll of dough from the refrigerator, sprinkle a sheet of waxed paper with little candies of many colors (nonpareils), chocolate shot (jimmies) or finely chopped nuts. Unwrap the roll of cookie dough and turn it around in these tiny candies to coat well. Then, slice and bake the cookies.

ROLLED COOKIES

Get out the rolling pin and cookie cutters before you start to make these cookies. They are a little more difficult to make than other cookies because you have to roll the dough, but this isn't hard if you chill the dough first and use the pastry cloth and stockinet-covered rolling pin (see How to flour a pastry cloth, page 20).

You can dress up rolled cookies in many ways. Just cutting them with various cookie cutters of many shapes gives them a different look. And you can sprinkle the unbaked cookie cutouts with sugar— white or colored—tiny candies or chopped nuts. Also you can spread the cooled, baked cookies with powdered-sugar icing—white or tinted with food color.

Bake these cookies only until they're light brown. Baking them longer will give you a tough, dry cookie.

EXTRA-GOOD SUGAR COOKIES

Sprinkle cookies with sugar before baking—they'll glisten

Slick Trick
To chill the dough for rolled cookies in a hurry, divide it into small portions and refrigerate.

⅔ cup soft shortening
¾ cup sugar
1 egg
¾ teaspoon vanilla
¼ teaspoon almond extract
2 cups sifted flour
1½ teaspoons baking powder
¼ teaspoon salt
4 teaspoons milk

1. Beat the shortening and sugar together until light and fluffy. Add the egg and beat to mix well. Add the vanilla and almond extracts. (You can use 1 teaspoon vanilla and omit the almond extract.) Mix thoroughly.

2. Sift the flour onto a square of waxed paper and then measure. Sift the measured flour with the baking powder and salt. Stir it into the sugar-shortening mixture along with the milk. Divide the dough in half and chill in the refrigerator 1 hour or until the dough is easy to handle.

3. Start heating the oven to 375° F. Grease a baking sheet with unsalted shortening or salad oil.

4. Roll the dough, half of it at a time, from the center to the edge until it is ⅛ to ¼ inch thick. (The thinner you roll the dough, the crisper the cookies will be.) Cut with a 3- or 4-inch round cookie cutter.

5. Use a wide spatula to place the cookies ½ inch apart on the greased baking sheet.

6. Bake on the rack in the center of the oven 8 to 9 minutes, or until the cookies are light brown.

7. Remove the pan from the oven at once and use a wide spatula to place the cookies on a wire cooling rack. Makes about 24 cookies.

For a change

· *Polka dot cookies:* Dot the tops of cooled Extra-Good Sugar Cookies with dabs of chocolate frosting.

· *Painted cookies:* Stir ¼ teaspoon cold water into 1 egg yolk. Divide the egg yolk among 3 or 4 small custard cups and tint each part a different bright color with food color of red, green, yellow and pink. Stir to mix the food color and egg yolk. When cookies are ready to bake, paint a design on the top of each with the tinted egg yolk. Use a small, clean, pointed brush for each color. If the egg yolk thickens while standing, add a few drops of cold water and stir.

· *Cookies on sticks:* Arrange popsicle sticks or wooden skewers with pointed ends on a greased baking sheet and place a round of cookie dough on the pointed end of each skewer. Allow at least ½ inch between each cookie. Bake like Extra-Good Sugar Cookies. Remove the pan from the oven and at once place a chocolate-coated candy mint on the center of each cookie. The candy will melt enough to stick to the cookie when it is cool. Use a wide spatula to place the cookies on wire racks to cool.

How to Flour the Cookie Cutter
Spoon a little flour into a small bowl. Dip the cookie cutter into the flour and tap it gently on the edge of the bowl to shake off the loose flour. The flouring keeps the rolled cookie dough from sticking to the cutter. Flour it as many times as you need to while cutting out the cookies.

Easy to hold—and eat

• *Funny face cookies:* While Cookies on Sticks are hot, you can decorate them with chocolate pieces instead of mints to make the features of a funny face. Let Funny Face Cookies cool before handling them so that the decorations will stay on. Or frost the tops of the cooled cookies and decorate them with little candies and nuts.

CHOCOLATE PINKS

Flatter everyone by writing his name on the dark chocolate cookies with pretty Pink Icing

2 (1-ounce) squares unsweetened chocolate
¾ cup soft shortening
1 cup sugar
1 egg
¼ cup light corn syrup
2 cups sifted flour
¼ teaspoon salt
1 teaspoon baking soda
1 teaspoon cinnamon
Pink Icing

Toothpick pen, frosting ink

1. Melt the chocolate in the top of the double boiler over hot, not boiling, water or in a saucepan over low heat. Cool until lukewarm.

2. Beat together the shortening, sugar and egg until light and fluffy. Stir in the chocolate and corn syrup.

3. Sift the flour onto a square of waxed paper or into a bowl and then measure. Sift the measured flour with the salt, baking soda and cinnamon into the chocolate mixture. Beat to mix well.

4. Divide the dough into three parts and chill it in the refrigerator at least 1 hour.

5. When you are ready to bake the cookies, start heating the oven to 350° F.

6. Place ⅓ of the dough on a lightly floured pastry cloth. Keep the rest of the dough in the refrigerator until you are ready to roll it.

Hold the shape

7. Roll the dough from the center to the edge ⅛ inch thick and cut it with a lightly floured cookie cutter. To avoid stretching the cookie cutouts, use a wide spatula to place them ½ inch apart on an ungreased baking sheet.

8. Bake on the rack in the center of the oven 10 to 12 minutes.

9. Remove the pan from the oven and take the cookies from the baking sheet with a wide spatula. Spread them on a wire rack to cool.

10. Roll, cut and bake the remaining two parts of the dough and the scraps, gathered together, in the same way.

11. When the cookies are cool, spread their tops with a creamy powdered sugar icing, tinted pink. Makes about 30 to 36 (3-inch) cookies.

PINK ICING

1 cup sifted powdered sugar
¼ teaspoon salt
½ teaspoon vanilla
1 to 1½ tablespoons cream or water
Red food color

1. Sift the powdered sugar onto a square of waxed paper or into a bowl and then measure. Put the measured powdered sugar, salt and vanilla in a small bowl. Add the cream or water and mix well with a spoon or with the electric mixer on low speed to make an icing that you can spread.

2. Tint the frosting pink with a few drops of red food color.

3. Spread it on the cookies with a spatula. Or make Pink Icing a little thicker, this way—use only about ¾ tablespoon of cold water or 1 tablespoon cream. Write names on the cookies with a toothpick dipped in the icing. Nice for a party.

GRANDMA'S MOLASSES COOKIES

They taste like molasses cookies Grandma used to make but they're topped with a sweet, shiny Sugar Glaze

4 cups sifted flour
1 teaspoon baking soda
½ teaspoon baking powder
1 teaspoon salt
2 teaspoons ginger
½ cup soft shortening
¾ cup sugar
¾ cup molasses
½ cup sour milk or buttermilk
Sugar Glaze

To Decorate Cookies
With a clean, small paintbrush cover the top or edges of rolled cookies with light corn syrup. Then dip the cookies or just edges in colored sugar or tiny candy decorettes that you buy at the supermarket.

Smart Look for Cookies
Cut the rolled dough with cutters of different sizes and shapes. Or make your own patterns. Draw bells, hearts, horses or anything you like on heavy cardboard. Cut out the drawing and grease one side of it. Place it greased side down on the rolled dough, and cut around it with the tip of a small, sharp knife.

See how to sour sweet milk, page 96

1. Sift the flour onto a square of waxed paper and then measure. Sift the measured flour with the baking soda, baking powder, salt and ginger into a medium bowl. Set aside.

2. Beat the shortening in a large bowl with the electric mixer on medium speed or with a spoon until light and fluffy. Gradually add the sugar and beat until very fluffy.

3. Stir in a little of the flour mixture, then a little molasses and sour milk. Keep adding the flour and the molasses and milk until you have used all of them. Start and end the mixing by adding some of the flour. Mix well.

4. Divide the dough into four parts. Cover and chill it at least 4 hours or overnight.

5. When you are ready to bake the cookies, start heating the oven to 400° F. Lightly grease a baking sheet with unsalted shortening or salad oil.

6. Roll out ¼ of the dough at a time from the center to the edge to ¼-inch thickness if you want fat, soft cookies, or to ⅛-inch thickness if you want thinner, more crisp cookies. Use a floured cutter to make the cutouts. To avoid stretching the cutouts, use a wide spatula to place them about ½ inch apart on the baking sheet.

7. Bake on the rack in the center of the oven 7 to 10 minutes.

8. Remove the pan from the oven and take the cookies from the baking sheet with a wide spatula. Spread them on a wire rack to cool. When partly cooled, spread with Sugar Glaze. Makes about 48 cookies.

SUGAR GLAZE

Put 2 cups sifted powdered sugar and 2 to 3 table-spoons milk in a medium bowl. Stir until smooth. Spread on tops of Molasses Cookies while they are slightly warm.

For a change

· *Gingerbread boys:* Cut the dough for Molasses Cookies, rolled ¼ inch thick, with a floured gingerbread-boy cutter. Lift the cutouts with a wide spatula or pancake turner onto a lightly greased baking sheet. Press raisins into the dough for the eyes, nose, a mouth with a smile and shoe and cuff buttons. Use bits snipped from red or green gumdrops with scissors for coat buttons. Bake like Molasses Cookies. You can move the legs and arms of the gingerbread boys

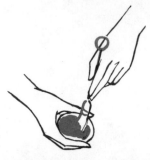

A Good Way to Frost Cookies

Spread Sugar Glaze over cookies with a pastry brush. Use a "runny" frosting—just mix in a little more milk. Place the cookie on a wire rack until the icing dries—with a paper towel underneath to catch the drip. You can tint the icing with food colors.

Run! Gingerbread boys

on the baking sheet, before baking, to make them look as
if they're dancing or running.

GIANT RAISIN COOKIES

Man-sized cookies big enough to satisfy the hungriest cookie
eaters. There's a hint of orange flavor

½ cup cut-up raisins
1½ cups soft shortening
1½ cups sugar
  2 large eggs
  2 teaspoons vanilla
  1 teaspoon grated orange peel
  4 cups sifted flour
  2 teaspoons salt
1½ teaspoons baking powder
⅓ cup milk
Raisins for tops of cookies

1. Cut the raisins coarsely with scissors.

2. Beat the shortening and sugar together in a large
bowl with the electric mixer on medium speed or with a
spoon until fluffy. Add the eggs, vanilla and orange peel.
Beat well.

3. Sift the flour onto a square of waxed paper and then
measure. Sift the measured flour with the salt and baking
powder. Stir a little of the flour into the shortening-sugar
mixture, then stir in a little milk. Mix well. Do this until
all the flour and milk are used.

4. Stir in the cut-up raisins.

5. Divide the dough into three parts and chill 1 hour or
longer in the refrigerator.

6. Start heating the oven to 375° F. Grease a baking
sheet with unsalted shortening or salad oil.

7. Roll one part of the dough at a time from the center
to the edge on a lightly floured surface until a little less
than ¼ inch thick.

8. Cut cookies with an empty 1-pound coffee can or its
lid. Place them 1 inch apart on greased baking sheets.

9. Sprinkle the circles of dough with sugar. Cut the
raisins in strips with scissors. Press the raisins into the
cookies to make initials or names.

10. Bake on the rack in the center of the oven 10 to 12
minutes, or until a light brown.

Raisin names or initials

Christmas Tree Cookies
After Chocolate Pinks or Extra-Good Sugar Cookies are on the baking sheet, push a 1-inch length of drinking straw into each unbaked cookie. You can cut the straws with scissors. Bake the cookies and remove the straws by gently twisting them out while the cookies are still hot. Frost the cooled cookies and decorate with little candies, or as you like. Pull narrow, bright-colored ribbons through the cooled cookies and tie them on the Christmas tree.

11. Remove the pan from the oven and lift the cookies from the baking sheet with a wide spatula. Place them on a wire rack to cool. Store them in a jar with a loose lid. Makes 35 (4-inch) cookies.

LEMON SNAPS

A crisp cookie that's just right for cutting in fancy shapes

1 cup soft butter or margarine
2 cups sugar
3 eggs
1 lemon, juice and peel
3 cups sifted flour

1. Beat the butter and sugar together with a spoon or the electric mixer on medium speed until light and fluffy. Gradually add the eggs and then the lemon juice and grated lemon peel. Beat thoroughly to mix.

2. Sift the flour onto a piece of waxed paper and then measure. Sift the measured flour into the lemon-egg mixture and beat with a spoon or on the mixer's low speed until the soft dough is workable. (You may need to add a little more flour.)

3. Divide the dough into three parts and place in the refrigerator to chill for at least 1 hour, or better still, 3 to 4 hours.

4. When you are ready to bake the cookies, start heating the oven to 375° F.

5. Take one part of the dough from the refrigerator and place it on a lightly floured pastry cloth. (Keep the rest of the dough in the refrigerator.)

6. Roll the dough from the center to the edge until it is ⅛ to ¼ inch thick. With floured cutters, cut as many cookies as possible from the rolled dough.

7. To avoid stretching the cutouts, use a wide spatula to place them about ½ to 1 inch apart on an ungreased baking sheet. Brush the cookie tops with a little cream or egg white mixed with a little cold water. Sprinkle the cookie tops with white or colored sugar.

8. Bake on the rack in the center of the oven about 10 minutes, or until a delicate brown.

9. Remove the pan from the oven and lift the cookies from the baking sheet with a wide spatula. Spread them on a wire rack to cool.

10. Roll, cut and bake the dough left in the refrigerator in the same way. At the last, gather up the scraps of dough, push them together, roll, cut and bake. Makes 40 to 48 (rolled ⅛-inch thick) cookies.

NO-BAKE COOKIES

Here are the easiest of all cookies to make. You don't bake them. So get out a saucepan, stirring spoon and your measuring tools and stir up a batch of cookies in a jiffy. We predict you'll have beginner's luck with them—that means *good* luck.

BUTTERSCOTCH CRUNCHIES

You can make these crunchy cookies with any ready-to-eat cereal flakes. So look in your cupboard and take your pick

  2 (6-ounce) packages butterscotch-flavored morsels
½ cup peanut butter
  6 cups corn flakes

1. In a large saucepan cook and stir butterscotch morsels and peanut butter over medium heat until the mixture melts. Remove from the heat and stir in the corn flakes with a spoon. Mix well.

2. Drop teaspoonfuls of the mixture onto a sheet of waxed paper. Let set. Makes 36 Crunchies.

NO-BAKE CHOCOLATE COOKIES

Stir these cookies up in a jiffy when something to nibble is in order. Let your guests help you make them

  2 cups sugar
½ cup milk
  1 stick butter or margarine (¼ pound)
  3 tablespoons cocoa
  1 teaspoon salt
  3 cups raw quick-cooking rolled oats
  1 teaspoon vanilla
½ cup broken walnuts
  1 cup coconut

1. Put the sugar, milk, butter, cocoa and salt in a large saucepan and bring to a boil. Remove from the heat and stir in the rolled oats, vanilla, nuts and coconut.

2. Drop from a teaspoon onto waxed paper to make 48 cookies.

SAUCEPAN PEANUT COOKIES

Top favorites of schoolboys, fathers and new cooks. No wonder—cookies have that wonderful peanut taste

      1 cup light corn syrup
      1 cup sugar
   1½ cups peanut butter
      4 cups cereal flakes

1. Mix the corn syrup and sugar in a medium saucepan. Bring the mixture to a full boil. Remove from the heat and stir in the peanut butter and cereal flakes. Mix well.

2. Drop heaping teaspoonfuls onto a buttered baking sheet. Makes 48 cookies.

Favorite cakes and frostings

BEAUTIFUL cakes bring lots of joy. What could take their place at birthday parties and wedding receptions? And what tastes better any time than homemade cake covered with pretty frosting?

There are two big cake families—traditional cakes made "from scratch" and cakes made with packaged mixes. The cook measures and mixes all the ingredients when she makes "from scratch" cakes, but with "box cakes"—the name she often gives to cakes made with a mix—much of the measuring and mixing is already done for her. We give you recipes for traditional or "from scratch" cakes to bake in layer pans, oblong pans, or in muffin pans to make cupcakes. You really do not need recipes for mix cakes. All you have to do is follow the directions on the packages.

The "from scratch" cakes in this Cookbook are favorites in *Farm Journal*'s Test Kitchens. They have that wonderful homemade taste, and they're made by quick, up-to-date methods. Before we give you the recipes, here's what good cakes are made of—what you put in the mixing bowl.

Ingredients for cakes

Flour is to cake what a foundation is to a house. Be sure to use the kind that the recipe calls for—cake or all-purpose flour. Cake flour is milled from soft wheat, which means it contains less gluten, a protein in flour, than all-purpose flour. It makes a lighter, higher cake, but you can bake good cakes with all-purpose flour if you use recipes designed for it.

Baking powder makes cakes light and somewhat porous instead of heavy.

Eggs add richness and some of the liquid, which binds or holds the ingredients together.

Sugar sweetens cakes and makes them tender and good-tasting.

Fats, such as vegetable shortenings (the kind that comes in 1- and 3-pound cans), butter, margarine and lard, also make cakes tender and rich. They give cakes what home economists call good eating quality. *Be sure to use the kind of fat listed in the recipe.*

Liquids, usually milk, bind the ingredients together.

Tips on mixing cake batters

Our recipes give the directions for mixing cakes with the electric mixer and/or a spoon. If you use an electric mixer, set the dial at the speed given in the recipe. Stop the beaters often and scrape them and the sides and bottom of the bowl with a rubber spatula (scraper). If you use a spoon, make vigorous strokes and count them—the recipes tell how many strokes are needed. Guessing may spoil the cake.

It is important to mix the ingredients as directed. Beating brings the flour and liquid together and develops enough gluten (a protein in flour) to make the cake hold its shape. And when the baking powder and liquid are mixed together in the batter and heated in the oven, carbon-dioxide bubbles form. They make the cake rise in the pan and make it light.

You can mix cake batters easier and better if you take the fat from the refrigerator ahead of time to warm to room temperature. One hour is long enough. It is especially important to warm hard fats, like butter and some margarines. Many of the vegetable shortenings are kept in the cupboard rather than in the refrigerator, so they will be ready to mix when measured. Eggs will beat up better, too, if at room temperature, but keep them in the refrigerator until a short time before you are ready to bake the cake. And unless the weather is very hot and humid, it's a good idea to let the milk from the refrigerator warm at room temperature with the eggs.

Measuring the right ingredients accurately is important but the cake will not be good unless they then are mixed properly, too. All you have to do is follow the recipes and for cake mixes, the label directions. Home economists have made hundreds of tests to work out the recipes and mixes, carefully balancing the ingredients. Remember that a cake recipe is like a doctor's prescription that the druggist must follow exactly.

Baking cakes

Before you mix the batter, always start the oven heating to the temperature given in the recipe. Put the pan of batter on a rack just below the center of the oven so that the top of the pan will be in the center of the oven. In this position, the cake has the best chance of browning just right—a golden brown.

When baking 2 cake layers, leave at least 1 inch of space between the pans and between the pans and the walls of the oven. Then the heat can circulate around them and bake the batter evenly. If your oven seems too fast or too slow, have the gas or electric company check the temperature control and adjust it. Cakes baked in an oven that is not hot enough are pale, the surface is pitted and the texture is coarse. If the oven is too hot, the cake browns too much and cracks and humps up in the center.

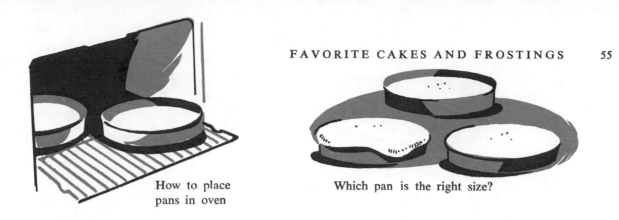

How to place
pans in oven

Which pan is the right size?

Use cake pans of right size

Use pans of the size suggested in the recipe. Pans that are too small make a lot of work—the batter runs over and oven cleaning is quite an unpleasant chore. Also the cake will look unattractive. Pans that are too large produce thin cakes that are pale in color. Cakes baked in pans of the right size have a golden brown crust, a slightly rounded top.

How to prepare cake pans

There are two ways to prepare cake pans so the cakes will not stick to them. Take your choice. (1) Set the pan on a sheet of *plain wrapping paper* and draw around the bottom with a pencil. Cut out the pattern you've made, and place the paper in the pan. It should lie flat and cover all of the bottom of the pan. You can buy packages of paper cake pan liners in many supermarkets. (2) Grease the bottom and sides of the pan with shortening, about 1 tablespoon shortening divided between 2 layer cake pans. Shake a little flour (about 1 tablespoon for 2 layer cake pans) in the greased pan to coat the sides and bottom. Then hold the pan upside down over the working surface and tap the bottom so all the loose flour will fall out.

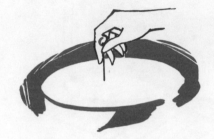

Tests for doneness

Keep the oven door closed until the baking time is up. (If you peek at the cake while it bakes, you may let cool air into the oven.) With the cake in the oven, touch its center lightly and quickly with a finger tip. If the mark or imprint made by the finger springs back or does not remain, the cake is done. You can double-check the doneness by sticking a cake tester or a wooden pick in the center of the cake. If it comes out clean and dry, the cake is done. When the cake does not test done by either method, bake it a little longer and test again.

How to cool cakes

Take the pan from the oven at once when the cake tests done and set it on a wire rack. Let it stand 10 minutes—hot cake is tender and breaks easily. When the 10 minutes are up, loosen the cake around the edges with a spatula. Place another cooling rack on top of the

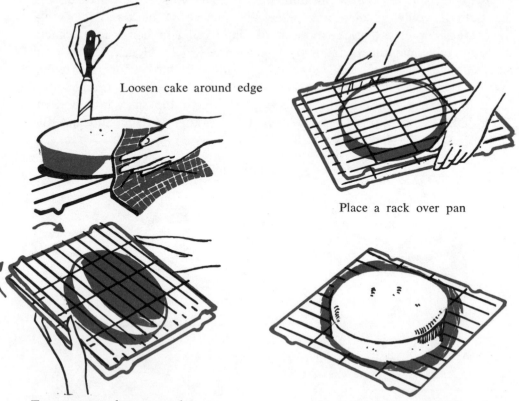

Loosen cake around edge

Place a rack over pan

Turn pan over between racks

Right side up to cool

cake and turn the pan of cake and the rack together upside down. Place the rack now holding the cake on the counter or work surface. Lift off the pan and peel off the paper lining if you used one. Then place another rack lightly on top of the cake and turn both racks (the cake between them) upside down. The top of the cake will be right side up. If you let a cake rest on its rounded top while cooling, it may crack. Complete the cooling and you'll be ready to frost the cake.

How to make oblong cakes

Mix cake batter as directed in recipes that follow; bake it in a 13×9×2-inch pan. If you want to remove the cake from the pan to frost it, you can line the bottom of the pan with paper cut to fit or grease and flour it as for layer cakes. If you want to leave the cake in the pan and frost only the top, just lightly grease the bottom of the pan with shortening (no need to line the pan with paper). Bake the oblong cake on the rack just below the center of the oven at 350° F. 35 to 40 minutes. Test for doneness. Set the cake on a wire rack to cool.

If you are going to remove the cake from the pan to frost it, loosen it around the edges with a spatula or a knife when it has cooled 10 minutes. Turn it out on a wire cooling rack and peel off the paper liner if you used one. Complete the cooling. If you want to store the cake in the pan, frost the top of the cool cake, cover and keep in a cool place.

How to make cupcakes

Place packaged paper liners (the kind you buy in supermarkets) in medium-size (2½-inch) muffin-pan cups. Or lightly grease the bottoms only of the muffin-pan cups. Fill the cups half full with the cake batter. Bake cupcakes on the rack just below the center of the oven at 350° F. 20 to 25 minutes. Test for doneness. If you used paper liners, lift cupcakes out of the pan and place them on wire cooling racks. Peel off paper liners when the cupcakes are cool or serve them in the paper liners. The liners will help keep them from drying out. If you did not use paper liners, let the pan of cupcakes cool 5 minutes on a wire rack, loosen them around the edges with a spatula and lift them out. Complete the cooling on wire racks.

How to freeze cakes

All of the cakes in this Cookbook covered with frostings made from our recipes may be frozen successfully. Cover a piece of cardboard with aluminum foil, place the cake on it and freeze, unwrapped, until firm. Then wrap the frozen cake. When you are ready to use the cake, unwrap it, place it on a wire rack and let it thaw at room temperature. It takes about 2 hours to thaw a frozen frosted cake and 30 minutes for cupcakes. If you want to freeze *unfrosted* cake and frost it just before serving, thaw it in its wrapper at room temperature. Layers will thaw in 1 hour.

If you want to freeze an oblong or loaf cake to use 2 or 3 days later, you can freeze it in the pan in which you baked the cake. If the cake pan has a cover, put it on, or make a cover for the pan with a piece of aluminum foil.

How to cut round cakes

Sooner or later everybody is asked to cut the cake. Learn how to do it right, and you'll then be ready when you're asked. Use a sharp knife with a thin blade. Stick the point of the knife into the cake, holding the handle straight up and the point down. Slice by pulling the knife toward you and use short, sawing motions. Do not press down on the cake. If the frosting sticks to the knife, rinse the knife in hot water (if you are cutting the cake in the kitchen) or wipe it off with a dampened clean towel or a paper napkin.

To follow the diagrams below for cutting cakes, first make the cut shown in color, next the cut indicated by a dotted line.

Start knife point in center

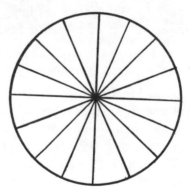

Easy-to-cut wedges

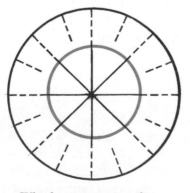

Wheel cut=more wedges

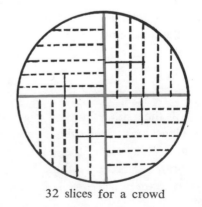

32 slices for a crowd

1. Cut the cake in wedges the size you want.

2. Or cut around the cake in a circle halfway between the center and the edge of the cake. You will have two circles. Cut pieces from the outer circle and remove them to a serving plate. Then cut pieces from the inner circle.

3. Or cut the cake into four quarters. Then cut each quarter into slices. The slices will not be exactly the same size, but you can cut the two pieces nearest the middle of each quarter in half to even up the servings. You get 32 slices.

How to cut oblong and square cakes

1. To cut an oblong cake in bars, first cut the cake into thirds lengthwise to make 3 strips of equal width (3 inches). Then cut the cake in half crosswise. Cut *each* half crosswise into fourths, making 12 bars. You will have a total of 24 servings.

2. To cut an oblong cake in diamonds, first cut diagonally across the cake from corner to corner. Then make 4 lengthwise cuts across the cake to divide it into 5 strips of equal width (almost 2½ inches). Start at one narrow side and cut diagonally (from end of each of the 4 lengthwise cuts) across the cake parallel to the first diagonal cut. Repeat, starting at the other narrow side of the cake. You will have 20 diamonds and 10 half diamonds.

3. To cut a 9-inch square cake in triangles, first make 2 vertical cuts across the cake to divide it into 3 equal strips. Then, without moving the cake, make 2 horizontal cuts to divide the cake into 3 equal strips. You will have 9 (3-inch) squares. Next, cut diagonally across each square. You will have 18 triangles.

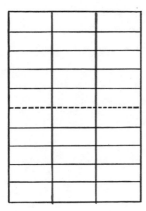

30 bars for 30 guests

Diamonds and triangles

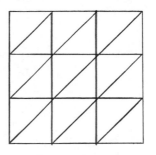

Cutting a square cake

TRADITIONAL CAKES

OLD-TIME YELLOW CAKE

You use cake flour, whole eggs and butter to make this cake by the Creaming Method

2¾ cups sifted cake flour
2½ teaspoons baking powder
1 teaspoon salt
½ cup butter
1½ cups sugar
3 eggs
1 teaspoon vanilla
1 cup milk

1. Take butter, milk and eggs out of refrigerator to warm to room temperature.

2. Start heating the oven to 350° F. Grease and flour or line 2 (9×1½-inch) round layer cake pans with paper cut to fit.

3. Sift the cake flour onto a sheet of waxed paper and then measure it into the sifter. Add the baking powder and salt; sift together 3 times. Set aside.

4. Place the butter in the large bowl of the electric mixer and stir until it softens.

5. Add sugar gradually, beating until light and fluffy.

6. Add eggs, one at a time, beating well after each. Add vanilla.

7. Add ¼ of the flour mixture to butter mixture and mix until smooth; add ⅓ of the milk and mix until smooth. Continue until all ingredients are used. Stop the electric mixer often and scrape the beaters and bowl.

8. Pour half the batter into one layer pan, the other half into the second pan. Be sure to divide the batter equally between the two pans.

9. Bake the cake layers on the rack just below the center of the oven 30 to 35 minutes. Leave space between the pans so the heat can circulate. Test for doneness.

10. Cool the cake.

For a change

· To make an oblong (13×9×2-inch) cake or 24 medium-size cupcakes from this recipe, follow directions at beginning of chapter.

COUNTRY LARD CAKE

You make this big yellow cake by a special Meringue Method, using lard and cake flour

    3 eggs
1½ cups sugar
    ⅓ cup lard
2¼ cups sifted cake flour
    3 teaspoons baking powder
    1 teaspoon salt
    1 cup milk
    1 teaspoon vanilla

1. Start heating the oven to 350° F. Grease and flour or line the bottom of 2 (9×1½-inch) round layer cake pans with paper cut to fit.

2. Separate egg yolks and whites in 2 bowls.

3. Beat the egg whites with a hand or electric beater until they are frothy. Then add ½ cup of the sugar gradually, beating until stiff, glossy peaks form.

4. Place the lard in the large bowl of the electric mixer and stir until it softens.

5. Sift the flour onto a sheet of waxed paper and then measure. Sift the flour with the baking powder, salt and the rest of the sugar (1 cup) over the lard.

6. Add ¾ cup milk and the vanilla. Mix on low speed of mixer until all the dry ingredients are dampened. Beat 1 minute more on medium speed of the mixer or 150 vigorous strokes by hand (count the strokes). Stop the mixer often and scrape the beaters and bowl with a rubber spatula.

7. Add the rest of the milk (¼ cup) and the egg yolks. Beat 1 minute more with mixer at medium speed or 150 vigorous strokes by hand (count the strokes). Stop the mixer often and scrape the beaters and bowl with a rubber spatula.

8. Fold the egg-white mixture into the batter. Use a rubber spatula (scraper) and cut down through the batter, across the bottom of the bowl, up on the opposite side. Turn the scraper upside down just below the top surface of the batter and move it across the bowl. Turn the bowl a little and repeat. Keep on mixing the batter in the same way, rotating the bowl a little each time, until the egg white is mixed into the batter.

Why Fold Egg Whites into Batters with Care
When you beat egg whites, you trap air in them. These air bubbles expand when they are heated in the oven and help make the cake light. That is why it is important to fold the beaten egg whites gently into the batter. You want to keep in as much of the air as possible.

Down, across, up and over

Turn bowl as you fold

Baking soda+acid=baking powder. When milk or other liquid touches the acid in baking powder, it starts action in the soda, which then gives off bubbles of carbon dioxide gas. The bubbles of gas and the air you beat into the batter make the cake rise. During the baking, the heat expands the bubbles and they form spaces. These spaces plus the steam that forms from the liquid when the batter gets hot in the oven make cakes light (also biscuits and other quick breads). Liquid expands greatly when it becomes steam—1 teaspoon liquid makes about 1600 teaspoons steam. Steam is vapor, so much of it evaporates from the batter, but enough is left to help make cakes light.

9. Pour half the batter into one layer pan, the other half into the second pan. Be sure to divide the batter equally between the two pans.

10. Bake the cake layers on the rack just below the center of the oven 30 to 35 minutes. Leave space between the pans. Test for doneness.

11. Cool the cake.

For a change

· To make an oblong (13×9×2-inch) cake or 30 medium-size cupcakes from this recipe, follow directions at beginning of chapter.

ONE-BOWL YELLOW CAKE

You use all-purpose flour and vegetable shortening to make this cake by the Quick Mix Method

½ cup vegetable shortening
2¼ cups sifted all-purpose flour
3½ teaspoons baking powder
1 teaspoon salt
1½ cups sugar
1 cup milk
1 teaspoon vanilla
3 eggs

1. Start heating the oven to 350°F. Grease and flour or line the bottom of 2 (9×1½-inch) round layer cake pans with paper cut to fit.

2. Place the shortening in the large bowl of the electric mixer and stir until it softens.

3. Sift the flour onto a sheet of waxed paper and then measure it into a sifter.

4. Add the baking powder, salt and sugar to the flour and sift the mixture over the shortening.

5. Add ¾ cup milk and vanilla. Mix on low speed of mixer until all the ingredients are dampened. Beat 2 minutes on medium speed of electric mixer or 300 vigorous strokes by hand (count the strokes). Stop the electric mixer often and scrape the bowl and beaters with a rubber spatula (scraper).

6. Add the rest of the milk (¼ cup) and the eggs and mix again on low speed. Beat 2 minutes more on medium

When to Buy New Baking Powder
If your baking powder is caked, it means that moisture has gotten in and it's lost its leavening power. Throw it out. Baking powder is one of the least expensive ingredients in your recipe. Don't take a chance on it and waste other ingredients.

speed or 300 strokes by hand. Stop the mixer often and scrape the beaters and bowl.

7. Pour half the batter into one layer pan, the other half into the second pan. Be sure to divide the batter equally between the two pans.

8. Bake the cake layers on the rack just below the center of the oven 30 to 35 minutes. Leave space between the pans. Test for doneness.

9. Cool the cake.

For a one-bowl yellow cake made with cake flour

Follow the directions for the cake made with all-purpose flour, but use 2½ cups cake flour and 3 teaspoons baking powder.

For a change

· To make an oblong (13×9×2-inch) cake or 24 medium-size cupcakes from this recipe, follow directions at beginning of chapter.

SNOWY WHITE LAYER CAKE

You will have 3 egg yolks left over when you make this cake. Use them in Chocolate Satin Frosting

See recipe for Chocolate Satin Frosting, page 71

½ cup vegetable shortening
2¼ cups sifted cake flour
3 teaspoons baking powder
½ teaspoon salt
1⅓ cups sugar
1 cup milk
1 teaspoon vanilla
3 egg whites

1. Start heating the oven to 350° F. Grease and flour or line the bottom of 2 (8×1½-inch) round layer cake pans with paper cut to fit.

2. Place the shortening in the large bowl of the electric mixer and stir until it softens.

3. Sift the flour onto a sheet of waxed paper and then measure. Add the baking powder, salt and sugar to the measured flour. Sift the mixture over the shortening.

4. Add ¾ cup milk and the vanilla and mix until all the ingredients are dampened. Beat 2 minutes on medium speed of electric mixer or 300 vigorous strokes by hand (count

About Cake Pans
When baking cake in heat-proof oven glass, use a temperature 25° F. lower than the recipe calls for. But use the same baking time called for in the recipe. The glass absorbs more heat than metal cake pans and passes it on to the cake. The cake will have a thicker, browner crust unless you bake it at the lower temperature.

So handy: an egg separator

the strokes). Stop the electric mixer often and scrape the bowl and beaters with a rubber spatula (scraper).

5. Add the rest of the milk (¼ cup) and the egg whites. Mix well. Beat 2 minutes more on medium speed of the mixer or 300 strokes by hand (count the strokes). Stop the mixer often and scrape the beaters and bowl with a rubber spatula.

6. Pour half the batter into one layer pan, the other half into the second pan. Be sure to divide the batter equally between the two pans.

7. Place the cakes on the rack just below the center of the oven. Allow some space between the pans.

8. Bake the cakes 25 to 30 minutes. Test for doneness.

9. Cool the cake.

For a change
· To make 24 medium-size cupcakes from this recipe, follow directions at beginning of chapter.

EASY CHOCOLATE FUDGE CAKE

Another Quick Mix recipe for cake that's fudgy and rich

    3 squares unsweetened chocolate
    ½ cup vegetable shortening
    1¾ cups sifted all-purpose flour
    1 teaspoon baking soda
    1 teaspoon salt
    1½ cups sugar
    1 cup milk
    1 teaspoon vanilla
    2 eggs

1. Start heating the oven to 350° F. Grease and flour or line the bottom of 2 (8×1½-inch) round layer cake pans with paper cut to fit.

2. Melt the chocolate in the top of the double boiler over hot, not boiling, water or in a saucepan set in a pan of hot water. Remove it from the heat and cool it slightly.

3. Place the shortening in the large bowl of the electric mixer and stir until it softens.

4. Sift the flour onto a sheet of waxed paper and then measure. Sift the measured flour, baking soda, salt and sugar together over the shortening.

5. Add ¾ cup of milk and the vanilla. Mix until all the dry ingredients are dampened. Beat 1 minute on medium speed of electric mixer or 150 vigorous strokes by hand (count the strokes). Stop the mixer often and scrape the bowl and beaters with a rubber spatula (scraper).

6. Add the melted chocolate. Beat 1 minute more with mixer at medium speed, or 150 strokes by hand (count the strokes). Stop the mixer often and scrape the bowl and beaters.

7. Add the rest of the milk (¼ cup) and the eggs. Mix well. Beat 1 minute more on the mixer, or 150 strokes by hand (count the strokes). Stop the mixer often and scrape the bowl and beaters.

8. Pour half the batter into one layer pan, the other half into the second pan. Be sure to divide the batter equally between the two pans.

9. Bake the cakes on the rack just below the center of the oven 30 to 35 minutes. Test for doneness.

10. Cool the cake.

For a change
· To make 24 medium-size cupcakes from this recipe, follow directions at beginning of chapter.

Flavor With Orchids
Pure vanilla that you buy in bottles is the extract of the seeds of an orchid that is native to Mexico. The ancient Aztec Indians there discovered how good the taste and fragrance of these seeds were when added to foods. Early Spanish explorers liked vanilla, too, and they introduced it to Europe. Imitation vanilla is made of entirely different substances that imitate the vanilla flavor.

CUPCAKES

QUICK COCOA CUPCAKES

Make these cupcakes when you want a treat—quick

½ cup vegetable shortening
½ cup sifted cocoa
1 cup milk
1½ cups sifted all-purpose flour
1 teaspoon baking soda
1 teaspoon salt
1⅓ cups sugar
2 eggs
1 teaspoon vanilla

1. Start heating the oven to 350° F. Grease the bottoms only of 24 muffin-pan cups. Or use paper liners (the kind you buy in supermarkets).

Measure and Be Sure
Never fill cupcake pans more than half full unless the recipe suggests otherwise. Here's how you can be certain your cupcake pan is exactly half full: measure depth of cup with ruler; make a pencil mark halfway between top and bottom; pour batter to this mark in each cup.

2. Stir the shortening in a large bowl to soften it. Sift the cocoa, measure and add it to the shortening. Measure the 1 cup milk, and add 2 tablespoonfuls of this milk to the cocoa-shortening. Beat carefully until the mixture is smooth and satiny.

3. Sift the flour onto a square of waxed paper and then measure. Sift the flour, baking soda, salt and sugar together over the cocoa mixture.

4. Add the rest of the milk and mix only until all the dry ingredients are dampened. Beat 2 minutes on medium speed of the electric mixer, or 300 vigorous strokes by hand (count the strokes). Stop the mixer often and scrape the beaters and bowl.

5. Add the eggs and vanilla. Stir to mix well. Beat 2 minutes more on medium speed of the mixer, or 300 strokes by hand (count the strokes). Stop the mixer often and scrape the beaters and bowl.

6. Fill the muffin-pan cups half full with batter and bake them 20 to 25 minutes. Test for doneness.

7. Lift cupcakes in paper liners from the pans and place them on wire cooling racks. Peel off paper liners when they are cool or serve the cupcakes in the liners. If you did not use paper liners, let the pan of cupcakes cool on a wire rack, loosen them around the edge with a spatula or a small knife. Lift them out and complete cooling them on wire racks. Makes 24 medium cupcakes.

THREE-TIER PARTY CAKE

Cupcakes are easy on the hostess because there's no cutting. Here's a neat way to serve them

1. Use the removable tube part of your angel food pan as a start for the tiers.

2. Cut 2 cardboard circles, one 7½ inches, the other 5½ inches in diameter. Cut holes in the center of the cardboard circles just large enough to slip over the tube to form tiers.

3. Place the tube part on a 12-inch cake plate. Cut a cross in the center of a 12-inch paper doilie and slip it over the tube to cover the bottom tier.

4. Twist a rubber band around the tube several times to form a secure base for the next tier, about 2½ inches from the bottom. Slip the 7½-inch cardboard circle over the tube.

Cover it with an 8-inch paper doilie the way you covered the plate.

5. Twist another rubber band around the tube several times to secure the third tier, about 2½ inches from the second tier. Slip the 5½-inch cardboard circle over the tube and cover it with a 6-inch paper doilie.

6. Arrange the frosted cupcakes on the three tiers. You can buy candy letters spelling "Happy Birthday" at the dime store and place them on the frosted cakes for decoration.

7. Place a slender bottle filled with a little water in the center of the tube and insert a cluster of fresh flowers in it. You can use artificial flowers in the wintertime.

Make a cupcake server

CAKES MADE FROM MIXES

When you are in a supermarket, take a look at the many packages of cake mixes lined up on the shelves. All you have to do is follow label directions *exactly* to make successful cakes. It is important that you not try to improve the mixes. If you add more eggs than called for on the label, your cake may be tough. Or if you use fewer eggs, your cake may be crumbly—eggs help hold together all the ingredients in a cake. And if you add milk when the directions call for water, your cake may be coarse and dry because the mix already contains dry milk.

PINK AND WHITE LOAF CAKE

Spread chocolate frosting on this pretty pink and white marble cake and serve with vanilla ice cream

 1 package white cake mix
½ teaspoon peppermint extract or 4 drops
    oil of peppermint
Few drops red food color
Creamy Chocolate Frosting

1. Start heating the oven to 350° F. Grease a 9×5×3-inch loaf pan and line the bottom with plain wrapping paper cut to fit.

2. Make the cake batter according to directions on the package. Divide the batter in half. To one bowl of batter add the peppermint flavoring and red food color, a drop at a time, to tint it a *delicate* pink.

Batter in two colors

Zigzag to marbleize

Plate over pan and turn

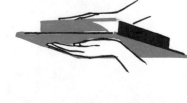

Now peaches are on top

3. Add a spoonful of white batter to the loaf pan and then one of the pink batter. Do this until you use all the batter. Then run the tip of a knife through the batter a few times in the shape of the letter *Z*. Or cut through the batter with the tip of a knife or spatula in zigzag lines, first one way and then the other. You can try both ways to see which design you like better. The knife mixes the white and pink batters—marbleizes them.

4. Bake the cake 45 minutes. Test for doneness by sticking a wooden pick or cake tester into the cake. If it comes out clean and dry, the cake is done.

5. Cool the cake. When it is cool, frost top and sides with chocolate frosting.

UPSIDE-DOWN PEACH GINGERBREAD

This peachy dessert is good hot or cold and so easy to make

1 (1-pound) can sliced peaches
3 tablespoons butter or margarine
½ cup brown sugar, packed firmly
1 package gingerbread mix

1. Drain the peaches in a sieve. Save and refrigerate the juice to use in making cold fruit drinks or gelatin salads.

2. Start heating the oven to 350° F.

3. Put the butter in a 9×9×2-inch pan. Set it in the oven until the butter melts. Remove the pan from the oven.

4. Sprinkle the brown sugar over the butter in the pan and arrange the drained peach slices on top. Make an even layer of the peaches.

5. Make the gingerbread batter as directed on the package. Pour the batter over the peaches.

6. Bake the gingerbread 40 to 45 minutes. Test for doneness. Remove from oven, allow to stand 5 minutes.

7. Place a serving plate on top of the pan and turn the pan and plate at the same time until the pan is on top. Let stand 1 minute, remove pan slowly.

8. Serve the gingerbread hot or cold, cut into 3-inch squares. You can top each serving with a scoop of vanilla ice cream, whipped cream or dessert topping in a pressure can. Makes 9 servings.

You can give the cakes you bake glamor by frosting them. And the frostings add the rich sweetness that makes cakes taste extra-good. All of our recipes are for frostings that are easy to whip up to a creamy, velvety spread.

Cool all cakes thoroughly on wire racks before frosting. Then brush the loose crumbs off the cake with a pastry brush.

Frosting 2-layer cakes

Line a large plate with 4 strips of waxed paper (see illustration). Set the plate on top of a mixing bowl that is at least 1 inch smaller across than the plate. This makes it easy to turn the cake when you're frosting it.

Place the bottom layer upside down on the plate, and with a metal spatula, spread about ⅓ of the frosting on top of it.

Place the top layer, right side up, on top of the frosted bottom layer. Then frost the sides of the cake. First, apply a thin layer of frosting, pulling the spatula around the cake to seal in the crumbs. Then add more frosting, using upward strokes. If the top layer slips or slides, stick a wire cake tester (a clean knitting needle will do) through both layers to hold them together. Bring the frosting up high on the sides— up to the top—and build up a *narrow* edge of frosting on top, all around.

Spread the frosting on top of the cake. Swirl it on just to the built-up edge. Don't just spread it in a smooth layer. You can sprinkle the top

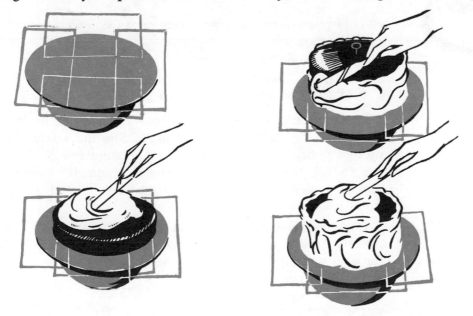

of the cake with chopped nuts, little candies or whatever decoration you like. The small chocolate candies that have coatings of several colors are very gay-looking. And for Halloween, candy corn makes a pretty trim. Candied cherries also are pretty. Use your imagination in adding decorations.

Let the frosting set a few minutes. Then carefully pull out the 4 strips of waxed paper. The cake plate will be clean.

Frosting oblong or loaf cakes

You can leave the cake in the pan and spread and swirl the frosting on top. If you take the cake out of the pan, first frost its sides and then swirl the frosting on the top the way you frost a layer cake.

Frosting cupcakes

The easiest way is to hold the cupcake in your hand and twirl it lightly in a bowl of frosting. Place the cakes on a wire rack and let the frosting set. If you want to add whole pecan or walnut halves to each cupcake, put them in the center of the cakes before the frosting sets.

Frosting Slick Trick

Sweet Arithmetic
The powdered sugar in a 1-pound package measures from 4 to 4½ cups when sifted.

BUTTER CREAM FROSTING

You won't go wrong on this frosting—it's delicious on all kinds of cake and it's buttery rich and easy to spread

    1 (1-pound) package powdered sugar
    ¼ teaspoon salt
    4 tablespoons milk or cream
    1 teaspoon vanilla
    6 tablespoons soft butter or margarine (¾ stick)

1. Empty the package of powdered sugar into a medium bowl. Add the salt, milk and vanilla. Stir the mixture to make a rather stiff, doughy paste. (If mixture is too stiff to stir and all the sugar is not dampened, add ¼ teaspoon milk at a time until you can stir the mixture and all the sugar is dampened.)

2. Add the butter and beat the mixture until it is smooth. Spread the frosting on cool cake. Makes enough for sides and tops of 2 (8- or 9-inch) round cake layers or about 30 cupcakes.

For a change
· *Orange butter cream:* Omit the milk and vanilla in Butter Cream Frosting and instead use ¼ cup orange juice and 1 teaspoon orange peel.
· *Lemon butter cream:* Omit the milk and vanilla in Butter Cream Frosting and instead use ¼ cup lemon juice and 1 teaspoon grated lemon peel.

CHOCOLATE SATIN FROSTING

A good frosting just right for Snowy White Layer Cake. It's the best way to use the leftover egg yolks

Frosting Trick
With a teaspoon: Turn the spoon upside down and press it gently into the frosting to make a scallop. Make rows of scallops over the top of the cake.

3 squares unsweetened chocolate
1½ cups sifted powdered sugar
3 tablespoons hot water
3 egg yolks
2 tablespoons soft butter

1. Melt the chocolate in the top of a double boiler over hot, not boiling, water.

2. Remove it from the hot water and add the powdered sugar and hot water. Stir the mixture until it is smooth.

See recipe for Snowy White Layer Cake, page 63

3. Add the egg yolks, one at a time, and beat after adding each egg until smooth.

4. Add the butter, 1 tablespoon at a time, and beat until smooth after each addition.

5. Cool the frosting, beating occasionally, until it is right for spreading. Makes enough frosting for 24 cupcakes or the sides and tops of 2 (8-inch) round cake layers.

BITTERSWEET CHOCOLATE FROSTING

Velvety and good—use this frosting on Country Lard Cake

See recipe for Country Lard Cake, page 61

3 squares unsweetened chocolate
1 (1-pound) package powdered sugar
⅛ teaspoon salt
½ cup evaporated milk
1 teaspoon vanilla
¼ cup soft butter or margarine (½ stick)

Too Thick or Too Thin?
If Chocolate Satin Frosting gets too stiff while you are spreading it on the cake, place it over hot water. If it gets too thin, set it over ice water.

1. Melt the chocolate in the double boiler over hot, not boiling, water.

2. Stir the powdered sugar, salt, undiluted evaporated milk

(just as it comes from the can) and vanilla in a medium mixing bowl to mix thoroughly.

3. Stir in the melted chocolate and the butter. Beat the frosting with a spoon until it is smooth and creamy. If the frosting is too stiff to spread smoothly, beat in a few drops of milk. Makes enough to frost the sides and tops of 2 (8- or 9-inch) round cake layers or 24 cupcakes.

PENUCHE FROSTING

Its rich butterscotch flavor makes all of our cakes super

½ cup dark brown sugar, packed firmly
3 tablespoons water
⅛ teaspoon salt
3 tablespoons soft butter or margarine
2 cups sifted powdered sugar

1. Mix the brown sugar, water and salt in a small saucepan. Stir the mixture over high heat just until the syrup comes to a full boil. Remove from the heat at once.

2. Add 1 tablespoon butter. Let the mixture cool about 10 minutes or until the bottom of the saucepan feels lukewarm, neither hot nor cold.

3. While the syrup cools, sift the powdered sugar onto a sheet of waxed paper. Then measure it into a medium bowl.

4. Pour the lukewarm syrup over the powdered sugar. Stir and beat until the frosting is smooth. Beat in the rest of the butter (2 tablespoons) and beat until the frosting spreads smoothly on the cakes. Makes enough to frost 18 to 24 cupcakes or an 8- or 9-inch square cake.

Skip the Sifting
When you use powdered sugar from an opened package, it may contain lumps. Sift the sugar or put it through a sieve to remove the lumps. If you use powdered sugar from an unopened package, it rarely has lumps. You can skip the sifting.

Pies that please

APPLE Pie . . . Cherry . . . Pumpkin . . . Lemon Meringue Pie. Which will you bake first? These are the Big Four in American pies, but there are many other favorites. Learn to bake good pies and you'll never have to ask yourself: What shall I fix for dessert?

You can serve pie proudly just as it is, but many cooks add a topping. Ice cream is a favorite on Apple Pie, whipped cream the traditional choice for Pumpkin Pie. For a change, serve sharp Cheddar cheese with these two pies, or with Cherry Pie—it's a tasty combination!

Kinds of piecrust

It's the crust that makes or breaks a pie, so let's start with it. We give you a choice of making your pastry with a solid fat, such as lard or vegetable shortening; with a vegetable oil or salad oil; and by the paste method, sometimes called Beginner's Pastry. All of these make excellent piecrust, and the kind you choose will depend on the ingredients you have and which method is easier for you. Many farm cooks, who are recognized as wonderful pie bakers, consider piecrust made with lard the most tender and flaky. Other superior cooks like best the pastry (slightly more mealy) made with salad oil. So take your choice, but follow the recipe you select and make no substitutions. Use all-purpose flour. You also can buy packaged piecrust mix ready to crumble into a bowl. You just add water, mix it and roll it out.

Then there are crumb crusts, often used for one-crust pies that chill in the refrigerator instead of baking. Follow whichever recipe you choose, down to the last word. That's the best insurance for good homemade pies.

Piepans

A glass piepan is ideal for baking pies because it absorbs the heat and browns the pastry attractively. You can use enamel, darkened tin or anodized aluminum piepans, but shiny piepans give pies a soggy bottom crust.

PASTRY MADE WITH SOLID FAT

For a 9-inch 2-crust pie:
 2 cups sifted flour
 1 teaspoon salt
⅔ cup plus 2 tablespoons lard or vegetable shortening
¼ cup cold water

1. Stir the flour and salt together in a medium bowl to mix. Then cut in the shortening with a pastry blender until the crumbs are the size of small peas.

2. Sprinkle the cold water (ice water is fine) into the flour mixture, 1 tablespoon at a time. Mix lightly with a fork until all the flour is moistened.

3. Mix the dough with a fork until it sticks together and leaves the sides of the bowl almost clean. Try not to mix it too much—that toughens pastry.

4. Take the pastry from the bowl and with cupped hands, smooth it into a ball. You are ready to roll it.

Pastry maker's friends

For an 8-inch 2-crust pie: Use 1½ cups sifted flour, ¾ teaspoon salt, ½ cup plus 2 tablespoons shortening and 3 tablespoons cold water. Mix like pastry for a 9-inch pie.

For an 8- or 9-inch 1-crust pie: Use 1 cup sifted flour, ½ teaspoon salt, ⅓ cup plus 1 tablespoon shortening and 2 tablespoons cold water. Mix like pastry for a 2-crust pie.

Cut dough in half, flatten

HOW TO ROLL PASTRY

This is important, so follow the directions carefully.

1. Use a pastry cloth and a stockinet-covered rolling pin to help you avoid adding too much flour, which will make pastry tough. Rub a little flour into pastry cloth.

2. For a 2-crust pie, cut the ball of pastry in half with a knife. On the pastry cloth flatten half of the pastry with

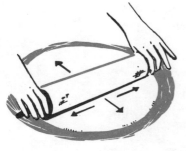

Roll from center to edges   Use piepan to measure   Fold crust to lift easily

your hands to make a circle. This will be the bottom crust.

3. Roll the pastry from the center of the circle in all four directions. When the rolling pin is near the edge of the circle, lift it up so all the pastry will be the same thickness. If the outer edge gets too thin, the pastry may tear and bake unevenly. To keep the dough in the shape of a circle and the edge from getting too thin, gently push the edge in with your hands. Lift the pastry occasionally to make it easier to roll into a circle of even thickness and to prevent pastry from sticking.

4. Roll the pastry to make a perfect circle 1 inch larger than the piepan. To measure the size, hold your piepan upside down over the pastry circle.

5. Fold the circle of pastry in fourths so you won't stretch or tear it. Place it loosely in the piepan and unfold it.

6. Carefully arrange the dough so it lines the piepan. If you tear the rolled pastry, press a patch of rolled dough over the hole so the filling can't seep through and make the undercrust soggy. You are ready to roll the top crust.

7. Roll the second half of the pastry just like the first one, but make it the same size as the piepan. Fold it in fourths and cut small slits in it so the steam in the filling can escape while the pie bakes.

8. Add the filling to the piepan and moisten the edge of the pastry with a little cold water. Put the pastry for the top crust over the filling. Gently press the top and bottom crusts together. Then fold the edge of the lower crust over the edge of the top crust. Use a fork to make a pretty design on the edge of the pie. Or flute the edge with a pinch and twist of your thumb and forefinger.

9. Cover the edge of the pie with a strip of aluminum foil, 1½ inches wide, to keep it from browning too much while it bakes. Bake as the pie recipe directs. Remove the foil after baking.

Slit Those Top Crusts
Steam forms in the pie during the baking. The slits let the steam escape. This keeps the top crust from bulging and breaking and helps to prevent the filling from bubbling over the edge.

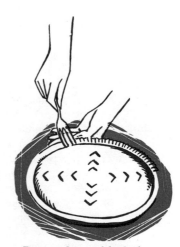

Press edges with fork

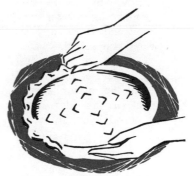

Or pinch and twist

Unfold dough; line piepan

Cut vents in top crust

Cover edge with foil

What Makes Pastry Tender?

When you add water or other liquid directly to flour and stir, beat or knead the mixture, strands of gluten (a protein) form. To keep too much gluten from forming in pastry, making it tough, you cut the solid shortening into the flour *before* you add water. The fat coats particles of flour so that the water cannot reach them. This keeps the gluten strands shorter and fewer in number because only the particles of flour that are not coated with shortening develop gluten.

The finer you cut the shortening into the flour, the more tender your pie crust will be. But larger pieces of shortening make pie crust flaky. So since pastry needs to be *both* tender and flaky, you cut the shortening into the flour until the mixture looks like peas—some small and some big peas. *After* you add the water, stir the pastry just enough to mix it and until the mixture almost cleans the sides of the bowl by itself. Avoid overstirring.

Chill the Pastry

After you roll the pastry between sheets of waxed paper, place it in the refrigerator while you fix the filling. Chilling makes it easy to peel off the paper and easier to handle.

For a change

· Bake pie without the top crust and then arrange pastry cutouts on it. To make the cutouts, cut the rolled pastry for the top crust in fancy shapes, such as stars, hearts or bells, using small cookie cutters or cardboard patterns as for cookies. Brush the cutouts with cold water and sprinkle with white or colored sugar. Put them on a baking sheet and bake in a very hot oven, 475° F., a few minutes or until a light brown. Watch them carefully—the pastry browns quickly. Remove cutouts from the baking sheet and cool them on wire racks. Put them on the top of the baked 1-crust pie.

UNBAKED 1-CRUST PIE SHELL (using solid fat)

For an 8- or 9-inch 1-crust pie:

Fit the rolled pastry into the piepan as for the bottom crust of a 2-crust pie, but make a higher edge and flute it with a pinch and twist of your thumb and forefinger.

BAKED 1-CRUST PIE SHELL (using solid fat)

For an 8- or 9-inch 1-crust pie:

1. Start heating the oven to 475° F.

2. Fit the rolled pastry into the piepan as for the bottom crust of a 2-crust pie, but make higher edges. Flute the edges like the unbaked pie shell.

3. Prick the pastry in the pan all over with a fork. The holes made by the fork let the steam out during the baking and the pastry will not puff up. (In a filled pie, the filling holds the pastry down while the pie bakes.)

4. Bake the pie shell on the rack in the center of the oven 8 to 10 minutes, or until it is a pretty brown. Watch it. The oven is very hot and it's easy to brown the pie shell too much.

PASTRY MADE WITH OIL

For an 8- or 9-inch 2-crust pie:
1¾ cups sifted flour
 1 teaspoon salt
 ½ cup salad oil
 3 tablespoons cold water

1. Mix the flour and salt in a medium bowl with a fork.

2. Mix in the oil thoroughly with a fork.

3. Sprinkle all the water over the mixture and mix well with a fork. Press the pastry firmly into a ball. If it is too dry to shape into a ball, add a few drops of oil.

4. Cut the pastry in half with a knife.

5. Dampen the board or other rolling surface with a little water and spread a sheet of waxed paper on it. The water keeps the waxed paper from slipping. Place half of the pastry on the waxed paper (set the other half aside). Place a sheet of waxed paper over the pastry on the board and roll it from the center to make a 12-inch circle.

6. Remove the top sheet of waxed paper from the pastry and place the pastry, paper side up, in the piepan. Peel off the paper. Fit the pastry loosely into the piepan and with a knife, trim it even with the edge of the piepan.

7. Roll the second half of the pastry between sheets of waxed paper, like the bottom crust. Peel off the top sheet of paper and cut small vents in the pastry so steam can escape while the pie bakes.

8. Add the filling to the pastry-lined piepan and place the pastry for the top over the filling, paper side up. Peel off the waxed paper. Trim the pastry for the top crust with scissors to ½ inch beyond the edge of the piepan. Fold the top crust under the lower crust and press to seal the bottom and top crusts. Flute the edge with a pinch and a twist of your forefinger and thumb. Cover the edge of the pie with a 1½-inch strip of aluminum foil to prevent browning too much while the pie bakes. (Remove foil from the baked pie.)

9. Bake as pie recipe directs.

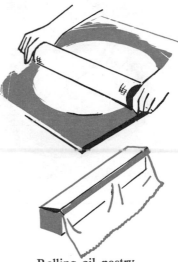

Rolling oil pastry

Into pan, peel off paper

For an 8- or 9-inch 1-crust pie: Use 1 cup plus 2 tablespoons sifted flour, ½ teaspoon salt, ⅓ cup salad oil and 2 tablespoons cold water.

UNBAKED 1-CRUST PIE SHELL (using oil)

For an 8- or 9-inch 1-crust pie:

1. Roll the pastry for a 1-crust pie between two sheets of waxed paper to make a 12-inch circle. Peel off the top sheet of waxed paper and fit the pastry loosely in the pie pan as for the bottom crust of a 2-crust pie. Trim off the pastry ½ inch beyond the edge of the piepan with scissors.

2. Fold under the edge of the pastry and flute it with a

To Measure Crust Size
Roll pastry made with oil between two 12-inch sheets of waxed paper. Roll it into a circle with the edge on the four sides even with the edge of the paper. The circle of pastry will be the right size.

Prick sides and bottom

pinch and a twist of your thumb and forefinger to make a higher edge than for 2-crust pies.

BAKED 1-CRUST PIE SHELL (using oil)

1. Start heating the oven to 450° F. Then fit the pastry for a 1-crust pie in the piepan and flute the edges.

2. Prick the pastry in the piepan all over with a fork. The holes you make will let the steam out during the baking and the pie shell will not puff up.

3. Bake the pie shell on the rack in the center of the oven 12 to 15 minutes, or until it is browned. Watch it. The oven is hot and it's easy to brown the pastry too much.

PASTRY BY THE PASTE METHOD— BEGINNER'S PASTRY

You will have good luck every time because you will not add too much water or flour and make your pastry tough

Use fork to make paste

2 cups sifted flour
1 teaspoon salt
⅔ cup vegetable shortening
4 tablespoons cold water

1. Stir the flour and salt in a medium bowl to mix. Cut in the shortening with a pastry blender until the mixture looks like coarse cornmeal.

2. Place ⅓ cup of the flour-shortening mixture in a small bowl. Add all the water to it and mix with a fork. Then add this to the rest of the flour-shortening mixture and mix with a fork, then with your fingers. Mix just until the pastry holds together so you can shape it into a ball with your hands.

3. Roll and fit it into a piepan as for Pastry Made with Solid Fat. Makes 1 (8- or 9-inch) 2-crust pie.

GRAHAM CRACKER CRUMB CRUST

Many pies that you make and chill in the refrigerator before serving have crumb crusts that are a snap to fix

Add paste to flour mixture

1⅓ cups graham cracker crumbs (16 to 18 crackers)
¼ cup sugar
¼ cup soft butter or margarine

1. Start heating the oven to 375° F.

2. Stir the graham cracker crumbs and sugar in a medium-size mixing bowl to mix well.

3. Rub in the butter with the back of a wooden spoon or the fingers until well mixed. (You can save out ⅓ cup of the crumbs to sprinkle on top of the pie if you like.)

4. Press the crumb mixture evenly on the bottom and sides of a piepan with the fingers. Do not put any of the mixture on the rim.

5. Bake on the rack in the center of the oven about 8 minutes, or until golden brown. Remove the pan from the oven and set it on a wire rack to cool before filling the crust. Makes one 8- or 9-inch crumb crust.

PIES EVERYBODY LIKES

APPLE PIE

Top-favorite American pie—good by itself or à la mode

Pastry for 1 (9-inch) 2-crust pie
  6 to 7 cups sliced, peeled apples (6 to 7 medium apples)
¾ to 1 cup sugar
  2 tablespoons flour
½ to 1 teaspoon cinnamon
⅛ teaspoon nutmeg
⅛ teaspoon salt
  2 tablespoons butter

See pastry recipes, pages 74–78

1. Use Pastry Made with Solid Fat, Pastry Made with Oil or Beginner's Pastry for a 2-crust pie. Mix pastry by recipe directions. Form it into a ball and cut it in half with a knife. Roll the bottom crust and line a 9-inch piepan with it, as the directions tell you. Put the pastry-lined pan in the refrigerator while you fix the filling. Set the other half of the pastry aside.

2. Cut apples in quarters, cut out the cores and cut the apples into slices ¼ inch thick. Place them in a large bowl.

3. Stir the sugar, flour, cinnamon, nutmeg and salt together to mix well. (The amount of sugar—¾ to 1 cup —you need to add depends on the tartness of the apples, and the amount of cinnamon—½ to 1 teaspoon—depends

For Apple Pie Bakers
If the apples you are using are not very juicy, sprinkle a little cold water on the slices. If they need more tartness, sprinkle them with 1 tablespoon lemon juice. Three medium apples weigh about 1 pound and make 3 cups sliced apples.

on how spicy you like apple pie.) Add the mixture to the apple slices and toss with 2 forks to mix well.

4. Start heating the oven to 425° F.

5. Roll the other half of the pastry for the top crust and cut small vents in it.

Hurry-up Pie
You can also make a good, hurry-up apple pie with canned apple slices for pies. Follow the directions on the can label.

6. Place the apple mixture in the pastry-lined piepan and spread it evenly. Dot it with butter.

7. Cover the apples with the top crust. Gently press the top and bottom crusts together. Then fold the edge of the lower crust over the edge of the top crust. Use a fork to make a pretty design on the edge of the pie, or flute edge with a pinch and twist of your thumb and forefinger. Then cover the edge of the pie with a 1½-inch strip of aluminum foil to prevent it from browning too much. (Remove the foil after the pie is baked.)

8. Bake on the rack in the center of the oven 50 to 60 minutes or until the crust is browned. Cool the pie on a wire rack. Serve it warm or cold. Makes 6 servings.

BLUSHING APPLE PIE

Red hots spice the applesauce with cinnamon and tint it red

See recipe for Graham Cracker Crumb Crust, page 78

1 (8-inch) Graham Cracker Crumb Crust
2½ cups thick applesauce
¼ cup red cinnamon candies (red hots)
Whipped cream

1. Bake and cool the Graham Cracker Crumb Crust.

2. Place the applesauce and cinnamon candies in a medium saucepan and stir over medium heat until the candies melt. Cool thoroughly.

3. Pour the mixture into the cool crumb crust. Chill the pie 1 hour or longer.

4. Serve the pie topped with whipped cream or vanilla ice cream. Makes 4 to 6 servings.

BLUEBERRY PIE

An around-the-year berry pie and a special winter favorite

See recipe for Graham Cracker Crumb Crust, page 78

1 (9-inch) Graham Cracker Crumb Crust
1 (3-ounce) package cream cheese
1 (1-pound) can blueberry pie filling
½ pint (1 cup) heavy cream
2 tablespoons sugar

1. Bake and cool the Graham Cracker Crumb Crust.

2. Beat the cream cheese with a little of the heavy cream added until it is soft and fluffy. Spread an even layer of cheese over the bottom of the crumb crust.

3. Spread an even layer of blueberry pie filling over the cream cheese and chill an hour or several hours.

4. At serving time, whip the rest of the cream, fold in the sugar and spread it over the pie. Makes 6 servings.

CHERRY PIE

Bake this favorite in February to honor George Washington and every other month because it tastes so wonderful

Pastry for 1 (9-inch) 2-crust pie
2 (1-pound) cans pitted tart cherries (water pack)
¼ cup flour
¼ teaspoon salt
1 cup sugar
4 drops almond extract
6 drops red food color
2 tablespoons butter

1. Use Pastry Made with Solid Fat, Pastry Made with Oil or Beginner's Pastry for a 2-crust pie. Mix pastry by recipe directions. Form it into a ball and cut it in half with a knife. Roll the bottom crust and line a 9-inch piepan with it, as the directions tell you. Put the pastry-lined pan in the refrigerator while you fix the filling. Set the other half of the pastry aside.

2. Drain the cherries in a sieve. Save the juice.

3. Mix the flour, salt and sugar in a medium saucepan and stir in ½ cup cherry juice. Stir and cook the mixture over medium heat until it thickens. (Be sure to let the mixture come to a full boil.) Remove it from the heat.

4. Add the almond extract, food color, butter and drained cherries (you will have about 3½ cups). Stir to mix and set aside while you roll the top crust. Cut small vents in the rolled pastry.

5. Start heating the oven to 425°F.

6. Pour the cooled cherry filling evenly into the chilled pastry-lined piepan and cover with the top crust. Gently press the top and bottom crusts together. Then fold the edge of the lower crust over the edge of the top crust. Use a fork to make a pretty design on the edge of the pie, or

How to Fit Pastry in a Piepan
When you line a piepan with pastry for the bottom crust, ease it gently and loosely into the pan to avoid stretching it. Then the pastry will be the same thickness all over. If stretched, the thin places may tear or bake faster than the thicker pastry.

See pastry recipes, pages 74–78

Be a Pie Crust Artist
Make different designs when you cut slits in your pie's top crust—a pattern of V's or a branch and leaves. Or trim a one-crust pie with pastry cutouts (directions on page 76).

Pretty Tops for Pies
For a shiny surface, brush the tops of 2-crust pies with a little milk before baking them. For a golden glazed top, brush the surface with water, then sprinkle evenly with sugar. Egg or egg yolk mixed with a little water and brushed on the unbaked pie will give you a glazed crust.

See recipe for Graham Cracker Crumb Crust, page 78

flute edge with a pinch and twist of your thumb and forefinger. Cover the edge of the pie with a 1½-inch strip of aluminum foil to prevent browning too much. (Remove the foil after the pie is baked.)

7. Bake the pie on the rack in the center of the oven 40 to 50 minutes, or until the crust is browned. Cool the pie on a wire rack. Makes 6 servings.

NORTH POLE CHERRY PIE

A beauty that looks like Christmas—a holiday special

1 (9-inch) Graham Cracker Crumb Crust
1 quart vanilla ice cream
1 (1-pound 6-ounce) can cherry pie filling

1. Bake and cool the Graham Cracker Crumb Crust.

2. Let the ice cream stand at room temperature until it softens *slightly*. Spread the ice cream evenly in the cool crumb crust. Freeze the pie for 3 or 4 hours. If you want to keep the frozen pie for a day or two before serving, put it in a plastic bag and store it in the freezer.

3. An hour before serving, spread the cherry pie filling over the ice cream in the pie. Return it to the freezer until time to serve. Makes 6 servings.

PUMPKIN PIE

Nothing tastes better for Halloween and Thanksgiving

See pastry recipes, pages 74–78

1 (9-inch) unbaked pie shell
2 eggs, slightly beaten
1 (1-pound) can pumpkin (2 cups)
¾ cup sugar
½ teaspoon salt
1 teaspoon cinnamon
½ teaspoon ginger
¼ teaspoon cloves
1⅔ cups evaporated milk or light cream

1. Make one 9-inch unbaked pie shell with Pastry Made with Solid Fat, Pastry Made with Oil or Beginner's Pastry. Put it in the refrigerator while you make the pie filling.

2. Start heating the oven to 400° F.

3. Beat the eggs slightly with a fork to mix the whites

Pumpkin Pie Spice
Instead of measuring the cinnamon, ginger and cloves separately when making pumpkin pie, use pumpkin pie spice. It is a mixture of the three spices.

and yolks. Stir in the pumpkin and add the sugar, salt, cinnamon, ginger and cloves. Stir in the milk or cream. Pour the filling into the pie shell.

4. Place the pie on the rack in the center of the oven (be careful not to spill the filling) and bake it 45 to 50 minutes, or until a knife inserted in the filling halfway between the edge and the center of the pie comes out clean. Makes 6 servings.

SUNNY LEMON PIE

A top favorite in the homes of California lemon growers— taste this pie and you'll know why. It's pretty, too

1 (9-inch) baked pie shell
4 eggs
Grated peel of 1 lemon
¼ cup lemon juice
3 tablespoons water
1 cup sugar

1. Bake one 9-inch pie shell, using Pastry Made with Solid Fat, Pastry Made with Oil or Beginner's Pastry. Cool on a wire rack.

2. Separate egg whites and yolks, putting the whites into the electric mixer's bowl, the yolks into the top of the double boiler.

3. Beat the yolks until thick; gradually stir in the lemon peel and juice, water and ½ cup sugar. Cook over hot, not boiling, water until thickened, stirring all the time. Remove the top of the double boiler from the hot water and set the egg-yolk mixture aside.

4. Start heating the oven to 350° F.

5. Beat the egg whites until stiff peaks form when you lift the beaters out of them. Then beat in the rest of the sugar (½ cup), 1 tablespoon at a time. Keep on beating until the egg whites are glossy and you can pile them up in mounds with a spoon.

6. Fold about half of the sweetened egg whites into the warm egg-yolk mixture with a spatula or spoon. Keep on folding until none of the egg whites show. Pour the mixture into the pie shell and spread evenly.

7. Spoon the rest of the sweetened egg whites around the edge of the pie to make a collar. Be sure the egg whites touch the crust all the way around.

Test for doneness

See pastry recipes, pages 74–78

How to Patch Pastry
If there are tears or holes in the pastry that lines the piepan, mend them with scraps of the pie dough so the juices cannot seep through and make the bottom crust soggy.

8. Put the pie on the rack in the center of the oven to brown the meringue lightly. It will take about 15 minutes. Cool the pie on a wire rack. Makes 6 servings.

LEMON CHEESE PIE

Make the Cherry Glaze and cool it after the pie is in the refrigerator. It glamorizes the pie dessert and adds flavor

See recipe for Graham Cracker Crumb Crust, page 78

1 (9-inch) Graham Cracker Crumb Crust
1 (8-ounce) package cream cheese
1 (15-ounce) can sweetened condensed milk
⅓ cup lemon juice
1 teaspoon vanilla
Cherry Glaze

1. Bake and cool the Graham Cracker Crumb Crust.
2. Soften cream cheese by beating with the electric mixer until light and fluffy. (Or let cream cheese stand at room temperature a few minutes and beat with a spoon.)
3. Gradually add the sweetened condensed milk to the cheese, beating all the time. Add the lemon juice and vanilla and stir to mix well.
4. Pour the cheese mixture into the cooled crumb crust. Put the pie in the refrigerator and chill 2 to 3 hours, or until ready to serve.
5. Cover with the Cherry Glaze. Makes 6 servings.

Read the Label
When a recipe calls for evaporated milk or sweetened condensed milk, read the label on the can to be sure you are using the right kind. Sweetened condensed milk is whole milk with sugar added, from which 60 per cent of the water was removed before it was canned. Evaporated milk is whole milk with nothing added, from which 50 per cent of the water was removed before canning. Some recipes use the thicker sweetened *condensed* milk; others the non-sweet *evaporated*. Makes a difference!
Once a can of evaporated or sweetened condensed milk is opened, cover it with aluminum foil pressed tightly over the top of the can and store it in the refrigerator.

CHERRY GLAZE

1 cup pitted drained tart cherries
½ cup cherry juice
3 tablespoons sugar
2 tablespoons cornstarch

1. Open a (1-pound) can tart cherries. (You will use about half of it to make this glaze.) Drain the cherries in a strainer or sieve and measure.
2. Stir the cherry juice (drained from the cherries), sugar and cornstarch together in a small saucepan. Cook over low heat, stirring all the time, until the mixture thickens and is clear.
3. Stir in the drained cherries. Cool.
4. Spread the cooled cherry mixture over the cool pie.

PECAN PIE

It's rich and it's yummy—also an easy pie to bake

1 (9-inch) unbaked pie shell
3 eggs
⅔ cup sugar
½ teaspoon salt
1 cup dark corn syrup
⅓ cup melted butter or margarine
1 cup pecan halves

See pastry recipes, pages 74–78

1. Make one 9-inch unbaked pie shell with Pastry Made with Solid Fat, Pastry Made with Oil or Beginner's Pastry. Put it in the refrigerator while you make the pie filling.

2. Start heating the oven to 375° F.

3. Thoroughly beat the eggs with the sugar, salt, corn syrup and melted butter with the electric mixer, or with a hand beater. Stir in the pecan halves with a spoon.

4. Pour the pecan mixture into the unbaked pie shell.

5. Bake the pie on the rack in the center of the oven until a knife inserted halfway between the center and edge of the pie comes out clean, 40 to 50 minutes. Cool. The pie will shrink a little as it cools. Serve slightly warm or cold. Makes 6 to 8 servings.

Don't Use Cake Flour in Pies
Cake flour is milled from softer wheats than all-purpose flour. It makes a mealy pie crust, which is so tender it falls apart. That's because the gluten in cake flour is not strong enough to hold the pie crust together. Use all-purpose flour for pie crust.

FRESH PEACH PIE

A simple pie to make when peaches are ripe—and so good

1 (9-inch) Graham Cracker Crumb Crust
18 large marshmallows
¼ cup milk
1 cup heavy cream, whipped
5 to 7 ripe fresh peaches, peeled and diced

1. Bake and cool the Graham Cracker Crumb Crust.

2. Put the marshmallows and milk in the top of the double boiler and heat over hot, not boiling, water until the marshmallows melt. Stir all the time so the marshmallows and milk will not separate. Cool.

3. While the marshmallow mixture cools, whip the cream.

4. Stir the diced peaches into the cool marshmallow mixture. Fold in the whipped cream. Pour the mixture into the

See recipe for Graham Cracker Crumb Crust, page 78

crumb crust and refrigerate the pie 4 hours or more before serving. Makes 6 servings.

GRATED CHOCOLATE PIE

This unusual chocolate pie is rich, luscious and easy to fix

See recipe for Graham Cracker Crumb Crust, page 78

1 (9-inch) Graham Cracker Crumb Crust
21 large marshmallows
½ cup milk
1 cup heavy cream, whipped
1½ squares semisweet chocolate, grated

1. Bake and cool the Graham Cracker Crumb Crust.

2. Put the marshmallows and milk in the top of a double boiler and heat over hot water, stirring all the time until the marshmallows melt. Remove the marshmallow-milk mixture from the heat and cool.

3. While the marshmallow mixture cools, beat the cream until it is fluffy and light. Grate the chocolate and save out 1 tablespoon of it for garnishing.

4. Fold the whipped cream and grated chocolate into the cool marshmallow mixture and pour it into the crumb crust. Sprinkle the 1 tablespoon grated chocolate over the top. Refrigerate the pie until time to serve. This pie also freezes well. Makes 6 to 8 servings.

Homemade breads

TAKE homemade bread from the oven and spread it with plenty of butter. Could anything taste better—smell better?

There are two great bread families—the quick breads and the yeast breads. Baking powder and/or baking soda make quick breads rise and increase in size—fast. Yeast makes yeast breads rise and grow bigger, but yeast works more slowly than baking powder and soda. For quick breads you handle the dough as gently as possible so that they will be tender—you try *not to* develop the gluten, a protein in flour. You knead or beat yeast breads to develop the gluten, which enables these breads to hold their shape.

Flour is very important in breadmaking. You can use all-purpose or instant-type flour in our recipes. You sift all-purpose flour in some of our recipes, but for others, you don't—just do what the recipe says. Instant-type flour is never sifted.

Quick breads

Let's start baking the quick breads—they're so easy and there are so many good ones, such as biscuits, muffins, pancakes, waffles and coffee breads. You'll find recipes for all of them in this book. And you'll notice a few recipes for desserts, such as cobbler and shortcake. These treats are made with biscuit dough.

After you've baked quick breads, you will want to try the yeast breads.

BISCUITS—DROP AND ROLLED

Biscuits taste best when they're so hot that butter spread on them melts quickly. So rush them from the oven to the table. It's a good idea to put them in a basket or dish lined with a napkin to keep them hot. For family meals, you can use a piece of aluminum foil, instead of a napkin, to trap the heat.

You may want to make your first biscuits from a packaged mix—just bake them as directed on the mix package. You'll also have good luck with our biscuit recipes. And they all are quick; that's living up to their family name—the quick breads. Drop biscuits are the easiest and quickest kind, so let's begin with them.

HOT DROP BISCUITS

Put them in to bake about 10 minutes before mealtime. Allow 10 minutes to get them ready to bake—serve hot

What Makes Rolled Biscuits Flaky?
When you pull a piece of a hot biscuit up from the top crust with the finger tips, the inside should peel off in long, thin sheets. This is a sign that the biscuits are flaky and good. The flakes are sheets of dough that the expanding steam separates into layers while the biscuits bake. Knead biscuit dough lightly to distribute the shortening evenly; this helps form the layers or flakes.

2 cups flour
3 teaspoons baking powder
1 teaspoon salt
¼ cup shortening
1 cup milk

1. Start heating the oven to 450° F.

2. Measure the flour, baking powder and salt into a medium bowl and stir to mix well.

3. Cut in the shortening with a pastry blender to mix it well with the flour. The mixture should look like coarse crumbs or coarse cornmeal. Make a "well" in the flour mixture.

4. Add all the milk to the "well" at once and stir with a fork until no flour shows and the soft dough forms a ball.

5. Drop tablespoonfuls of the dough 1 inch apart on an ungreased baking sheet. Or drop the dough into greased muffin-pan cups. Fill the cups ⅔ full.

6. Put the baking sheet or the greased muffin-pan cups on the rack in the center of the oven. Bake them 10 to 12 minutes or until the biscuits are golden brown. Makes about 20 biscuits.

HOT ROLLED BISCUITS

Roll or pat out biscuit dough half as thick as you want your biscuits. They double in height during the baking

2 cups flour
3 teaspoons baking powder
1 teaspoon salt
¼ cup shortening
¾ cup milk

Dip in flour, then cut

1. Start heating the oven to 450° F.

2. Measure the flour, baking powder and salt into a medium bowl and stir to mix well.

3. Cut in the shortening with a pastry blender to mix it well with the flour. The mixture should look like coarse crumbs or coarse cornmeal. Make a "well" in the flour mixture.

4. Add all the milk to the "well" and stir with a fork until none of the flour shows and the dough makes a ball that follows the fork around the bowl.

5. Turn the dough onto a lightly floured, cloth-covered board and roll it around 3 or 4 times to coat it lightly with flour. Knead the dough gently 5 to 6 times. Kneading helps mix all the ingredients and makes flaky, light biscuits.

6. Pat the dough (with your hands) or roll it out (with a rolling pin) about ½ inch thick. You can measure the thickness with a ruler. If you like thin, crusty biscuits, pat or roll out the dough ¼ inch thick.

7. Cut out the biscuits with a lightly floured 2-inch cutter (use a smaller cutter if you like small biscuits). Cut straight down—be careful not to twist cutter. Cut circles of dough as close together as possible so you will have few scraps. Push the scraps together—do not knead them—and cut out the biscuits.

8. Lift the circles of dough to the ungreased baking sheet with a wide spatula to keep them round. Allow 1 inch between dough circles if you like biscuits with crisp sides. If you like biscuits with soft sides, put the circles of dough close together on a ungreased baking sheet or bake them in an ungreased round layer cake pan.

9. Put the pan on the rack in the center of the oven and bake 10 to 12 minutes or until golden brown. Makes about 20 biscuits if dough is rolled or patted ½ inch thick.

For a change

· *Rich biscuits:* Use recipe for Hot Rolled Biscuits but increase shortening to 6 tablespoons and use ⅔ cup milk instead of ¾ cup.

· *Cheese biscuits:* Make like Hot Rolled Biscuits but add ½ to ¾ cup grated Cheddar cheese to the flour, baking powder and salt mixture.

· *Orange biscuits:* Make like Hot Rolled Biscuits but add the grated peel of 1 orange to the flour, baking powder and salt mixture.

How to Prevent Lopsided Biscuits
If you twist the cutter when you cut biscuit dough, it stretches some of the strands of gluten (a protein in flour) out of shape, and the sides of the biscuits will be uneven. Push the cutter straight down into the dough, and pull it straight up.

Your choice: crusty or soft

See how to grate orange peel, page 18

· *Cheese topped biscuits:* When Hot Rolled Biscuits or Hot Drop Biscuits are on the baking sheet ready for baking, top each round of dough with a teaspoon of this mixture: Melt 1 (3-ounce) package pimiento cream cheese with 2 tablespoons of butter.

HURRY-UP CHERRY COBBLER

Use ½ cup sugar instead of ⅔ cup and canned apricots, blackberries or sliced peaches instead of the cherries

    1 (1-pound 4-ounce) can pitted tart cherries
⅔ cup sugar
    1 tablespoon cornstarch
    2 teaspoons butter
¼ teaspoon cinnamon
    1 cup flour
    1 tablespoon sugar
1½ teaspoons baking powder
½ teaspoon salt
    3 tablespoons shortening
½ cup milk

1. Start heating the oven to 400° F.

2. Open the can of cherries and place them in a colander or sieve to drain. Save the juice.

3. Mix the ⅔ cup sugar and cornstarch in a medium saucepan. Gradually stir the juice drained from the cherries into the sugar-cornstarch mixture. Stir and bring to a boil over high heat and then lower heat and stir and boil 1 minute. The mixture will thicken. Add all the cherries at one time.

4. Pour the hot cherry mixture into a 6-cup (1½-quart) casserole. Dot the top of the fruit with the butter and sprinkle with the cinnamon. Set the casserole in the oven to keep hot while you make the biscuit topping.

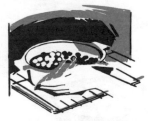

Keep cherries hot in oven

5. Measure the flour, 1 tablespoon sugar, the baking powder and salt into a medium bowl and stir to mix. Add the shortening and mix with a pastry blender until the mixture looks like coarse crumbs. Make a "well" in the mixture.

6. Add all the milk at one time to the "well" and stir with a fork until no flour shows and the soft dough forms a ball.

Drop biscuit dough on top

7. Remove the cherry filling from the oven. Drop tablespoonfuls of the biscuit dough on the top.

8. Bake on the rack in the center of the oven 25 to 30 minutes.

9. Remove the cobbler from the oven and serve warm. Pass a pitcher of cream to pour over it. Makes 6 servings.

SUPER STRAWBERRY SHORTCAKE

Some good cooks butter both halves of the biscuits and use the tops, crusty side down, for the shortcake's top layer

So handy: a strawberry huller

1 quart fresh strawberries (4 cups)
1 cup sugar
2 cups sifted flour
3 tablespoons sugar
3 teaspoons baking powder
1 teaspoon salt
½ cup shortening
1 egg
⅓ cup milk (about)
Butter or margarine
Heavy cream, whipped

1. Pick over the berries to remove any badly bruised ones. Wash and drain the berries. Remove the hulls. Crush the berries lightly with a potato masher or slice them. Add 1 cup sugar. (Or add enough sugar to make the berries as sweet as you like them. Taste to find out how much sugar to add.) Cover and put them in the refrigerator while you make the shortcake.

2. Start heating the oven to 450° F.

3. Sift the flour onto a square of waxed paper or into a bowl and then measure. Sift the measured flour with the 3 tablespoons sugar, baking powder and salt into a medium bowl.

4. Cut in the shortening with a pastry blender or 2 table knives, scissor-fashion, until the mixture looks like coarse crumbs.

5. Beat the egg in a small bowl with a fork, whisk or rotary beater to mix yolk and white. Stir in the milk. Then stir the wet mixture into the flour-shortening mixture with a fork and mix well. You should have a soft dough, but one that's not too wet to handle. (Add a little more milk if necessary.)

6. Turn the dough onto a lightly floured surface and pat or roll it to ½-inch thickness.

Make a 3-story shortcake

7. Cut the dough with lightly floured 3-inch cutter. If you have enough dough left over, you can cut it in 1½-inch circles to make an extra topping on the shortcake.

8. Place the circles of dough 1 inch apart on an ungreased baking sheet and bake on the rack in the center of the oven about 10 minutes or until the shortcakes are a golden brown.

9. Remove the shortcake circles from the oven and split them in half. Spread both halves with butter. Place one in each serving dish. Spoon half the sweetened berries over the buttered halves. Put the top halves of the shortcake on top of the berries (buttered side down) and spoon the rest of the berries on top. If you have the extra-small circles of baked shortcake, put them on top of the berries.

See how to whip cream, page 19

10. While the shortcakes are baking, whip the cream. Serve the shortcakes warm with spoonfuls of whipped cream on top. Makes 6 shortcakes.

IN & OUT COFFEE CAKE

The trick in this recipe is to bake half of the cinnamon-nut topping in the coffee cake and the other half on top to brown

Divide the topping

Topping:

¾ cup brown sugar, packed firmly
⅓ cup butter or margarine
2 tablespoons cinnamon
½ cup chopped nuts

Cake:

1 egg, slightly beaten
1⅓ cups milk
3 cups packaged biscuit mix
¼ cup sugar

1. Start heating the oven to 400° F. Grease a 9×9×2-inch pan with shortening.

2. Mix the ingredients for the topping and divide in half.

3. Stir the egg, beaten slightly with a fork or a wire beater, into the milk.

Fold half of it into batter

4. Stir the biscuit mix and sugar together in a large bowl to mix well. Make a "well" in the center of the flour

and add the egg-milk mixture. Stir with a fork or spoon to mix thoroughly. Then fold in half of the topping.

5. Spread the batter evenly in the pan and sprinkle the other half of the topping on top.

6. Bake the cake on the rack in the center of the oven 25 minutes. Serve it warm, cut into 3-inch squares. Makes 9 servings.

Sprinkle on topping

THE FIRST COOKBOOK

The world's oldest known cookbook was written in ancient Greece, where good food was considered an important part of good living. The cookbook, written for the wealthy people, was in several volumes and dealt with other things than cooking, including the etiquette of eating.

PANCAKES, WAFFLES AND MUFFINS

Pancakes, waffles and muffins are great favorites. All of them are fast to fix and tasty—especially if served piping hot. If you have a good basic recipe for each of the three breads, you can make many kinds of pancakes, waffles and muffins from them. The trick is to add different foods to them, such as cheese, nuts and blueberries.

Both pancakes and waffles are tops in good eating when served with plenty of butter or margarine and a sweet syrup, honey, or shaved maple sugar. Heat the syrup and butter or margarine in a saucepan until piping hot and serve in a pitcher—cold syrup would cool the pancakes and waffles. Muffins are best spread with butter or margarine and jelly or jam.

Waffles make excellent desserts—like our Coconut Waffles with chocolate syrup (the kind you pour over ice cream). With creamed chicken, turkey or tuna or chilli con carne spooned over them, they are a satisfying main dish.

Electric skillets and griddles are fine for baking pancakes because they have even, controlled heat. And they're easy on the cook—you can sit at the dining table and do the baking and serving. Many of today's griddles have smooth surfaces that you don't have to grease. If you do grease your griddle, rub it with a little shortening on a paper towel. Follow the directions for heating and using your waffle iron, electric skillet and griddle.

You can buy excellent packaged pancake and muffin mixes. Look them over the next time you're in a supermarket. And you can make good waffles from packaged pancake, biscuit and waffle mixes. Read the labels for directions.

FAVORITE PANCAKES

Don't crowd pancakes on the griddle—you'll find it's difficult to turn them. Use a wide spatula or pancake turner

When Water Dances
The griddle is heated just right for baking pancakes if a few drops of cold water dropped on it form little beads that dance on the surface.

1¼ cups sifted flour
2½ teaspoons baking powder
 2 tablespoons sugar
 ¾ teaspoon salt
 1 egg
1¼ cups milk
 3 tablespoons melted butter, margarine or salad oil

1. Set the griddle over low heat. Or if you use an electric griddle or skillet, start heating it to the temperature the manufacturer recommends (see booklet of instructions).

2. Sift the flour onto a piece of waxed paper or into a bowl and then measure. Sift together the flour, baking powder, sugar and salt into a wide-mouthed pitcher, a quart measuring pitcher or a medium bowl. Or stir together to mix thoroughly.

3. Beat the egg in a small bowl with a wire or hand beater. Add the milk and melted butter. (For thicker pancakes, use ¾ cup instead of 1¼ cups of milk.) Slowly stir into the flour mixture and mix with a spoon only until the flour is wet. The batter will be a little lumpy.

4. When the griddle is hot enough, pour the batter from the pitcher or drop it from a large spoon or a ¼-cup measure onto the griddle to make a pancake. Lightly spread the pancake out with the back of a spoon. One-fourth cup of batter makes a pancake about 4 inches in diameter. For pancakes the size of silver dollars, use 1 tablespoon batter for each cake. Bake 3 pancakes at a time, or more if your griddle is large enough.

Measure for same-size cakes

5. Cook until the cakes are full of bubbles, the edges are dry and the pancakes are golden brown underneath. Then loosen and turn each pancake with a wide spatula or pancake turner. Turn only once or they will not be light. Brown on the underside—it will take about 2 minutes.

6. Serve at once with butter or margarine and syrup or honey or a pitcher of heated syrup mixed with butter. If the pancakes must wait a few minutes, spread them on racks or between towels in a low oven with the door open. Makes about 12 (4-inch) pancakes.

For a change: dollar cakes

For a change
· *Blueberry pancakes:* When the pancake batter is on the griddle, sprinkle 1 tablespoon of washed and drained fresh blueberries or unthawed frozen blueberries on each cake. Or stir ¾ cup fresh blueberries into the batter.
· *Apple pancakes:* Stir 1 cup finely chopped, cored and peeled apples into the batter for Favorite Pancakes. You can sift a touch of cinnamon, about ¼ teaspoon with the flour for a delicate spicy taste.
· *Pecan pancakes:* Stir 1 cup chopped or broken pecans or walnuts into the batter for Favorite Pancakes.
· *Frankfurter pancakes:* Just before turning pancakes, top each cake with a few thin frankfurter slices.
· *Sausage pancakes:* Just before turning pancakes, top each cake with a little cooked and crumbled pork sausage.
· *Banana pancakes:* Place 3 banana slices on griddle for each pancake. Pour on batter for Favorite Pancakes and bake until golden on both sides. Serve with butter and honey or butter and powdered sugar.
· *Rolled pancakes:* Just before you begin baking the pancakes, start heating the oven to 400° F. When the pancakes come off the griddle, spread each cake with about 2 tablespoons of cream-style cottage cheese. Roll the warm pancake and put it in a shallow baking pan. When all the pancakes are baked, filled and rolled, cover the pan with a lid or a sheet of aluminum foil and put the pan in the heated oven for 10 minutes. Use 2 rolled cakes for a serving. Serve topped with a spoonful of tart jam or with canned cherry pie filling. If you like spicy cottage cheese, mix 1 tablespoon sugar, ¾ teaspoon cinnamon, ¼ teaspoon nutmeg, ⅛ teaspoon salt into 1¼ cups of cottage cheese.

Spread with cheese, roll up

WHIPPED BUTTER

This fluffy topping is popular in pancake houses

Put 1 stick or ½ cup butter (¼ pound) in electric mixer's small bowl. If butter is not at room temperature, let it stand ½ hour. Beat at low speed until smooth. Then beat at high speed until light and fluffy. The beating will take about 10 minutes. Pile in a small bowl and serve with pancakes or waffles without chilling. Makes about 1 cup.

For a change
· *Honey butter:* Gradually add ¼ cup honey to Whipped Butter. Beat until smooth.

How to Sour Sweet Milk
Often when you want to use a recipe that calls for sour milk or buttermilk, you find only sweet milk in the refrigerator. You can make your own sour milk. Pour 1 tablespoon vinegar or lemon juice into a cup and fill the cup with sweet milk. Let it stand a few minutes and the milk will be sour. The acid of the vinegar or lemon juice sours the milk. You will notice the milk looks thicker after you add the vinegar or lemon juice. That's because the acid thickens (coagulates) the protein in the milk.

Batter 1 inch from edge

Lift out with a fork

BUTTERMILK WAFFLES

If you have no buttermilk or sour milk, make your own or use the recipe for Sweet Milk Waffles

2 cups sifted flour
3 teaspoons baking powder
1 teaspoon baking soda
1 teaspoon salt
4 eggs
2 cups buttermilk or sour milk
1 cup melted butter or margarine or salad oil

1. Start heating the waffle iron.

2. Sift the flour onto a sheet of waxed paper or into a bowl and then measure. Sift the measured flour, baking powder, baking soda and salt into a medium bowl.

3. Beat the eggs until light with a hand beater or electric mixer on high speed, and stir in the buttermilk. Pour over flour mixture and beat with a hand beater or the electric mixer on high speed until the batter is smooth.

4. Stir in the butter.

5. By this time the waffle iron should be heated. Pour batter from a cup or pitcher into center of lower half of waffle iron until it spreads to about 1 inch from the edges. It takes about ½ cup batter for a waffle. Keep the waffle iron open no longer than necessary. Gently bring the cover down.

6. Bake the waffle until no steam shows around the edges and the signal on the waffle iron tells you the waffle is done. Lift up the top and gently loosen the edges of the waffle with a fork. Remove the waffle and serve at once. Reheat the waffle iron before baking the next waffle. Makes about 6 waffles.

For a change
· *Sweet milk waffles:* Make like Buttermilk Waffles but use 2 cups sweet milk instead of the buttermilk. Omit the baking soda and use 4 teaspoons baking powder instead of 3. Separate the eggs and beat the whites until stiff. Fold them into the batter at the last.
· *Blueberry waffles:* Scatter 2 tablespoons washed and drained fresh blueberries on the waffle batter as soon as you pour it on the waffle iron.
· *Nut waffles:* Scatter 2 tablespoons broken pecans or

walnuts on the waffle batter as soon as you pour it on the waffle iron.

· *Corn waffles:* Fold 1 cup drained whole-kernel corn, canned, into the waffle batter for Buttermilk or Sweet Milk Waffles at the last.

· *Cheese waffles:* Fold ½ cup grated process American cheese in the batter for Buttermilk or Sweet Milk Waffles.

· *Coconut waffles:* Fold 1 cup fine, grated coconut (packaged) into the batter for Buttermilk or Sweet Milk Waffles.

BEST-EVER MUFFINS

Nine from one! Use this recipe and you can make nine different kinds of muffins with it. All of them are delicious

```
2 cups sifted flour
3 teaspoons baking powder
½ teaspoon salt
¼ cup sugar
1 egg
1 cup milk
¼ cup melted shortening or salad oil
```

1. Start heating the oven to 400° F. Grease bottoms of medium muffin-pan cups with shortening.

2. Sift the flour onto a square of waxed paper or into a bowl and then measure. Sift the measured flour with the baking powder, salt and sugar into a large bowl. Make a "well" in the center.

3. In a 2-cup measuring cup or a small bowl, beat the egg with a fork or a wire whisk. Stir in the milk and shortening. Pour all at once into "well" in flour mixture.

4. Mix quickly and lightly with a fork until all the flour is moistened, but do not beat. The batter will be lumpy.

5. Quickly fill the greased muffin-pan cups ⅔ full with the batter. Wipe off any spilled batter.

6. Bake on the rack in the center of the oven about 25 minutes or until the muffins are golden. Or insert a cake tester or wooden pick in the center of a muffin. If it comes out clean, the muffin is done.

7. Remove the pan from the oven and place it on a wire rack. Run a spatula around the outside edge of each muffin to loosen. Lift out and serve at once. Makes 12 medium muffins.

How Baking Soda Works Recipes for quick breads, such as waffles, sometimes call for baking soda. These recipes also use some ingredient containing acid, such as sour milk, buttermilk, molasses and vinegar. The acid and the baking soda together form carbon dioxide gas that helps make the batter or dough light. The gas also destroys the bitter taste of soda. You do not need to have an acid ingredient when you use baking *powder,* because it contains some acid already and also some soda. The two work together when liquid is added.

Wipe up the spills!

Perfect Muffins

Muffins must be very light when you lift them in your hand. On the outside they are pebbled, not smooth, and their tops are slightly rounded. Cut one in half from top to bottom and you will see little holes scattered evenly inside. They are tender when they look like this.

Knobby Muffins With Tunnels

If you mix muffin batter too much, you will have small, tough muffins with peaks or knobs on top. Inside them, you'll find long holes, called tunnels. The overmixing develops the gluten, a protein in flour, too much—and makes it harder for the baking powder to do its work. Thus, overmixed batter rises very little during the first part of the baking. After the muffin batter heats through, steam and carbon dioxide gas (formed by baking powder and liquid) push between the toughened strands of gluten, making the tunnels in the muffins. The steam and gas also push some of the batter out at the soft center top of the muffins, making the knobs.

For a change

· *Blueberry muffins:* Wash and thoroughly drain 1 cup fresh blueberries in a colander or on paper towels. Fold them into the batter for Best-Ever Muffins with the last few strokes of mixing.

· *Raisin muffins:* Add 1 cup finely cut-up raisins to the batter for Best-Ever Muffins with the last few strokes of mixing.

· *Date muffins:* Add 1 cup finely cut-up dates (see directions for chopping dates) to the batter for Best-Ever Muffins with the last few strokes of mixing.

· *Coconut muffins:* Add 1 cup shredded coconut to the batter for Best-Ever Muffins with the last few strokes of mixing.

· *Cranberry muffins:* Cut 1 cup washed and drained fresh cranberries in halves. Place in a small bowl and add ⅔ cup powdered sugar. Let stand while mixing the batter for Best-Ever Muffins. Stir the cranberries into the batter with the last few strokes of mixing.

· *Cheese muffins:* Fold ½ cup grated, sharp yellow cheese into the batter for Best-Ever Muffins with the last few strokes of mixing.

· *Bacon muffins:* Fold ¼ cup crisp cooked bacon, broken in bits, into the batter for Best-Ever Muffins with the last few strokes of mixing. (Use the leftover bacon from breakfast.)

· *Chive muffins:* Snip chives in small pieces with scissors. Add ½ cup of them to the batter for Best-Ever Muffins with the last few strokes of mixing. The muffins are especially good with fish.

CORN MUFFINS

Too good to give up. American Indians made corn breads thousands of years ago with meal they ground between rocks

    1 cup sifted flour
    2 tablespoons sugar
    4 teaspoons baking powder
    1 teaspoon salt
    1 cup cornmeal
    2 eggs, slightly beaten
    1 cup milk
    ¼ cup melted shortening or salad oil

1. Start heating the oven to 425° F. Grease bottoms of muffin-pan cups.

2. Sift the flour onto a square of waxed paper or into a bowl and then measure. Sift the measured flour with the sugar, baking powder and salt into a large bowl. Stir in the cornmeal. Make a "well" in the mixture.

3. Add the eggs to the milk and stir in the shortening. Pour all at once into the "well" in the dry ingredients. Stir with a fork just to mix and until all the dry ingredients are moistened. The batter will not be smooth.

4. Fill muffin-pan cups ⅔ full with batter. Bake on the rack in the center of the oven 15 to 20 minutes or until the muffins are golden.

5. Remove the pan from the oven and place it on a wire rack. Run a spatula around the outside edge of each muffin to loosen. Lift out and serve at once. Makes 12 muffins.

For a change
· *Bacon corn muffins:* Add ⅓ cup crisp cooked bacon, broken in bits, to batter for Corn Muffins with the last few strokes of mixing.

Save on Dishwashing
If you grease more muffin-pan cups than you fill with batter, fill the empty cups half full with water. If you don't, the grease will burn on the cups and they will be difficult to wash. You can also use paper liners instead of grease in your muffin-pan cups. Teflon-lined muffin-pan cups are easy to wash. You need not grease them after the first greasing or "seasoning" of the new pans. Follow the manufacturer's directions for seasoning the pans with salad oil. The muffins will not stick in these pans.

Wonderful yeast breads

There are two kinds of yeast breads—kneaded bread and no-knead bread. No-knead breads are newer and faster to make—they are usually called batter breads. When you make them, you beat the batter (dough) instead of kneading it. Both kneaded and no-knead breads contain yeast—that's what makes them rise.

Yeast—active dry and compressed

In making yeast bread, you can use either active dry yeast, which comes in little packages, or cakes of compressed yeast that are wrapped in foil. Our recipes call for active dry yeast because it is available every place and can be stored many weeks longer than compressed yeast. The expiration date on the label of active dry yeast tells you if the yeast is "young" enough to make good bread.

Compressed yeast is perishable. It must be kept in the refrigerator, and no longer than a week or two, though you can keep it in the freezer up to 6 months. Thaw frozen compressed yeast at room temperature and then use it at once. Sometimes compressed yeast dries out and turns a light brown around the edges. Rub the yeast between your fingers—if it crumbles, it still is fresh enough to use even if it is a little discolored. You can use a cake of compressed yeast instead of a package of active dry yeast in our recipes, but dissolve it in lukewarm, not warm, water.

How yeast works

Yeast is a living plant and it needs three things to grow—*moisture, warmth* and *food*. (As it grows it produces more yeast and makes breads light.) Water provides the moisture. You dissolve the yeast in water before mixing it with the other ingredients. The water is warm, not hot (105° to 115°F.) for active dry yeast and, as mentioned, lukewarm (85°F.) for compressed yeast. If the water is too hot, it kills some of the yeast; if it is too cold, it either slows down or stops yeast growth. The first few times you bake yeast breads, use a candy thermometer to learn the temperature of the water before you add the yeast to it. Drop a little of the water on the inside of your wrist. You soon will learn to judge the right temperature without a thermometer.

Sugar is the food that encourages yeast to grow quickly, and as you'll notice, sugar is an ingredient in all our yeast bread recipes. It is especially important in the Dough for Refrigerator Rolls, a no-knead bread that contains more sugar than most doughs. The additional sugar feeds the yeast plants a longer time and they can be stored for several days in the refrigerator. The cold temperature holds back the growth of the yeast, too. When you bring out the dough, shape it and set it aside to rise, the yeast plants warm up and start to grow—there's plenty of sugar left in the dough for food. Yeast also feeds on the sugars in flour, but the extra sugar you add is ready to use and hurries the growth of yeast. But add only the amount of sugar given in the recipe—too much or too little sugar slows down the action of yeast.

Besides the warmth from the water, yeast is also provided with warmth by placing the dough in a warm place (85°F.) to rise. It is important to keep it out of drafts so the temperature will be steady, even. Cold drafts of air chill the dough and delay the growth of yeast. Here are three good ways to give yeast doughs a fine chance to grow:

1. Set the bowl of dough or batter on the rack of an unheated oven that has no pilot light. Place a large bowl of hot water on the oven floor beneath the bowl. The water adds heat and the oven protects the dough or batter from drafts. This is especially fine for the first rising. If you put the dough in the oven for the second rising, you will have to take it out before the dough is yet light enough to bake, because you must start heating the oven for the baking.

2. Or fill a large bowl about ⅔ full of warm water. Place a wire cooling rack on top of the bowl and set the bowl of batter or dough on the rack. Cover completely with a clean dish towel to hold in the heat. Empty the bowl of water, as it cools, and add more warm water.

3. Or set the bowl of batter or dough in a deep pan of warm water. Drop some of the warm water on the inside of your wrist. It should feel warm (not hot) 105° to 115° F. on the candy thermometer.

Watch the bread dough and shape it into loaves when it has risen enough. Then bake the loaves of dough when they are light. The general rule is to put these doughs in the pan and the oven when they have about doubled in bulk or size—every recipe tells how much to let the dough rise. If you let it rise too much, the bread will fall, become coarse and have big holes; it also will be dry. If you bake the dough before it is light enough, the bread will be heavy, the loaves small.

Make the Finger Tip Test with kneaded yeast doughs. With a finger press the dough lightly near the edge of the pan. If the dent made by the finger stays, the dough is ready for the oven.

For baking loaf breads, use glass, dark tin or dull aluminum (anodized) loaf pans, which are not shiny. A shiny metal reflects the heat away from the bread and crust does not brown by the time the bread is done.

We mentioned the importance of putting the dough in the heated oven at once when it is ready (light enough). Make sure also that the oven is heated to the temperature given in the recipe. The dough should rise very fast the first 5 to 10 minutes it's in the oven. The temperature must be hot enough to give the yeast the boost in growth. The bread should not brown until later. Whenever breads brown too fast while baking, lay a piece of aluminum foil or brown paper over them and complete the baking.

Where to keep bread

You may have to hide the bread you make—it will taste that good. But if you do have more rolls or bread than you eat at the first serving, wrap them (after cooling) in waxed paper and place them in a metal breadbox with holes for ventilation. If you do not have a bread-box, wrap them in waxed paper, saran or aluminum foil. In hot, humid summer weather, store the wrapped bread in the refrigerator to prevent mold. The bread will stale more quickly than bread kept in a breadbox.

Wrapped bread put in the freezer doesn't mold and it stays really fresh. But don't expect the freezer to freshen bread that was stale before freezing. Aluminum foil is ideal for wrapping bread because it molds tightly around the loaf and crowds the air out. And it seals itself.

Thaw frozen bread without unwrapping at room temperature on a wire rack. It will take at least 2 to 3 hours to thaw it, depending on the size of the bread and how warm the room is. If the bread is wrapped in foil, put it without unwrapping in an oven heated to 375° F. It will thaw and warm in 20 minutes. If you want it to have a crisp crust, open the foil the last 5 minutes.

SHORTCUT BATTER BREADS

Let's start making the no-knead breads. Then try the no-knead Refrigerator Rolls. Before you start to mix the batter, you will collect the tools and utensils you need. It is a good idea to get out both a mixing spoon and the electric mixer. While you can mix the batter with a spoon, a combination of spoon and electric mixer is ideal—there's lots of beating to do.

Batter breads rise twice, once in the mixing bowl and then in the baking pan, and it is important to put the batter into the pans and later, the pans into the oven *at the right time*. When the batter in the bowl has about doubled in size, looks moist and rough or pebbled and has tiny bubbles under the surface, it is time to put it in the baking pan. When the batter is in the pans, watch it and do not let it rise too much. If it does rise too much, turn it back into the bowl and beat it 25 hard strokes to remove the big bubbles of carbon-dioxide gas made by the yeast. Then put it back in the pans and let it rise again until *almost* doubled in size. If it has risen too much and you bake it without beating it and letting it rise again, the loaf will sag in the center.

Batter breads, when baked, have a dark brown crust that is somewhat rough or pebbled. Inside the breads are quite open in texture (the holes are larger than in kneaded breads). But these quick yeast breads have a nutlike, yeasty flavor that's delicious.

WHOLE WHEAT BATTER BREAD

You can bake a loaf of this bread in about 2 hours— almost half the time it takes to bake a loaf of kneaded bread

1¼ cups warm water (not hot, 105° to 115° F.)
  1 package active dry yeast
  2 tablespoons brown sugar
  1 cup whole wheat flour
  2 cups white flour
  2 teaspoons salt
  2 tablespoons soft shortening

1. Rinse out a large bowl with hot water to warm it. Pour the 1¼ cups of warm water into the warmed bowl, sprinkle on the yeast and stir until it dissolves.

2. Add the brown sugar, ½ cup whole wheat flour, 1 cup white flour, the salt and shortening. Beat 2 minutes with the electric mixer on medium speed (or 300 vigorous strokes with a long-handled wooden spoon). Stop the beaters a few times and scrape the sides and bottom of the bowl with a rubber spatula. The batter will be soupy.

3. With the spoon, beat in the other ½ cup of whole wheat flour and 1 cup of white flour. Scrape the batter from the sides and bottom of the bowl with a rubber spatula. Cover the bowl with a clean dish towel or waxed paper, and set it in a warm place (85° F.), away from drafts, until it doubles in size. This will take about 30 minutes.

4. Grease an 8- or 9-inch loaf pan.

5. Stir the batter back down with 25 strokes of the spoon or until it is about the same size it was when you set it aside to rise. This removes some of the gas bubbles made by the yeast and produces a loaf of bread that's more uniform in shape and has a finer texture (not large holes). It also brings the yeast in contact with more sugar (food). Pour the batter into the loaf pan. Flour your hand lightly

How to Slice Breads
The best way is to use a knife with a saw-toothed edge. Use a sawing motion and try not to press down on the loaf. A cooled loaf cuts more neatly than a warm one. Cut batter breads in thicker slices than the sliced bread you buy in supermarkets. They'll have more of a homemade look and taste and they're easier to slice.

Measure rise with a ruler

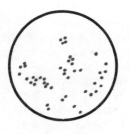

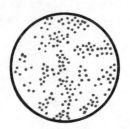

How Yeast Works
Here are two pictures of
yeast under a microscope.
The one on the top shows
how yeast looks when
taken from the package.
The other shows yeast
after it has had warmth,
liquid and food. Notice
how the yeast cells have
increased in number.
When yeast grows, it gives
off tiny bubbles of
carbon dioxide gas. It's
these bubbles that make
breads rise.

and smooth the top of the batter. Push the batter into the
corners of the pan with a rubber spatula. Cover with a
clean dish towel and set the pan of bread in a warm place
(85° F.) to rise the second time.

6. Let it rise until the batter is ¼ inch from the top
of an 8½-inch loaf pan or 1 inch from the top of a 9-inch
loaf pan. This will take about 40 minutes.

7. When the batter has risen 30 minutes, start heating
the oven to 375° F.

8. Bake the bread on the rack in the center of the oven
40 to 50 minutes, or until the crust is a deep brown. To
test for doneness, tap the crust with your fingers. If it has a
hollow sound, the bread is done.

9. Remove the pan from the oven and take the loaf out
of the pan. Brush the top of the loaf with a little shortening
or butter. Cool the bread right side up on a wire rack away
from drafts. It slices best if cut a little thicker than the
sliced bread you buy.

For a change
· *Rye batter bread:* Use 1 cup rye flour instead of the
whole wheat flour in the Whole Wheat Batter Bread recipe.
And use ½ cup more white flour (2½ cups instead of
2 cups). If your family likes caraway seeds, stir 1 tablespoon of them into the batter when you add the flour the
first time.

DOUGH FOR REFRIGERATOR ROLLS

Make rolls any time up to 3 to 5 days after the dough
has chilled 2 hours. Keep tightly covered in refrigerator

1¾ cups warm water (not hot, 105° to 115° F.)
 2 packages active dry yeast
 ½ cup sugar
 1 tablespoon salt
5½ to 6 cups flour
 1 egg, unbeaten
 ¼ cup soft shortening, butter or margarine

1. Pour warm water into a large warm bowl and sprinkle on the yeast. Stir until the yeast dissolves.

2. Add the sugar, salt and about half the flour. Beat
with an electric mixer on medium speed 2 minutes or beat
hard with a wooden spoon until the mixture is smooth.

3. Add the egg and soft shortening. Beat to mix. Mix in the rest of the flour with your hands or a spoon until the soft dough is easy to handle. Shape it into a ball.

4. Wash, dry and grease the large bowl; put the ball of dough, the smooth or top side down, in the clean bowl; then turn the greased side up. Cover tightly with waxed paper or aluminum foil, or place the bowl of dough in a plastic bag.

5. Put the dough in the refrigerator and let it rise at least 2 hours or until doubled in size before using it. Use it within 3 to 5 days, but punch the dough down every day until you use it. And punch down before shaping into rolls.

6. Make the rolls by these directions.

Bag it—to keep out air

PAN ROLLS

1. About 2 hours before you want to serve hot rolls, grease an 8- or 9-inch round pan.

2. Remove the Dough for Refrigerator Rolls from the refrigerator. Take out ⅓ of the dough and place it on a lightly floured surface. Cover and put the unused cold dough back in the refrigerator.

3. Shape the dough with your finger tips into 12 smooth balls of the same size. Place the balls close together in the pan, brush each ball top with a little melted butter, cover with a clean dish towel or waxed paper and let rise in a warm place (85°F.), away from drafts, until doubled in size. It usually will take about 1½ hours.

4. When the rolls are almost, but not quite, doubled in size, start heating the oven to 400°F.

5. Bake on the rack in the center of the oven 12 to 15 minutes, or until golden brown.

6. Remove the pan from the oven and brush the tops of the rolls with 1 tablespoon of soft butter or margarine. Serve warm. Makes 12 rolls.

What Gluten Does
Gluten is the protein that develops in flour when you add water or milk and beat bread batter or knead bread dough. The gluten stretches and surrounds the gas bubbles made by the yeast, and as the gas expands, the batter or dough rises along with it. During the baking, steam and air also help the bread rise.
The oven heat hardens the gluten—that's why bread holds its shape when removed from the pans in which it baked.

THREE-LEAF CLOVER ROLLS

1. About 2 hours before you want to serve hot rolls, grease 12 (2½-inch) muffin-pan cups.

2. Take the Dough for Refrigerator Rolls from the refrigerator and place ⅓ of it on a lightly floured surface. Cover and put the unused cold dough back in refrigerator.

Three balls make a cloverleaf

3. Divide the dough into two equal parts and roll each half with palms of hands to make ropes 16 inches long.

4. Cut each rope into 18 pieces of the same size. Shape each piece of dough into a smooth ball. Tuck the edges under to make a smooth top.

5. Put 3 balls of the dough in each muffin-pan cup. Brush the tops of the rolls with melted butter. Cover with a clean dish towel or waxed paper and let rise in a warm place (85° F.), away from drafts, until doubled in size.

6. When the rolls are almost, but not quite, doubled in size, start heating the oven to 400° F.

7. Bake like Pan Rolls 12 to 15 minutes or until golden brown. Serve warm. Makes 12 rolls.

KNEADED BREADS

Kneading does three things. It develops the gluten, a protein in flour, so that it can stretch and increase in size when you add the yeast; it mixes in the flour; and it distributes the ingredients throughout the dough. Here's how to do it:

1. Rub a little flour on your hands and on the board or on the cloth covering the board. Press the dough until it is flat. Pick up the edge that is farthest from you and fold it over on the edge that is nearest to you.

2. With the heels of your hands, push the dough away from you with a rocking, rolling motion. Press the dough lightly as you push it.

3. With both hands, give dough a quarter turn around on the board.

Flatten dough on board

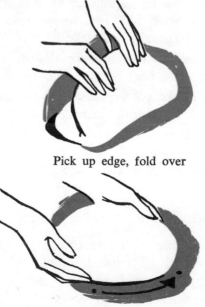

Pick up edge, fold over

Push with heels of hands

Give dough a quarter turn

Now fold, push and turn again. Keep doing this until the dough is smooth and elastic. This will take you at least 10 minutes at first, but after you have baked bread several times, you can do it in 5 to 8 minutes.

If the dough becomes sticky, spread 1 teaspoon of flour on the board under the dough and flour your hands again. Do this only when necessary. Scrape up any dough that sticks to the board. The kneading is done when the dough is almost as smooth as a rubber ball, feels springy, elastic and like satin to the hands. It no longer sticks to your hands or the board.

4. Shape the dough into a ball and let it rest on the board while you wash, dry and lightly grease the large bowl in which you mixed the dough. Put the ball of dough, with its smooth top down, into the bowl. Then turn the dough over so its top is up. This turning greases the surface of the dough so that it stays soft and stretches easily as the dough rises. Cover with a clean dish towel. Dough is ready to rise.

When the dough is ready for the pans, you shape it into loaves.

How to shape loaves

1. Turn the raised dough onto a lightly floured surface and cut it in half with a knife. Cover one of the halves with a clean dish towel while you work with the other half. Let the dough rest while you grease 2 (9×5×3-inch) loaf pans.

2. Flatten the uncovered dough with your fingers and press it into an oblong 9×7×1 inches. You can use a rolling pin to make the dough into the oblong. The width of the dough will be about the same as the length of the loaf pan. Try to make the dough of even thickness.

Cut ball of dough in half

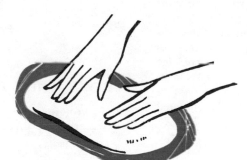

Flatten dough with fingers

Press into oblong, 9×7×1″

3. Fold each 7-inch end of the oblong of dough to the center and overlap these ends slightly. With both hands, press the folded sides down firmly.

4. Now seal the dough by pinching the center seam and ends. Roll to make loaf smooth. Place the loaf in the greased pan with the sealed seam down. Then shape the second half of dough the same way and place it in a greased loaf pan.

Flatten Bread Dough
Before you shape bread dough into loaves, you press it flat. This removes some of the larger gas bubbles made by the yeast and helps make a loaf with small, even holes.

Fold ends to center, overlap   Pinch center seam and ends

Which Milk in Yeast Breads?
You can use fresh, dry or evaporated milk. If you use fresh milk, scald it by heating it until tiny bubbles appear around the edge of the saucepan. Do not let it boil. The heating destroys chemicals called enzymes that would make the dough sticky and hard to handle.
Reconstitute dry milk by adding warm water as directed on the package and scald it.
Add an equal amount of hot water to evaporated milk to dilute it.
Always cool milk until lukewarm (85° F.) before using in yeast breads.

Into pan, seam side down

PERFECT WHITE BREAD

When it comes to baking good white bread, think of the old saying: Practice makes perfect. It's really true

Why Use Milk in Breads?
Milk makes bread more nutritious and gives it softer crusts and a velvety, creamy crumb, or texture. Breads made with milk brown beautifully when toasted.

½ cup warm water (not hot, 105° to 115° F.)
2 packages active dry yeast
1¾ cups milk, scalded
3 tablespoons sugar
1 tablespoon salt
3 tablespoons soft shortening
7 cups flour (about)

1. Pour warm water into a large bowl and sprinkle the yeast in it. Stir until yeast dissolves.

2. Pour the milk into a medium saucepan and scald it by heating over medium heat until small bubbles show around the edge. Do not let it come to a boil. Set it aside to cool until lukewarm. (You can substitute lukewarm water for the scalded and cooled milk.)

3. Add the sugar, salt, shortening and the lukewarm milk to the yeast mixture and beat in about 3 cups of flour with a spoon. Beat until the mixture is smooth and falls from the spoon in ribbons or "sheets."

4. With a spoon and one hand, mix in enough of the rest of the flour to make a dough that pulls away from the sides of the bowl in a mass and leaves only a small amount sticking to the bowl. (It will be a little sticky to handle, but stiff enough to hold its shape when turned onto a lightly floured board.) You will have some flour left, the exact amount depending on how dry the flour is—how much liquid it absorbs. Part of it you will use on the board when you knead the dough.

5. Turn the dough onto a lightly floured board. Then wash, dry and grease the bowl.

6. Now it's time to knead the dough.

7. When the dough is kneaded, put it in the clean greased bowl and turn it once to grease all sides. Cover it with a clean dish towel or waxed paper and set it in a warm place (85° F.), away from drafts, (so the temperature will be steady or even and the yeast will grow all the time) to rise until doubled in size. This will take 1 to 2 hours.

8. Punch the dough down until it is about the same size it was when you put it into the bowl to rise and turn it over in the bowl, smooth side up. Cover again with the clean dish towel or waxed paper and let it rise as before, until it is doubled in size. This second rising will take from 45 minutes to an hour.

9. Punch the dough down again and turn it onto a lightly floured surface. Cut it in half with a large knife or kitchen scissors and let it rest a few minutes while you lightly grease 2 (9×5×3-inch) loaf pans.

10. Shape the dough into 2 loaves.

11. Cover with the clean dish towel or waxed paper and let rise in a warm place again until doubled in size. This will take about 1 hour. To test if the bread is ready to bake, press the edge of the dough in one of the pans

Cover dough, let it rise

Punch down with fist

Cover and let rise again

See directions for kneading, pages 106–7

See how to shape loaves, pages 107–8

Prizewinning Crust
For a tender crust, brush warm baked rolls or bread loaves with shortening, melted butter or margarine. Then cover with a clean dish towel for a few minutes. For a crisp crust, do not grease or cover rolls or bread loaves. But cool them out of drafts to prevent crust from cracking. For a glazed shiny crust, brush the dough before baking with 1 egg yolk mixed with 2 tablespoons of cold water.

lightly with your little finger. If the dent made by the finger stays, the dough is ready to bake. Do not let it rise too much or it will fall while baking.

12. Start heating the oven to 425° F. after the dough has risen 40 minutes in the pans. Be sure the oven is heated before adding the bread.

13. Put the loaf pans on the rack in the center of the oven. Leave at least 2 inches between the two pans and between the pans and the walls of the oven so the heat can move around the dough and bake it.

14. Bake 25 to 30 minutes or until the loaves are a deep golden brown. Remove the pans from the oven and take the loaves from the pans at once; place them on a wire rack, right side up, to cool. Brush the tops with a little melted butter or margarine if you like a tender crust. Cool the bread away from drafts so the crust won't crack.

GARLIC FRENCH BREAD

Buy a loaf of crusty French bread to make this hot bread for dinner, or for a cookout

So handy: a garlic press. Put the garlic clove in the press and crush, holding it over the food you want to season with garlic.

1 loaf French bread
1 clove garlic, crushed, or ½ teaspoon garlic powder
½ cup soft butter or margarine

1. Start heating the oven to 350° F.

2. Cut the bread in half lengthwise. Peel garlic, cut in half and crush by pressing with a spoon.

3. Mix the butter and crushed garlic in a small bowl. Spread the butter mixture on the cut surface of each bread half, removing the garlic pieces.

4. Put the bread back together to form a loaf and wrap it tightly in aluminum foil.

5. Place the bread in the oven and heat it 10 to 12 minutes or until the butter melts and the bread is hot. Cut slantwise into serving pieces.

For a change
· *Parsley garlic bread:* Add 2 tablespoons snipped parsley to the garlic butter.
· *Cheese garlic bread:* After you spread the garlic butter on the bread, sprinkle on evenly 3 tablespoons grated Parmesan cheese.

How to slice Garlic Bread

Desserts—pride of good cooks

IF YOU counted all the choice recipes in home kitchens, you'd find more for desserts than for other parts of the meal. Almost all good cooks like to make desserts, so they always are on the lookout for new dishes to try. This Cookbook has many excellent dessert recipes—cookies, cakes, pies and homemade ice cream, to name a few. But here is a collection of other types of desserts you'll want to make. Many of them are simple, but they all taste wonderful.

You'll find some of the great country fruit treats on the next few pages—desserts to make when fresh fruit is in season. Then there are some puddings that always win compliments. Many of them are made with convenient packaged mixes and are a snap to fix.

The custards deserve a special mention because they are so delicate and delicious. If you've heard that custards are difficult to make, just try our recipes and see how untrue the rumor is. Custards are milk thickened with eggs and sweetened with sugar, and it's important to use low heat in cooking them so the protein in the milk and eggs will not become tough. You'll notice we suggest surrounding our custards with water or steam—that's to keep the temperatures low while they cook, and make them tender.

Waffles always are fun for dessert. You can bake them at the table while everybody watches and waits enthusiastically. Our two recipes are different and decidedly good. So are all of the recipes that follow!

BAKED APPLES

Baked apples and molasses cookies are a country dessert

  6 medium cooking apples
¾ cup sugar
  1 cup water

    1. Start heating the oven to 350° F.

Peel the stem end

2. Wash and core the apples with a paring knife or apple corer.

3. Starting at the stem end, peel the apple, a third of the way down. This will keep the steam that forms in the apples, when they are cooking, from bursting the skins. Place the apples, peeled end up, in a shallow baking pan.

4. Mix the sugar and water in a small saucepan and bring the mixture, stirring all the time, to a boil over medium heat. Then simmer over low heat 10 minutes. Pour this hot syrup over the apples.

6. Bake the apples until they test tender when you stick a kitchen fork into them. It will take from 30 minutes to 1 hour, depending on the apples. Some cook quicker than others.

7. Take the apples from the oven and serve warm or cold with cream or ice cream. Makes 6 servings.

How to make baked apples different

· *Broiled tops:* Sprinkle 1 teaspoon sugar over each apple when you take the baked apples from the oven. Then run them in the broiler, under low heat, for 5 minutes or until they brown lightly. It's a good idea to spoon a little of the juice over the apples three or four times while they are broiling. Or use a baster if you have one.

Surprise baked apples: Stuff a marshmallow, a cut-up pitted date, 1 teaspoon of canned mincemeat, a little currant jelly or orange marmalade, flaked coconut mixed with brown sugar or raisins into the cavity (where the core was) of each apple before baking.

APPLESAUCE

There's nothing better than applesauce when apples are fresh from orchards, but the sauce is tasty any time

8 cooking apples (2½ pounds)
½ cup water
½ to ⅔ cup white or brown sugar, packed firmly
½ teaspoon vanilla

1. Peel apples, cut into quarters and remove the cores. Put them in a medium saucepan. You will have almost 8 cups of apples.

2. Add the water, cover the saucepan and cook the apples over medium heat until they come to a boil. Then

So handy: a food mill

simmer over low heat until the apples test tender when you stick them with a fork—about 20 to 25 minutes. Stir the apples a few times, adding more water if they cook dry. This is important, for the apples might scorch and would not taste good.

3. Beat the tender apples smooth with a spoon. Or if you have a food mill, cook the apples, without peeling them, until tender and then put them through the food mill.

4. Stir ½ cup sugar into the smooth, hot applesauce. Stir until the sugar dissolves. Then taste the sauce—you may want to add more sugar. Some apples are more tart than others.

5. Stir in the vanilla. Serve warm or cold. Makes 6 servings.

For a change
· *Pine-apple sauce:* Add ½ cup crushed canned pineapple to the apples before cooking.

Ways to serve applesauce
· *Applesauce à la mode:* Serve applesauce in individual dishes and top with vanilla ice cream.
· *Marshmallow applesauce:* Top servings of applesauce with a spoonful of marshmallow creme.

APPLE CRISP

You can use white instead of brown sugar in this pudding

```
6 cups peeled, sliced apples
1 tablespoon lemon juice
1 tablespoon water
¾ cup brown sugar, packed firmly
½ cup flour
¼ cup quick-cooking rolled oats
⅓ cup soft butter or margarine
1 teaspoon cinnamon
```

1. Start the oven heating to 375° F.

2. Spread the sliced apples in an 8-inch square baking pan. Sprinkle the lemon juice and water over the apples.

3. Stir together the brown sugar, flour, rolled oats, butter and cinnamon. Sprinkle this mixture evenly over the apples.

4. Bake for 40 to 45 minutes. Serve warm or cold with cream or milk. Makes 6 servings.

BAKED PEACHES

When you tire of sliced peaches and cream, bake them

6 large ripe fresh peaches
3 tablespoons lemon juice
½ cup honey
Cream, ice cream or raspberry sherbet

1. Start heating the oven to 350° F.

2. Wash and peel peaches. Cut them in half and remove the pits. Place the peach halves in an 8-cup (2-quart) casserole.

3. Mix the lemon juice and honey and pour the mixture over the peaches.

4. Cover and bake until tender when tested with a kitchen fork. It will take about 30 minutes.

5. Serve warm or cold with cream poured over or topped with vanilla ice cream or raspberry sherbet. Makes 6 servings.

STRAWBERRY PINK RHUBARB SAUCE

This proves rhubarb and strawberries are a great food team

3 cups cut-up rhubarb
1 cup sugar
1 tablespoon water
1 (10-ounce) package frozen strawberries

1. Wash the rhubarb. Do not peel off the skin unless it is tough. Cut the stalks into 1-inch pieces.

2. Place the rhubarb in a medium saucepan. Add the sugar and water. Cover and cook it over low heat until it is tender, about 25 minutes.

3. Remove it from the heat. Stir in the frozen strawberries. Stir the mixture until the strawberries thaw. Serve the sauce warm or chilled. Makes 2½ cups.

STRAWBERRIES AND CREAM

For a gourmet dish use dairy sour cream instead of heavy cream, but don't whip the sour cream—use from the carton

1 quart fresh strawberries
½ cup light brown sugar
1 cup heavy cream

1. Wash the strawberries gently in cold water and drain in a strainer or sieve. Then hull them into a large bowl.

2. Add the brown sugar to the berries and toss gently to mix.

3. Whip the cream and sweeten. Take out 6 tablespoons of it. Fold the rest of the whipped cream into the sugared berries.

4. Divide the berries among 6 dessert dishes and top each serving with 1 tablespoon of the whipped cream saved out. Makes 6 servings.

AMBROSIA

Top this Christmas dessert with a sliced banana at mealtime

4 large oranges
6 tablespoons sugar
1 (3½-ounce) can flaked coconut
3 tablespoons orange juice

1. Peel the oranges with a knife the way you peel apples, taking care to cut off the white part under the orange-colored skins. Navel oranges, which have no seeds, are excellent in this dessert, but you can use any other kind. If there are seeds, discard them.

2. Slice the oranges thinly crosswise. The slices should be ⅛ inch thick or as thin as you can make them.

3. Spread ⅓ of the orange slices in a medium serving bowl—a glass one is pretty. Sprinkle with 2 tablespoons sugar and then with ⅓ cup coconut and 1 tablespoon orange juice. Repeat, making two more layers of orange slices and sprinkle them with the sugar, coconut and orange juice.

4. Cover the bowl and chill the dessert several hours, or at least 1 hour. Serve at the table in dessert dishes. Garnish with drained maraschino cherries if you like. Makes 6 servings.

BANANA SUNDAE

One of the best-tasting ways to dress up bananas

1 cup frozen sliced strawberries
3 large bananas
1½ pints vanilla ice cream

How to Store Coconut
Once you open a can or package of coconut, keep it in a covered airtight container, either in the refrigerator or freezer. Coconut is the fruit of the tropical coco palm tree. Like all fruits, coconut is perishable.

Freckled Bananas
When bananas are covered with little brown spots, they are just right for mashing and mixing into puddings, breads and cakes. To hold ripened bananas a few days, refrigerate them. But be sure to wrap them tightly in a plastic bag, or they'll smell up the refrigerator. Their skins will turn brown in the refrigerator, but the inside will stay the same for a few days. Keep unripe bananas at room temperature until they ripen the way you like them.

Spade the Ice Cream
When you take ice cream from the freezer, it's frozen so hard and firm that you scarcely can dip it up for serving. An ice cream spade really helps. That's because it's so strong!

Scoop the Ice Cream
If you want to serve ice cream in neat rounded servings, use an ice cream scoop. You'll play no favorites. All the mounds of ice cream will be the same size.

1. Partly thaw the strawberries.

2. At serving time, peel the bananas and cut them into lengthwise halves. Place each half, cut side down, on a serving plate.

3. Put a scoop of ice cream inside the banana curve. Spoon the partly thawed strawberries on top. Makes 6 servings.

For a change

· *Banana caramel sundae:* Omit the strawberries and pour caramel sauce over the ice cream and bananas. You can buy the sauce in jars in the supermarket or make your own by the recipe that follows.

CANDY CARAMEL SAUCE

This sauce, hot or cold, tastes good on vanilla ice cream

½ pound caramel candy pieces (about 28)
½ cup hot water

Place the caramels and water in the top of the double boiler. Heat over boiling water, stirring frequently, until the caramels melt and make a smooth sauce. Serve hot or cold. Makes 1 cup.

PINEAPPLE TAPIOCA PUDDING

When you fold in the whipped cream, you can spoon the pudding into dessert dishes to chill until served

1 (6-ounce) can frozen pineapple juice
¼ cup sugar
3 tablespoons quick-cooking tapioca
⅛ teaspoon salt
1 (8¾-ounce) can crushed pineapple
⅓ cup heavy cream (whipping cream)

See how to whip cream, page 19

1. Thaw the pineapple juice, but do not add water to it. Just pour it from the can into a measuring cup. Add enough cold water to make 2 cups of liquid.

2. Pour the water-pineapple juice mixture into a medium saucepan and stir in the sugar, tapioca and salt. Mix well.

3. Bring the mixture to a boil over medium heat, stirring all the time. Remove it from the heat. Cool until lukewarm, about 20 minutes, and then stir in the crushed pineapple undrained.

4. Place the pudding in the refrigerator for 30 minutes. Then whip the cream, but do not add sugar or vanilla to it. Fold the whipped cream into the pudding. Put the pudding back in the refrigerator and chill it at least an hour, or longer if you wish to serve it later. It needs no garnish, but a few fresh mint leaves on top of each serving are attractive. Or if you like, pass a pitcher of light cream to pour over the pudding. Makes 6 servings.

SPICE DUMPLINGS IN APPLESAUCE

Delicious! And a dessert that's simple to make. Try it at home and again over coals at a cookout

　2 (1-pound 2-ounce) cans applesauce or 4 cups
　　homemade applesauce
½ package spice cake mix

1. Heat the applesauce in a heavy skillet until it is bubbling hot.

2. Make the spice cake by package directions (remember, you are using only half a package). Pour the batter slowly over the top of the hot applesauce.

3. Cover the mixture and cook over medium heat 20 to 30 minutes. Serve it hot with milk or light cream. Makes 8 servings.

CRANBERRY CRUNCH À LA MODE

Just the dessert to "wind up" a chicken dinner in fine style

　1 cup raw quick-cooking rolled oats
½ cup flour
　1 cup brown sugar, packed firmly
½ cup butter or margarine
　1 (1-pound) can cranberry sauce (whole or jellied)
Vanilla ice cream

1. Start heating the oven to 350° F. Grease an 8×8×2-inch pan with shortening.

2. Mix the rolled oats, flour, brown sugar and butter with a pastry blender until crumbly. Spread half of this mixture evenly to cover the bottom of the pan.

3. Spread the cranberry sauce evenly over the crumbs. Cover the top with the rest of the crumbs.

Cranberry Bounce
Cranberries are the only fruit that bounce like rubber balls. The growers use the bounce test to find out if their berries are of high quality and ready for the market. They give the red berries 4 chances to bounce over boards 4 inches high. The firmer the fresh berries are, the higher they bounce. When cranberries are overripe or bruised, they do not bounce—they plop.

Skating on Cranberry Bogs
Cranberry growers keep their bogs covered with water during the winter to prevent the vines from freezing. The bogs provide safe ice skating because the water underneath the ice layer is only deep enough to cover the low vines.

4. Bake the dessert 25 minutes. Serve it hot, cut into bars, with a scoop of vanilla ice cream on top. Makes 6 servings.

WAFFLES À LA MODE

Try butterscotch or caramel sauce instead of the chocolate

1¼ cups sifted cake flour
1 tablespoon sugar
½ teaspoon salt
1 teaspoon baking powder
2 eggs
1 cup light cream
1 tablespoon melted butter or salad oil
¼ cup chopped nuts
Ice cream
Chocolate Sauce

1. Sift the flour onto a square of waxed paper or into a bowl and then measure. Sift the measured flour with the sugar, salt and baking powder.

2. Separate the egg yolks from the whites. Stir the cream, egg yolks and melted butter together in a large bowl. Beat well. Add the nuts and the flour mixture and mix well.

3. Beat the egg whites until stiff and fold them into the batter.

See how to bake waffles, page 96

4. Bake the batter on the hot grids of a waffle iron. You will have 2 waffles to break into 8 sections.

5. Serve the waffles at once with each section topped with a scoop of vanilla or your favorite ice cream. Pour on fudge sauce from the supermarket or make your own Chocolate Sauce (recipe follows). Makes 8 servings.

CHOCOLATE SAUCE

Keep this sauce in the refrigerator—it comes in handy

1 (6-ounce) package semisweet chocolate pieces
½ cup light corn syrup
¼ cup milk
1 tablespoon butter or margarine
¼ teaspoon vanilla

1. Put the chocolate pieces, corn syrup, milk and butter into the top of the double boiler. Place it over hot water

to heat, stirring until the chocolate melts and makes a smooth sauce.

2. Remove the sauce from the heat, stir in the vanilla and serve hot or chilled. Makes 1½ cups.

PECAN COOKIES À LA MODE

Bake these cookie-waffles with the gang gathered round and serve them hot—they'll make a hit with everybody

  1 (4-ounce) package chocolate pudding and pie filling mix
¼ cup sugar
  1 cup flour
  1 teaspoon baking powder
½ teaspoon salt
  2 eggs, separated
½ cup milk
½ cup melted butter or margarine
  1 cup chopped pecans
Vanilla ice cream

1. Sift together, in a large bowl, the pudding mix, sugar, flour, baking powder and salt.

2. Separate the egg whites and yolks. Beat the yolks and add the milk to them. Stir the egg-yolk mixture and melted butter into the dry ingredients. Add the pecans.

3. Start the waffle iron heating.

4. Beat the egg whites until stiff and fold them into the batter. Put the batter into a wide-mouthed pitcher.

5. Pour the batter from the pitcher onto the waffle iron. Bake and serve at once with vanilla ice cream on top. Makes 6 servings.

STEAMED CUSTARDS

A new, easy way to fix velvety custards—they never weep

1½ cups milk
  3 eggs
  3 tablespoons sugar
¼ teaspoon salt
½ teaspoon vanilla
Nutmeg, if you like it

1. Heat the milk in the top of the double boiler over

Why Custard Weeps
When you cook custard at too high a temperature, the protein in the milk and eggs shrinks and forces out the liquid. The cook says: The custard is weeping.

hot, not boiling, water or heat it in a saucepan over low heat. Heat the milk until it bubbles around the edge, but do not let it boil or simmer.

2. Beat the eggs slightly (don't overbeat), add the sugar, salt and vanilla and stir to mix. Add the milk slowly and stir slowly.

3. Pour the custard mixture into 5 (5-ounce) cheese glasses. Sprinkle the tops with nutmeg.

4. Place the glasses on a rack or on folded paper towels in a kettle with a tight-fitting lid. Do not let the glasses touch.

5. Pour cold water into the kettle to ⅓ the height of the glasses. Cover the kettle.

6. Bring the water to a boil over high heat and turn off the heat at once. Be sure not to remove cover. Leave the custards in the covered kettle to steam 8 to 10 minutes before removing the lid.

7. Cool the custards until lukewarm. Cover the tops with pieces of foil and refrigerate them until time to serve. Makes 5 servings.

Cover tightly and steam

For a change

· *Custard cup custards:* If you do not have the 5-ounce cheese glasses called for in the recipe for Steamed Custards, you can use 4 (5-ounce) custard cups, which are shorter and larger across than the taller cheese glasses. You'll need a larger kettle (6-quart) with a tight lid.

Pour 1 inch of boiling water into the kettle and set the filled custard cups in it on two layers of paper toweling. Bring the water to a boil, cover the kettle with a tight lid and cook over *very low heat* 10 to 12 minutes. Remove the custard cups from the kettle, cool and then cover them with foil and chill in the refrigerator. Makes 4 servings.

Beef and pork

WHEN you plan a meal, you think first about what kind of meat to have. Then you decide what other foods—vegetables, salad and dessert—will go with what you select.

When meat comes to the kitchen, store it in the coldest part of the refrigerator. It is a good idea to wrap it loosely in waxed paper, but leave the paper open at both ends so the cold air can quickly reach the meat and keep it cool enough to prevent spoilage. If your refrigerator has a meat compartment, the wrapping is not so important. Cool cooked meats in the refrigerator within 2 hours after cooking so the bacteria that cause spoilage will not have time to grow. Use cooked refrigerated meats within 4 days or freeze them.

Smart cooks want to fix meat to taste its best, and this is easy to do. There are only two ways to cook meats—in dry heat, called roasting and broiling, and in moist heat, with water or other liquid, such as tomato juice, added. Cook meats, other than those you broil, at a low temperature (325° F.) if roasting, and at simmering (just below boiling) if cooking in moist heat. There will be less shrinkage of the meat and flavor will be best if it is cooked slowly and gently in or over low heat.

Beef . . . top favorite meat

DIFFERENT KINDS OF BEEF ROASTS

There are two kinds of beef roasts—those you always cook, uncovered, in the oven in dry heat (without adding water or other liquid) and pot roasts that you cook, tightly covered, in a pot, such as a Dutch oven, and to which you add water or other liquid. You can cook pot roasts on top of the stove or in a slow oven.

The best cuts of beef for dry roasting are rolled rib roasts (bones removed) and standing rib roasts, and the rump and sirloin tip. All of these cuts must be of top quality. The best cuts for pot roasts are boned rump, sirloin tip, arm (from chuck) and blade (from chuck). The meat does not need to be of top quality because liquid is added to make steam, which tenderizes the connective tissue. You will find that the pot roast tastes better if the lean meat is covered with fat and has streaks of fat in it.

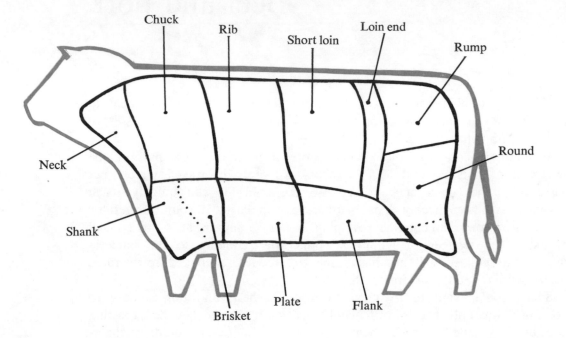

Timing an oven roast

Tender, juicy oven-roasted beef! It tastes so good and it's easy to fix. You don't need to watch roasts while they cook. You don't even have to turn them. But you must start with good, tender beef, and you simply can't hurry the roasting.

There can be no accurate time for cooking roasts because two cuts of the same weight often differ greatly in size, shape and the amount of fat they contain.

You can cook all beef roasts, regardless of their size, shape and weight, exactly the way you like beef—rare, medium or well done. The secret is to use the meat thermometer. It will tell you when the meat is done the way you like it.

Here are timetables for roasting a 4-pound rolled rib roast, measuring about 5 inches across, and a 4-pound standing rib roast, measuring about 6 inches from the tip of the rib to the backbone. A longer standing rib roast of the same weight will cook more quickly. The number of hours and minutes is a guide to give you an idea of how long before mealtime you need to put the roast in the oven to cook.

Rolled Rib Roast (4-pound)

Temperature on Thermometer		Roasting Time (about)
Rare	140° F.	2 hours, 45 minutes
Medium	160° F.	3 hours, 15 minutes
Well done	170° F.	3½ hours

Standing Rib Roast (4-pound)

Rare	140° F.	1 hour, 45 minutes
Medium	160° F.	2 hours, 15 minutes
Well done	170° F.	3 hours

The bones in the standing rib roast help carry the heat to all parts of the roast—therefore it cooks more quickly than a rolled roast.

HOW TO COOK A 4-POUND ROLLED RIB ROAST

1. Look at the timetable to find out about how long your roast will need to cook to the doneness you like. That will tell you when to put it in the oven to be ready by mealtime. If you want to cook your roast to medium doneness, you will want to get it in the oven at least 3½ hours before you will serve it. This allows time for it to "set."

2. Start the oven heating to 325° F.

3. Take the roast from the refrigerator and put it fat side up on a rack in a shallow pan. Do not add water or rub the meat with flour.

4. You can sprinkle on a little salt and pepper, but seasonings cannot penetrate the meat for more than ¼ inch. That's why most cooks let everybody season his own serving of meat the way he likes it.

5. With a skewer, make a hole through the fat side to the center of the roast. Then carefully push the meat thermometer into this hole, trying to make sure the small, pointed end doesn't rest on fat.

6. Put the roast in the oven. Do not cover it—a cover would collect steam in the pan. Do not turn the meat during the cooking. Look at the thermometer occasionally when the roasting time is about up.

7. When the roast is almost done, remove the pan from the oven and let the meat "set" 15 to 30 minutes. Roasts of all kinds slice more easily if you let them "set" after taking them from the oven. While they "set" in a warm place,

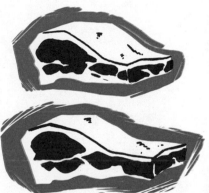

Two Rib Roasts
These two roasts weigh the same but they are a different size and shape. The thicker roast on the top will take more cooking time.

See how to use a meat thermometer, page 18

you can put the last-minute touches on the rest of the meal. Even though the meat is out of the oven, it will keep on cooking while it "sets." That's why many good cooks remove the roast from the oven when the thermometer reads 5 to 10° lower than the one in the timetable—130 to 135° F. for rare, 150 to 155° F. for medium and 160 to 165° F. for well-done roasts.

8. Serve the roast on a warm platter with the large end down. Garnish with sprigs of parsley or water cress or with a cooked vegetable, such as carrots or beets, if there is room on the platter—it's hard to carve the roast if the platter is crowded. The roast will make 8 to 12 servings. The leftover meat, sliced, is good cold or used in sandwiches or many dishes.

STANDING RIB ROAST

Cook a standing rib roast like a rolled rib roast, but stand it on the rib ends in a shallow, open pan. Buy at least a 2-rib roast and have the meatman saw across the ribs close to the backbone so that you can remove it when the roast is cooked. It will carve more easily with the backbone removed.

POT ROAST WITH VEGETABLES

All the meal is in one pot. Just add a fruit or lettuce salad and apple or pumpkin pie for a true American feast

    2 tablespoons flour
    2 teaspoons salt
    ⅛ teaspoon pepper
    3½ pounds arm, blade or rump pot roast
    3 tablespoons shortening
    ½ cup water
    1 bay leaf
    6 small onions, peeled
    6 medium carrots, peeled
    3 stalks celery, sliced
    4 medium potatoes, peeled and cut in halves

1. Mix the flour, 1 teaspoon of the salt and the pepper and spread on a sheet of waxed paper. Roll the meat in this to coat on all sides. Or rub the seasoned flour into the meat on all surfaces with your hands.

2. Heat the shortening in a heavy Dutch oven or large skillet and brown the meat on all sides over medium heat. This will take from 15 to 20 minutes.

3. Add the water and bay leaf, cover tightly and simmer over low heat about 2½ hours. Add a little more water if the liquid cooks down.

4. Add the prepared vegetables, tucking them into the liquid around the beef. Sprinkle them with the other 1 teaspoon of salt. Cover tightly and simmer 45 minutes to 1 hour or until all the vegetables are tender.

5. Remove meat (use a meat lifter) and vegetables to a warm platter. Set the platter in a very low oven to keep warm while you make the gravy. Makes 6 servings.

POT ROAST GRAVY

Measure all ingredients carefully—that's the secret

1. When the meat is on the warm platter, pour all the fat and meat juices from the pan into a bowl. The fat will rise to the top.

2. Spoon off 4 tablespoons fat and put it back in the cooking pan. Heat it over low heat and gradually stir in 4 tablespoons of flour to make a smooth mixture, slightly brown. The best tool for stirring gravy is a wire beater. Stir with a flat, circular motion.

3. Gradually stir in 2 cups of the cooking liquid from the bottom of the bowl. If there's not enough, add water or canned beef bouillon to make 2 cups.

4. Cook and stir the gravy over low heat until smooth and thickened. This takes only a few minutes, not more than 5. As you stir, loosen any brown particles of meat that may have stuck to the pan. They add flavor.

5. Season the gravy to taste with salt and pepper and pour it into a bowl. Serve piping hot. Makes 2 cups.

Smooth Gravy
When you make pan gravy, you stir the flour into the fat. The fat separates the particles of starch in the flour and keeps them from forming lumps. When you thicken a hot liquid, such as stew, you first mix the flour with cold water to separate the particles of starch. If you don't do this, the starch grains do not have a chance to separate. They form lumps that cannot be broken up no matter how long and hard you stir.

SIR LOIN

History records that a king of England, King Charles II, was so fond of the loin of beef, roasted, that he knighted it. He touched his sword to the cut of beef and said: "I hereby name thee Sir Loin." The name stuck to a cut we enjoy today: broiled sirloin steak.

So handy: meat mallet, tongs

Why Do You Pound Steak?
Steaks used for Swiss steak have lots of connective tissue called collagen (call'ah-jen). Pounding helps break up this tissue, making the meat more tender.

SWISS STEAK

All steaks, cut 1½ to 2 inches thick, will cook fork-tender this way. Do brown the meat well first to get rich flavors

2 to 3 pounds round steak, chuck or rump steak, cut 1½ to 2 inches thick
¼ cup flour
1 teaspoon salt
¼ teaspoon pepper
2 tablespoons salad oil or fat
1 large onion, peeled and thinly sliced
1 stalk celery, cut up
1 (1-pound) can tomatoes (2 cups)

1. Start heating the oven to 350° F.

2. Trim off the excess fat. If using round steak, cut a gash just through the fat border every 3 inches. This prevents the meat from curling up during cooking.

3. Mix the flour, salt and pepper and sprinkle half of the mixture over one side of the meat. Pound it in with a meat mallet or the edge of a heavy saucer or plate. Turn the meat, sprinkle with the remaining flour mixture and pound on the other side.

4. Heat the salad oil in a heavy skillet or Dutch oven over medium heat. Add the meat. Cook until well browned on both sides, turning once with tongs if you have them. (Tongs are better than a fork because you can get a firmer grip. Also, you don't put holes in the meat to let the juices run out.) This will take at least 20 minutes.

5. Top meat with the onion slices and celery and pour on the tomatoes. Cover and bake until tender when you stick a fork into the meat, about 2 hours. Remove the cover and bake 30 minutes longer. Serve on a warm platter with the sauce poured over the meat. Makes 6 to 8 servings.

For a change

· *Western style:* Use 1½ cups hot water, 3 tablespoons ketchup and ¾ teaspoon prepared mustard instead of the tomatoes.

· *Mixed vegetables:* Use canned vegetable juice cocktail instead of tomatoes.

· *Individual Swiss steaks:* Make like Swiss Steak recipe, but cut the meat into 6 or 8 pieces before cooking. Add ⅛ teaspoon dried thyme with the salt and pepper.

STEAKS—OVEN- AND PAN-BROILED

Broil tender cuts of top quality—no cook ever won compliments on a tough steak. For oven-broiling, you need a steak at least 1 inch thick. Thin steaks, ½ to ¾ inch thick, are best pan-broiled.

The favorite cuts of steak are: *porterhouse* (from large end of short loin), which has a T-shaped bone; *T-bone* (from center of short loin), which looks like porterhouse but is smaller; *club* (smallest steak in the short loin), which is triangular in shape; *rib* (sliced from the rib section); *filet mignon* (from tenderloin), which is boneless; and *sirloin* (from the loin end), which is less expensive than most steaks and makes a good choice for families because it is large (if it's a full cut).

The number of servings you get from a steak depends on how thick it is cut and the size of the animal. Cuts from big beef are larger than those from small animals.

Timetable for oven-broiling steaks

The cooking time depends on how thick the steaks are cut, and timetables are only a guide to give you an idea how long before mealtime to start the broiling. Steaks vary so greatly in size and the amount of bone and fat they contain that no exact timing can be given. When you think the steaks are done the way you like them, cut a small slit in the meat near the bone with a sharp knife and look at the color of the meat to see if it is a red to a deep pink (rare), pale pink (medium) or gray (well done).

Cuts	Thickness	Total Cooking Time	
T-bone, Club, Filet Mignon, Rib	1 inch	rare	10 minutes
		medium	12 minutes
		well done	16 minutes
	1½ inches	rare	18 minutes
		medium	20 minutes
		well done	25 minutes
	2 inches	rare	32 minutes
		medium	36 minutes
		well done	40 minutes
Sirloin or any large steak	1 inch	rare	20 minutes
		medium	24 minutes
		well done	28 minutes
	1½ inches	rare	24 minutes
		medium	28 minutes
		well done	32 minutes

Cut to test for doneness

OVEN-BROILED STEAK

1. About 10 minutes before you start broiling the steak, set oven regulator for broiling. If your range does not have a broiling regulator, turn the oven regulator on full.

2. Cut off the extra fat from the steak or if it is lean, like filet mignon, brush both sides of it with salad oil.

3. Slash through the fat edge every 2 inches with scissors or a sharp knife, but do not cut into the lean meat. This will keep the steak from curling while it broils.

4. Rub the heated broiler rack with a piece of fat from the steak to prevent the meat from sticking to it. Put the steak on the rack.

5. Put the broiler pan in the oven about 2 inches from the heat if the steak is thin, 3 to 5 inches from the heat if the steak is thick. Or follow the range manufacturer's directions.

6. Broil the steak for half of the time given in the time-table. Then turn it over with tongs. If you stick a fork into it, some of the juices that taste so good will escape and the steak may be dry. Cook on the second side until done. Frozen steaks, even if hard-frozen, take little more broiling time than the same cuts of fresh meat. The thicker cuts require at least one fourth more broiling time or sometimes even more. For a medium T-bone steak, 1½ inches thick, the cooking will take from 25 to 35 minutes. Test the doneness with a knife.

7. Lift the steak to a warm platter, sprinkle it lightly with salt and pepper and, if you like, dot it with butter or margarine. Garnish with sprigs of parsley or water cress if you have it.

8. Serve at once.

PAN-BROILED STEAK

1. Rub a skillet, large enough to hold the steak without crowding, with a piece of fat (suet) cut from the meat. This will keep the steak from sticking.

2. Heat the skillet over high heat and add the steak, cut ½ to ¾ inch thick, and brown on both sides. Do not cover and do not add water.

3. Turn the heat down and continue cooking and turning with tongs until the meat is done. Spoon off the fat as it collects in the skillet. If you have a baster, use it to remove the fat.

Minute Steaks
Minute steaks are thin cuts from the round that are scored (cut) by a special machine that breaks the connective tissue. Pan-broil them but only 2 minutes on each side.

So handy: a baster

4. It takes about 8 minutes to cook the steak rare, 10 to 12 minutes for medium and 15 to 20 minutes for well-done steak.

5. Season steak with salt and pepper, lift it onto a warm platter and serve at once.

GOOD BEEF STEWS

A beef stew is cooked like a pot roast, only the meat is cut into 1- to 2-inch pieces. You use the less tender beef cuts, which have wonderful flavors: the *chuck* (shoulder), *bottom round, neck meat, shank meat, flank* and *plate*. The chuck cooks tender more quickly than the other cuts, but it costs more.

You can cook stews in the oven or on top of the range. If you cook your stew on top of the range, look at it a few times while it cooks to see if you need to add more water—sometimes it gets low.

BAKED BEEF STEW

It takes about 3 hours to make this stew, but it's almost a whole meal. Stir with fork before serving so meat will show

¼ cup flour
  2 teaspoons salt
¼ teaspoon pepper
  2 pounds lean beef, cut in 1½-inch pieces
¼ cup salad oil
2½ cups water or tomato juice
  6 small onions
  4 carrots
  6 medium potatoes

What Makes Pot Roasts and Stews Tender?
The combination of the hot liquid and steam changes the tough connective tissue in meats to gelatin, which is tender.

1. Start heating the oven to 350° F.

2. Put the flour, salt and pepper in a paper sack. Add the pieces of meat, about 6 at a time, to the sack and shake until the meat is coated with the seasoned flour. Continue until all the meat pieces are coated. Save the sack with whatever flour is left in it.

3. Heat the oil in a heavy medium skillet. Add the beef cubes and cook and stir over medium heat until the meat is browned on all sides. This will take about 20 minutes. It's all right if some of the browned flour sticks to the skillet, but watch it and don't let it burn.

4. Remove the meat and place it in a 12-cup (3-quart) casserole.

5. Stir the flour mixture from the sack into the skillet until smooth. Then slowly stir in the water or tomato juice. Cook and stir until the mixture comes to a boil, scraping the browned flour from the bottom of the skillet. Pour this over the meat in the casserole.

6. Cover and bake 1½ hours.

7. During the last half hour of baking, fix the vegetables. Peel and slice the onions (you can use 2 medium onions, cut in fourths, if you do not have small onions). Peel the carrots and cut lengthwise in quarters. Peel the potatoes and cut them in halves. (You can also add 3 stalks of celery, cut up, with the vegetables. And for color and flavor, you can add 1 (10-ounce) package or 2 cups of frozen peas during the last 15 minutes of cooking.)

8. When the meat has cooked 1½ hours, remove it from the oven (use a pot holder!) and add the vegetables. Cover the casserole and put it back in the oven. Bake 1 hour longer, or until the vegetables are tender when you pierce them with a kitchen fork.

9. Serve the casserole. Makes 6 servings.

For a change
· *Lamb stew:* Use 2 pounds of lamb, cut into 1½- to 2-inch pieces, instead of the beef in Baked Beef Stew. Trim off all the fat you can. Boned lamb shoulder makes a good stew. Before serving the stew, spoon off the fat from the top and then stir to bring some of the meat up from the bottom of the casserole.

GROUND BEEF—HAMBURGERS

Ground beef is a favorite of many people. It cooks quickly and tastes wonderful, and there's almost no end to the ways you can fix it.

All ground beef is lean meat mixed with some fat meat or suet. It is made from the less tender cuts of beef, which have fine flavor. If you buy ground beef at meat counters, you usually have three kinds from which to make your selection. The kind labeled *hamburger* usually contains 20 to 25 per cent fat and it costs the least. *Ground chuck* has less fat, from 10 to 20 per cent, and *ground round steak* usually has 10 per cent fat added. Some fat is desirable because it gives the meat a good taste and juiciness.

If you have your meat or locker-plan man grind beef to order, meat ground once and rather coarsely is best for hamburger sandwiches. It tastes more like steak. Meat ground twice is tighter or more compact and solid. It is good in meat balls or loaves.

Store ground beef like other fresh meats in the coldest part of your refrigerator. It usually will keep in good condition 2 days.

Hamburgers top the list of popular sandwiches. There are two basic kinds: in one, you shape the meat in patties and in the other, you use "loose" or unshaped ground beef and cook it with canned soup, ketchup or something added that makes it soupy, like Sloppy Joes. You spoon this hot hamburger mixture over buns.

Then there are many dishes made with hamburger. Let's start with sandwiches, and then end up with main dishes that contain ground beef.

SKILLET HAMBURGERS

For juicy, tender hamburgers, shape patties lightly, turn once and don't spank with spatula while cooking

1 pound ground beef
1 teaspoon salt
⅛ teaspoon pepper
2 tablespoons finely chopped onion

1. Put all the ingredients into a medium bowl and toss lightly with a fork to mix well.

2. Divide the mixture into four equal parts with a fork and gently shape them into 4 thick patties. Or divide the mixture into eight equal parts and shape them into 8 thin patties.

3. Heat 2 tablespoons salad oil or fat in a heavy skillet or on a griddle and add the meat patties. Cook patties the way you like them—rare, medium or well done. It will take about 8 minutes for the thick patties and 3 to 6 minutes for thin patties, but if you like them rarer or better done, shorten or lengthen the cooking time. Turn the patties once with a wide spatula while cooking. Makes 4 to 6 servings.

For a change
· *Pan-broiled hamburgers:* Heat a heavy skillet or griddle until sizzling hot. Rub *lightly* with a little fat or salad oil or sprinkle with salt to prevent sticking. Brown the patties on both sides quickly. Then lower the heat and cook like Skillet Hamburgers.

So handy: a hamburger press

For Moist Hamburgers Add ¼ cup water or evaporated milk to 1 pound of ground beef before shaping the meat into patties. Your hamburgers will be extra-juicy.

Make the patties thin

Seal the filling inside

Square Hamburgers
If you want to make hamburger sandwiches with bread slices instead of buns, shape the meat patties into squares instead of rounds to fit the bread.

· *Cheeseburgers:* When the patties are cooked, spread the tops thinly with prepared mustard and then place a slice of Cheddar cheese on top. Do this right away while the patties are hot so the cheese will melt.

· *Hamburgers with pockets:* Use the recipe for Skillet Hamburgers. Shape the meat mixture into 8 thin patties. Place a thin tomato slice on 4 of the patties. Sprinkle with salt or onion salt and then with a little grated or cut-up cheese. Top with the other 4 meat patties; press edges together to seal and cook like Skillet Hamburgers. Instead of using the thin tomato slices and cheese, you can use thin onion slices, spread with prepared mustard and a little pickle relish or shredded process cheese mixed with ketchup.

BARBECUED HAMBURGERS

It takes about 1 hour to make these from start to finish, but you can make them ahead and reheat

Barbecue Sauce
1½ pounds ground beef
 ¾ cup evaporated milk
 ¾ cup dry bread crumbs
  1 egg
1½ teaspoons salt
 ⅛ teaspoon pepper
  3 tablespoons finely chopped onion
  1 tablespoon fat

1. Make the Barbecue Sauce (recipe follows).

2. Mix the beef, milk, bread crumbs, egg, salt, pepper and chopped onion together and shape into 12 large patties. You will use about ¼ cup of the meat mixture for each hamburger.

3. Melt the fat in a large, heavy skillet and brown the meat patties in it, on both sides.

4. Pour the Barbecue Sauce over them, cover the skillet and simmer gently 45 minutes. Serve a spoonful of the sauce on each hamburger. Makes 12 hamburgers.

BARBECUE SAUCE

3 tablespoons vinegar
2 tablespoons sugar
1 cup ketchup
5 tablespoons chopped onion

Cook all ingredients together in a small saucepan until the mixture comes to a boil. Then pour it over the hamburgers.

HAMBURGER GOO

Prize winner to fix in 30 minutes. A 4-H Club girl won blue ribbons with the sandwiches in her first demonstration

    1 pound ground beef
    1 cup cut-up celery
    ½ cup chopped onion
    1 tablespoon brown sugar
    2 tablespoons vinegar
    ½ teaspoon dry mustard
    ¾ cup ketchup
    2 tablespoons flour
    6 sandwich buns

1. Put the beef in the skillet. Stir and brown it over medium heat. Pour off the fat. Add the celery, onion, brown sugar, vinegar, mustard and ketchup. Sprinkle the flour on the mixture. Stir to mix well. Simmer about 20 minutes.

2. Cut buns in half and put them together with the beef mixture in between. Makes 6 sandwiches.

RANCH BEEF LOAF

You're lucky if there are leftovers to use in sandwiches

    1½ cups soft bread crumbs
    ¾ cup milk
    2 pounds ground beef
    2 teaspoons salt
    ⅛ teaspoon pepper
    1 medium carrot, peeled and grated
    1 small onion, peeled and minced or cut fine
    2 eggs, beaten
    ¼ cup ketchup
    3 tablespoons brown sugar
    2 tablespoons prepared mustard

1. Start heating the oven to 325°F.

2. Put the bread crumbs in a large bowl and pour the milk over them.

Lining the Pan
You can pack the mixture tightly into a 9×5×3-inch loaf pan if you wish. The loaf is more difficult to remove from the pan, though, if it touches all the edges. To loosen it more easily, you can line the bottom and ends of the pan with a strip of aluminum foil. Let the foil extend over the edge of the pan 2 inches to help you lift out the loaf after cutting around the pan edges to loosen it.

Garlic on a Pick
Run a toothpick through a peeled garlic clove when you add it to chili con carne and other dishes while cooking. It then is easy to remove the garlic and throw it away before serving the food it helped to season. It would be disastrous to have someone bite into the whole clove of garlic!

3. Stir in the ground beef, salt, pepper, grated carrot, onion and beaten eggs. Mix thoroughly with a spoon or fork.

4. Lightly shape the meat-loaf mixture with your hands to make an oval loaf. Put it in a shallow baking pan, such as a 13×9×2-inch pan. Gently smooth the loaf to make it even and neatly shaped. The loaf will be juicier if you handle the mixture very little.

5. Mix the ketchup, brown sugar and mustard and spread it over the top of the loaf.

6. Bake it 1½ hours.

7. Remove the meat loaf from the oven. Loosen the bottom of the loaf from the pan and lift it onto a warm platter with a wide spatula. Slice to serve. It is good hot or cold. Makes 8 servings.

CHILI CON CARNE

The "State Dish" of Texas, where it's served with and without the beans and often with piping-hot corn bread

1 pound ground beef
1 (15-ounce) can red beans or kidney beans
1 (1-pound) can tomatoes (2 cups)
1 (⅛-ounce) package instant onion
1 small clove garlic
2 tablespoons chili powder (or less)
½ teaspoon salt
¼ teaspoon cumin seeds

1. Stir the ground beef in a skillet until it starts to brown. Add the beans, tomatoes and onion.

2. Add the clove of garlic, chili powder, salt and cumin seeds to the beef mixture and stir to mix.

3. Cover the skillet and simmer 15 to 20 minutes. Remove the garlic. Makes 6 servings.

Hot or Mild—Which?
Chili peppers, those with pointed ends, are hot, while bell peppers, those with rounded ends, are mild. You discard the seeds of peppers when using the vegetable in cooking because they're really hot. The pointed peppers are used to make Tabasco and chili—they're both hot! Use them in small quantities.

THAT GOOD BARBECUED TASTE

The Peruvians, who were barbecuing food when the first Spanish explorers arrived, used the pit method—the food was buried on ashes and hot coals in a pit dug in the earth and covered to cook the food long and slowly. They still use this method and say that cooking in the earth is what makes barbecued food really taste good.

MEAT BALLS IN TOMATO SAUCE

Serve on spaghetti, and all you'll need for the main course is garlic bread and a green salad

Tomato sauce:

    2 tablespoons salad or olive oil
    1 clove garlic, minced
    ¾ cup chopped onion
    2 (10-ounce) cans tomato purée (2½ cups)
    1 teaspoon salt
    ⅛ teaspoon pepper
    1 bay leaf
    2 teaspoons sugar

1. Heat salad oil in a saucepan. Add the garlic and onion. Cook over low heat to a golden brown.

2. Add the tomato purée (pronounced pew-ray'), salt, pepper, bay leaf and sugar. Bring to a boil over medium heat and simmer 45 minutes. While the sauce simmers, fix the meat balls.

Meat Balls:

    3 slices white bread
    ⅓ cup milk
    1 pound ground beef
    2 eggs
    1 teaspoon salt
    ⅛ teaspoon pepper
    1 clove garlic, minced
    2 teaspoons dried parsley
    2 tablespoons shortening

1. Break the bread in pieces into a medium bowl. Add the milk and let stand about 5 minutes or until the bread takes up all the milk.

2. Add the beef, eggs, salt, pepper, garlic and parsley.

3. Mix well with a spoon. Shape with your hands into 12 balls of equal size.

4. Melt the shortening in the skillet. Add the meat balls and brown on all sides.

5. Pour the tomato sauce on, cover and simmer 45 minutes. If you wish to serve on spaghetti, cook it while the Meat Balls simmer in the Tomato Sauce.

The Lily, Garlic
Garlic belongs to the lily family. And garlic cloves are the bulbs from which the plant grows. The cloves are crushed or minced and added to many dishes for seasoning. Then there is garlic powder made by grinding the dried garlic cloves. Another useful seasoning is garlic salt, which cooks add to many dishes instead of salt. It contains garlic powder, salt and a chemical that keeps the salt from caking—makes it pour from a shaker.

So handy: a meat ball former

Pork is a tender meat

You don't have to worry about the pork you cook being tender—it's a very tender meat. You'll know good pork by its soft gray-pink flesh and white fat. When pork is cooked, the meat is gray and the juices are clear.

Loin cuts are great favorites. The loin reaches from the shoulder to the leg, and it makes elegant roasts, which are almost as good cold as warm. It also contains the popular pork chops.

Among the other cuts that are fine for roasting are the fresh leg, with lots of lean meat, and the shoulder cuts. The fresh leg is not always available because this cut usually is cured—then it's called ham. The shoulder roasts are the Boston butt—boned or with bones—and the picnic roast, with or without bones. Sometimes the boned picnic cut is rolled and tied in shape with string.

Pork chops are very popular. Rib loin chops (usually with 1 bone) and the loin chops (sometimes boned) with tenderloin are great favorites. Blade loin chops are cut from the shoulder end of the loin and sirloin chops from the ham end.

Pork steaks are slices of the leg (with a little round bone), arm steaks (also with a little round bone) and blade steaks (with a small piece of blade bone). Arm steaks come from the picnic, blade steaks from the shoulder. Look at the pork chart to see where on the animal these cuts are located.

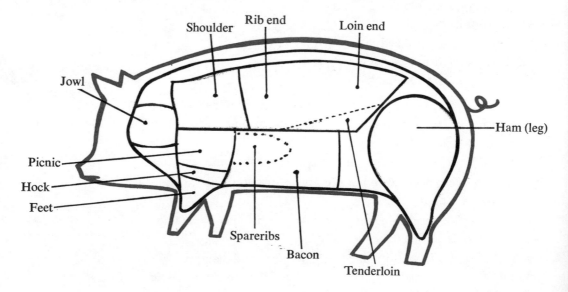

GLAZED PORK ROAST

Apricot and peach preserves are also good spread on the roast. Use the kind you have on the cupboard shelves

  1 (4- to 5-pound) pork loin roast (loin end)
  1 teaspoon salt
  ½ teaspoon ground cloves
  ¼ teaspoon pepper
  ½ cup cherry preserves

1. Start heating oven to 325° F.

2. Put the roast fat side up on a rack in a shallow pan. Insert the meat thermometer.

See how to use a meat thermometer, page 18

3. Put the roast in the oven. Do not cover or add water.

4. Cook the roast until the meat thermometer reads 170° F. The roast will need to cook about 30 minutes per pound, or about 2 to 2½ hours.

5. About a half hour before the roast is done, remove the pan from the oven and sprinkle the roast with the salt, ground cloves and pepper. Spread on the cherry preserves. Put it back in the oven. Roast until the meat is done. Makes 8 servings.

BAKED PORK CHOPS

Be sure to brown the pork chops first to make them and the gravy taste really good and look attractive

  6 rib or loin pork chops, 1 inch thick
  1 tablespoon flour
  1 (1½-ounce) package onion-soup mix
2½ cups boiling water
  ½ pint dairy sour cream

1. Brown the pork chops on both sides in a hot skillet. Put the chops in a single layer in the baking pan.

2. Start heating the oven to 350° F. about 45 minutes before mealtime.

3. Pour the fat from the skillet into a bowl or cup. Measure 1 tablespoon of fat and place in the skillet. With a wire beater or spoon, stir in the flour and onion-soup mix to make a smooth paste. Slowly stir in the boiling water. When the mixture is smooth, pour it over the pork chops.

Dairy Sour Cream
Many recipes today call for dairy sour cream. You buy it in ½- and 1-pint cartons or bottles. It is a smooth light cream, which means it contains only about 18 per cent butterfat. (Heavy cream for whipping contains at least 30 per cent butterfat.). The dairyman adds a "starter" (bacteria) to the light cream which sours it and gives it a flavor many people like. You can depend on the same results every time when you use a recipe calling for *dairy* sour cream because its fat content is always about the same. Creams soured at home vary more in their amount of fat.

4. Cover the pork chops. (You can cover them with a sheet of aluminum foil if your baking pan doesn't have a lid. Or you can put them back in the skillet to bake, if your skillet doesn't have a wood or plastic handle that would burn.)

5. Place them in the oven and bake 30 minutes.

6. Remove the pork chops from the oven and place them on a warm platter.

7. Make the gravy. Using a wire beater or spoon, slowly stir the dairy sour cream into the liquid in the baking pan. Heat it, if the sour cream has cooled the mixture, but do not let it boil or the cream will separate. Serve in a gravy boat or bowl. Makes 6 servings.

PORK CHOPS WITH BEANS

Pork Is Leaner These Days
The servings of pork you eat today contain more body-building protein and fewer fat calories than the pork of even a few years ago. That's because farmers have been producing meat-type hogs with less fat. Also more fat is trimmed from the pork at meat counters in our markets and locker plants.

No matter how hungry everybody is this main dish will fill each one up—just right to serve on a cold winter day

1 tablespoon fat
6 loin pork chops or shoulder steaks, ¾ inch thick
½ teaspoon salt
⅛ teaspoon pepper
¼ cup finely cut-up onion
1 clove garlic, minced
2 teaspoons sugar
½ teaspoon dry mustard
¼ cup ketchup
1 tablespoon vinegar
1 (1-pound) can kidney beans
1 (1-pound) can green lima beans

1. Start heating the oven to 350°F. about 1 hour before mealtime.

2. Melt the fat in a large skillet. (You can cut fat from the pork chops or shoulder steaks and heat it in a skillet over low heat until you get 1 tablespoon melted fat. Discard the cracklings—the unmelted fat.)

3. Put the pork chops in the skillet and brown them on both sides. You may need to brown 3 chops at a time, depending on the size of the skillet. It takes about 20 minutes to brown the chops. Sprinkle with the salt and pepper, and remove them from the skillet.

4. Put the onion and garlic in the skillet and cook over

low heat until soft. Stir in the sugar, mustard, ketchup and vinegar.

5. Drain the liquid from the kidney and lima beans in a sieve or colander. Add the drained beans to the skillet. Stir to mix well.

6. Pour the bean mixture in an 8-cup (2-quart) casserole and arrange the pork chops over the top. Cover and put it in the oven.

7. Bake 45 minutes or until the pork chops test tender when you stick a kitchen fork into them. Makes 5 or 6 servings.

PORK SAUSAGE, COUNTRY STYLE

Fresh pork sausage, shaped into little patties, is just the thing for breakfast. Cook the patties in a skillet until brown on both sides and no longer pink inside. Make the patties about ½ inch thick and cook them over low heat. Turn them with a wide spatula a few times while they cook and spoon out the fat as it collects in the skillet. It takes about 15 minutes to cook sausage properly.

Because fresh pork sausage is seasoned, it's a fine meat to add to many other foods to add flavor. Here is a recipe you will enjoy making.

SAUSAGE-CORN BAKE

No need to watch this dish while it bakes and there's no dishing up for serving—just carry casserole to the table

4 medium potatoes, peeled and thinly sliced
2 medium onions, peeled and thinly sliced
1 pound bulk pork sausage
1 (1-pound) can cream-style corn
1 (8-ounce) can tomato sauce
Salt
Pepper

1. Peel, wash and slice the potatoes and onions.

2. Start heating the oven to 350°F. Grease an 8-cup (2-quart) casserole.

3. Shape the sausage into 8 thin patties. Place in a heavy skillet and cook over medium heat to brown on both sides, turning once. This will take about 8 minutes.

4. While the sausage cooks, put a layer of potatoes, onions, corn and tomato sauce, using half of each, in the casserole. Then add a second layer of each (the potatoes, onions, corn and tomato sauce). Sprinkle each layer with salt and pepper.

5. Top with the sausage patties, drained. Spoon over the top 3 tablespoons of the sausage fat from the skillet.

6. Cover the casserole and bake 45 minutes. Uncover it and bake 15 minutes longer. Makes 6 to 8 servings.

HAM—A FAVORITE CURED PORK

There are two kinds of ham sold in almost all supermarkets—the fully cooked and the cook-before-eating kinds. Ask the meatman from whom you buy the ham or your locker man which kind you are buying or which kind was cured for you at the processing plant. If you buy a whole ham, the label tells which kind it is.

PAN-BROILED HAM

If you want to cook a slice of ham, a good thickness is ½ inch, although you can use a ¼-inch slice. Heat a heavy skillet and rub a little piece of the ham fat over it. Add the ham slice and lower the heat. Heat fully cooked ham 4 minutes on each side over low heat, the cook-before-eating kind 6 to 8 minutes on each side. Remove the ham to a warm platter.

TWIN HAM LOAVES

Serve one loaf warm, the other cold. It's good both ways

```
    2 eggs
    1 cup milk
    1 cup bread crumbs
    1 cup corn flakes
 1½ teaspoons salt
   ¼ teaspoon pepper
    1 pound ground ham
 1½ pounds ground fresh pork
```

Topping:

1 cup brown sugar
½ teaspoon dry mustard
¼ cup vinegar
¼ cup water

1. Start heating the oven to 350° F.

2. Break the eggs into a large bowl and beat them slightly with a fork or wire beater. Stir in the milk, bread crumbs, corn flakes, salt and pepper. Thoroughly mix in the ground ham and pork.

3. Form 2 loaves in a 13×9×2-inch pan.

4. Make the topping. Mix the brown sugar, mustard, vinegar and water in a small saucepan. Heat the mixture to boiling and stir until the sugar dissolves. Pour the topping over the ham loaves.

5. Bake the ham loaves 1 hour and 10 minutes. Baste the loaves several times with the brown-sugar mixture during the baking. Slice the loaves to serve. Makes 12 servings.

BAKED BEANS AND HAM

Cinnamon is the unusual touch in this quick main dish. It gives a special flavor that surprises and pleases people

1 tablespoon brown sugar
½ teaspoon cinnamon
2 (1-pound) cans pork and beans
6 pieces (serving-size) fully cooked ham slices, ½ inch thick
1 (8½-ounce) can pineapple slices, drained

1. Start heating the oven to 350° F.

2. Stir half of the brown sugar (1½ teaspoons) and cinnamon (¼ teaspoon) into 1 can of the beans. Spread the bean mixture in the bottom of a 6-cup (1½-quart) shallow baking dish.

3. Arrange the ham slices on top of the beans. Top them with the drained pineapple slices.

4. Add the rest of the brown sugar (1½ teaspoons) and cinnamon (¼ teaspoon) to the second can of pork and beans. Spoon over the pineapple and ham.

5. Cover and bake the beans and ham 45 minutes. Makes 6 servings.

Cinnamon, Spice Queen
Cinnamon is the most popular spice in cooking. It's the dried reddish brown bark of an evergreen tree that belongs to the laurel family. Its first home was China and places in Southeast Asia. The young shoots that grow on tree stumps are cut and peeled twice a year. To cut down on the breakage in shipping, workers roll the bark in what they call quills—we call them sticks. We use the sticks in making pickles. They are ground to powder and packaged for use in cooking.

How to Curl Bacon
Bacon curls are a pretty
and tasty garnish
(decoration). To make
them, pan-fry the bacon
as usual. Just before it is
thoroughly cooked, roll
each slice around the
tines of a fork and stand
it on end to crisp. Drain
on paper towels. Good on
scrambled eggs.

HAM SCALLOPED POTATOES

If you want to fix a dish to please meat-and-potato fans
—and that's most fathers and brothers—this is a sure bet

4 cups (1 quart) thinly sliced potatoes
⅔ cup finely chopped onions
2 cups cooked ham, cut in small strips
2 tablespoons flour
1 teaspoon salt
⅛ teaspoon pepper
3 tablespoons butter
1½ cups scalded milk

1. Start heating the oven to 375° F. 1 hour before meal-time. Grease an 8-cup (2-quart) casserole.

2. Peel the potatoes, slice them thinly and measure. Arrange a layer of the potatoes in the casserole and top with a layer of the onions. Arrange a layer of the ham strips on top. Stir the flour, salt and pepper together to mix and sprinkle some of the mixture over the ham. Dot with some of the butter. Arrange more layers in the casserole until all the potatoes, onions and ham, and flour mixture are used. Dot the top of the casserole with the remaining butter.

3. Heat the milk in the top of the double boiler over boiling water or in a saucepan over low heat until small bubbles show around the edge of the pan. Do not let the milk boil.

4. Pour the hot milk over the food in the casserole.

5. Place the casserole, covered, on the rack in the center of the oven and bake 45 minutes. Then remove the cover and bake 15 minutes longer or until the potatoes test tender when you stick a fork into them. Makes 4 to 5 servings.

RIBBONS OF PAN-FRIED BACON

Bacon is so well liked for breakfast that many people call the meat "breakfast bacon." But it's good in all the daily meals and as an ingredient in many dishes. Nothing could be easier to cook just right. That's why it's surprising so much bacon comes to the table too brown and brittle or undercooked. Here's how to handle it to get perfect results.

1. Put the amount of bacon you want to cook in a *cold* skillet or on a cold griddle. A heavy skillet or griddle is

Pan Shelf
A pan shelf is a handy
attachment for your
frypan. As bacon cooks,
move it to the shelf to
keep warm. The fat will
drain back into the skillet.

best. If you take the bacon slices from a package, don't try to separate them now or they may be so cold that they will break.

2. Put the skillet or griddle over low heat. As the bacon heats, it is easy to separate the slices with two forks. See that the slices lie flat.

3. Cook slowly over low heat, turning the slices with tongs or two forks, until the bacon is crisp—about 8 minutes. Don't let it get brittle or it will lose much of its good flavor.

4. Remove each slice of bacon when it is cooked and place it flat on paper toweling or pan tray to drain. When all the slices are cooked and drained, serve the bacon on a warm platter.

It's easier with two forks

QUICK QUIZ

Ask anyone who made the first sauerkraut and see if you get the correct answer. The word itself is German, but the answer is: the Chinese. It's called sour cabbage in China.

Oh boy! hot dogs

Call them hot dogs, frankfurters or franks for short—they're favorites by any name. They're all made of meat with seasonings. Some of them are all-beef and others are beef and pork. A few kinds also contain some wheat or soy flour.

All of them are cooked before they ever reach your kitchen. Because they are ready-to-eat, you can slice them into salads, sandwiches and soups. But most everybody likes them best hot and served in split and buttered Coney buns (long buns). Here are three ways to heat them.

Heated in water: Heat the franks about 8 minutes in hot, not boiling, water to cover. Remove from water with tongs, and serve at once.

Heated in a skillet: Melt about 1 tablespoon of fat in a heavy skillet. Add the franks and turn until they brown on all sides. Or split them lengthwise in half and brown the cut side first. Or cut short slanting slits in franks an inch apart before browning them. Be careful not to brown them too much—they'll get dry and tough.

Broiled: Preheat broiler 10 minutes. Rub each frank with salad oil, melted butter or margarine. Broil in pan about 2 to 3 inches from heat, turning once. It will take about 8 minutes to broil franks.

BARBECUED FRANKS

Lightning quick—you can fix it in 20 minutes. Serve with lettuce salad, hot garlic bread and pineapple slices

1 pound frankfurters
½ cup ketchup
2 tablespoons prepared mustard
½ teaspoon ground cloves
2 tablespoons salad or cooking oil
1 (3⅓-ounce) can French-fried onions

What Makes Hot Dogs Burst in Cooking If you let the water boil rapidly when you are heating frankfurters, the skins will burst. That's because the steam in the meat expands more than the skins. So use medium heat and bring the water to simmering, not the boiling, point.

1. Drop frankfurters into a kettle of simmering water. Cover and heat (do not let them boil) 5 minutes. Drain. Place them in a skillet.

2. Mix together the ketchup, prepared mustard, cloves and salad oil. Pour the mixture over the frankfurters. Simmer over low heat about 5 minutes.

3. Heat the onions as directed on the can label.

4. Turn frankfurters onto a warm platter. Garnish with the onions. Makes 6 servings.

FRANKS AND BEANS

Easy main dish to fix for supper—bake it in a casserole

1 (1-pound) can pork and beans
1 (1-pound) package frankfurters
2 tablespoons ketchup
1 teaspoon dry mustard
1 tablespoon brown sugar
3 slices bacon

1. Start heating the oven to 350° F.

2. Spread one third of the beans in a 6-cup (1½-quart) casserole.

3. Slice the frankfurters crosswise and spread half of them over the beans in the casserole. Cover them with another third of the beans. Dot with the ketchup and sprinkle on the dry mustard and brown sugar. Spread the rest of the frankfurter slices on top and then cover them with the last of the beans.

4. Cut the bacon in small pieces with the kitchen scissors. Sprinkle the pieces over the top of the beans.

5. Bake the casserole on the rack in the center of the oven 30 minutes. Serve hot. Makes 5 to 6 servings.

Chicken for dinner

A COUNTRY chicken dinner! The thought of such a meal makes many people hungry. The cook first remembers how good chicken can taste—that inspires her. Then she starts thinking about what kind to fix.

There are three types of chicken available almost every place. *Broiler-fryer chickens* are all-purpose because you can cook them any way you like. They are tender chickens that weigh from 1½ to 4 pounds, ready to cook. *Roasting chickens* are a little larger than broiler-fryers—that means they are a little older. They weigh from 3½ to 6 pounds, ready to cook, and are good for roasting or oven-frying. *Stewing chickens* or hens are less tender and they weigh from 2½ to 5 pounds, ready to cook. They have more fat than broiler-fryer and roasting chickens and are best when cooked slowly with water added.

In addition, many supermarkets sell chicken parts—chicken breasts, thighs, legs, wings, etc., packaged separately. This helps the cook. She can select the parts that she thinks will most please the people who are going to eat the chicken.

OVEN-FRIED CHICKEN

If Oven-Fried Chicken must wait before you serve it, brush it with melted butter and leave it in a very low oven

1 (2- to 3-pound) broiler-fryer, cut in serving pieces
1 cup flour
2 teaspoons salt
¼ teaspoon pepper
2 teaspoons paprika
½ cup butter

1. Start heating the oven to 375° F.

2. Wipe the chicken pieces with a damp cloth and then dry with paper towels. Remove pinfeathers with small tweezers.

Frozen Chicken
Frozen chicken is best thawed before cooking. Leave it in the wrapper and let it thaw in the refrigerator—it will take from 12 to 24 hours. If you want to thaw the chicken more quickly, leave it wrapped and put it in the sink under a slow stream of cold water. It will thaw in an hour or less. Wipe thawed chicken dry with paper towels before cooking.

Pan for Oven-frying Chicken
A jelly roll pan is ideal for oven-frying chicken because it is large and shallow. If you measure it with a ruler, you'll find it is 15½ ×10½ ×1 inches. Any shallow, large pan, such as one measuring 13×9×2 inches, will do, though. Or you can make your own pan with aluminum foil. Use 2 layers of regular foil or 1 layer of heavy-duty foil. Shape like a jelly roll pan, grease it and set it on a baking sheet. Then put the chicken pieces on it and bake.

3. Put the flour, salt, pepper and paprika in a strong paper bag and shake to mix. Add a few pieces of chicken at a time and shake the bag to coat the chicken pieces thoroughly with the flour mixture.

4. Melt the butter in a 13×9×2-inch pan set in the oven.

5. Add the chicken pieces and turn each piece to coat it with the melted butter. Then arrange them, skin side down, in one layer in the pan. Do not let pieces touch.

6. Place the pan on the rack in the center of the oven and bake 1 hour or until chicken is tender when you stick it with a fork. Makes 4 to 5 servings.

For a change
· *Oven-fried drumsticks:* Wipe 12 drumsticks with a damp cloth. Push the skin of each drumstick over the top—the broad end. Roll in ½ cup flour mixed with 1½ teaspoons salt and 1 teaspoon paprika and oven-fry like Oven-Fried Chicken. Makes 5 to 6 servings. If you want to give the chicken a different taste, season it with ¾ teaspoon salt, instead of 1½ teaspoons and add ¾ teaspoon garlic salt. Or mix 1 teaspoon poultry seasoning with the flour used to coat the chicken.

SKILLET BARBECUED CHICKEN

If dinner must wait after it's ready, this barbecued dish is just right, but reheat the chicken in the sauce to serve

Barbecue Sauce
  1 (3- to 3½-pound) broiler-fryer, cut up
⅔ cup flour
  1 tablespoon salt
  1 teaspoon paprika
  3 tablespoons butter

1. Make the Barbecue Sauce and set aside.

2. Wipe the pieces of chicken with a damp cloth and dry with paper towels. Remove all the pinfeathers with small tweezers.

3. Put the flour, salt and paprika in a paper bag. Drop 3 or 4 pieces of the chicken at a time into the bag. Shake the bag to coat the chicken well with the seasoned flour.

4. Melt the butter in the skillet and add the chicken

So handy: a strawberry huller or tweezers to remove pinfeathers from chickens.

pieces. Cook over medium heat until the chicken is browned on all sides. Turn the chicken with tongs; don't pierce with a fork or you'll lose some of the flavorful juices.

5. Pour the Barbecue Sauce over the chicken. Cover and cook slowly for 40 to 50 minutes. Turn the pieces several times during the cooking. Serve on a platter with the sauce poured over. Makes 4 servings.

BARBECUE SAUCE

1 teaspoon salt
¼ teaspoon pepper
1 teaspoon paprika
1 tablespoon sugar
½ clove garlic, minced
½ cup cut-up onion
½ cup water
1 cup ketchup
¼ cup lemon juice
2 tablespoons butter

1. Mix the salt, pepper, paprika, sugar, minced garlic clove, onion, water and ketchup in a small saucepan.

2. Heat it over medium heat to a boil. Lower the heat and simmer, uncovered, for about 20 minutes. Remove the sauce from the heat and stir in the lemon juice and butter. Mix well. Makes 2½ cups.

OVEN-FRIED PECAN CHICKEN

There's no spattering of fat when you oven-fry chicken and there are so many different seasonings—pecans in this one

1 (2½- to 3-pound) broiler-fryer, cut in serving pieces
1 cup biscuit mix
1½ teaspoons salt
2 teaspoons paprika
½ teaspoon poultry seasoning
½ cup finely chopped pecans
½ cup evaporated milk
½ cup melted butter or margarine

1. Start heating the oven to 375° F. Grease a 13×9×2-inch pan.

2. Wipe chicken pieces with a damp cloth and dry with

Dry Chicken First
When oven-frying chicken, wipe it with a damp cloth and then with paper towels before coating it with flour. If the pieces are dry, the flour will stick to the chicken better. Some good cooks place the floured chicken on a rack and let it dry a half hour before cooking it.

Pretty Color
When you add paprika to the flour in which you roll the chicken before cooking, it adds a rosy tinge to the brown— makes the cooked chicken very attractive. Paprika is made from dried sweet red pepper, ground very fine.

Cereal Coatings for Chicken
Roll chicken pieces for oven-fried chicken in crushed corn flake crumbs, or crushed crisp rice cereal or equal parts of crushed shredded wheat biscuits and fine dry bread crumbs, instead of in the flour.

To Oven-fry 2 Chickens
You will need 2 large,
shallow pans. Set each
pan on a rack in the
oven. After the chicken
has cooked 30 minutes,
shift the pans—move the
pan from the bottom rack
to the top rack and vice
versa. Then both pans of
chicken will have the same
chance to brown.

paper towels. Remove all the pinfeathers with small tweezers.

3. Put the biscuit mix, salt, paprika, poultry seasoning and pecans in a paper bag and shake to mix. Pour the evaporated milk into a bowl. Dip the chicken pieces in the evaporated milk to coat all sides. Then add 3 or 4 chicken pieces at a time to the paper bag containing the biscuit mix and shake to coat thoroughly. Repeat until all the chicken pieces are coated.

4. Place them in the pan, skin side down. Do not let the pieces touch. Pour the melted butter over the chicken.

5. Bake the chicken 1 hour or until it is tender when you test it with a kitchen fork. If it's easier for you, you can bake the chicken 2 hours in a 200°F. oven. Makes 4 to 5 servings.

CREAMED CHICKEN

There's no better way to use the leftover scraps of chicken than this—do try this easy dish

1 can condensed cream of chicken soup
⅓ cup chicken broth, canned or homemade
2 cups diced cooked chicken
¼ teaspoon salt
6 slices buttered toast

Why Chicken Darkens Around the Bones in Cooking
Sometimes chicken turns a reddish brown around the bones when it is frozen. This color darkens with cooking. Don't worry about it for it's a sign the chicken is good—a young bird. What happens is that some of the hemoglobin (red blood cells) in the marrow of the bones moves out—migrates, the poultryman says.

1. Mix the soup and broth in a saucepan. Add the chicken and salt. Heat the mixture until it is piping hot.

2. Spoon the hot chicken over the toast. Makes 6 servings.

For a change
· *Creamed turkey:* Use cooked turkey instead of the cooked chicken.

Fish is available everywhere

No MATTER where you live, you can get good fish now that it's quick-frozen, packaged and shipped about the country. Among the kinds you can find in most supermarkets are halibut, flounder, sole, cod, haddock, ocean perch, pike, catfish, salmon and whiting.

Fish steaks are cut crosswise of the fish, usually from large fish like halibut, haddock, cod, salmon and swordfish. Fish fillets are cut lengthwise from the sides and other parts of the fish and they are boned. All or most of the skin is removed. Some of the favorite fish fillets are those from cod, haddock, flounder, ocean perch and sole.

All you have to do to get frozen fish ready to start cooking it is to thaw it enough that you can separate the pieces—fillets or steaks. Thaw it in its wrapper in the refrigerator for a couple of hours.

In many places you can buy fresh fish cut in fillets or steaks. And you may be fortunate in living near a source of good fish that you or someone in the family catches. If you must store this fish before cooking it, wrap it in waxed paper and keep it in the coldest place in the refrigerator. Use it within a day if possible—or wrap it and put in the freezer. For 4 servings you will need about 1½ pounds of fresh fish fillets and 2 pounds of fresh fish steaks.

Does fish flake? It's done

Cook all fish just until it is done. The test for doneness is to pull it apart with a fork. If the fish flakes and still looks moist, it is ready for the platter. If you cook it longer, the flesh looks dry and it also tastes dry.

Herb Cookery
Use a light hand when adding herbs, but do experiment by using them in cooking to give dishes a gourmet taste. Remember that 1 teaspoon of a dried herb equals about 3 tablespoons of the fresh herb. Dried herbs are the leaves (never the stems) of low-growing shrubs.

Cut 6 wedges from 1 lemon

BAKED FISH STEAKS OR FILLETS

Baking is one of the easiest and best ways to cook frozen or fresh fish—thaw frozen fish as label directs

1. Mix ½ cup butter or salad oil with ¼ cup lemon juice and 2 teaspoons minced onion in a piepan or shallow dish.

2. Season both sides of the fish pieces with a little salt.

3. Start heating the oven to 350° F.

4. Dip the fish pieces in the butter-lemon mixture and arrange them in a shallow baking pan lined with aluminum foil. The size of the pan depends on how much fish you are cooking. Spread the pieces out in one layer. (If you have washed celery leaves in the refrigerator, it's a good idea to cover the foil with a layer of them before adding the fish. It not only flavors the fish but it also helps keep the fish from sticking.) If you have any of the butter-lemon mixture left, pour it over the fish in the pan.

5. Put the pan on the rack in the center of the oven and bake the fish without covering for 25 to 30 minutes.

6. Remove the fish from the oven and lift it to a warm platter with a wide spatula. Sprinkle the fish with paprika. Garnish the platter with quarters of lemons and snipped parsley or chives.

OVEN-FRIED FISH

Kitchen miracle: There's no fish odor in the kitchen when you oven-fry fish—and you don't have to watch or turn fish

¼ cup milk
 2 teaspoons salt
 2 pounds fish fillets
 1 cup corn flake crumbs
Lemon slices

1. Start heating the oven to 500° F. Grease a baking sheet.

2. Mix the milk and salt in a small bowl and stir.

3. Dip the fillets in the milk mixture and roll them in corn flake crumbs (or bread crumbs) to coat. (You can use fish steaks or small dressed fish instead of the fillets.) Place them on the baking sheet, lined with foil and greased with butter, margarine or salad oil. Don't let fillets touch.

4. Bake the fish on the rack in the center of the oven 15 minutes. Garnish with lemon slices. Makes 6 servings.

FISH PIQUANT

The French dressing is the surprise flavor—faint, but good

2 pounds frozen fish fillets, like haddock, flounder or perch
½ cup French salad dressing
2 tablespoons butter
1 small onion, cut fine
1 lemon
Tartar sauce

1. Thaw fish as directed on package.
2. Dip fish pieces in the French dressing.
3. Heat the butter in a skillet. Add the fish and sprinkle the onion over the top.
4. Cook over moderate heat 8 minutes on each side, turning only once.
5. Serve on a warm platter with wedges of lemon and tartar sauce. Makes 6 servings.

QUICK TARTAR SAUCE

2 tablespoons pickle relish
1 tablespoon finely chopped onion
1 tablespoon snipped parsley
1 tablespoon chopped canned pimiento (optional)
1 cup mayonnaise

Stir the ingredients into the mayonnaise in the order listed above. Chill in the refrigerator. Makes 1½ cups.

PINK SALMON LOAF

It's a toss-up which way this loaf is best—hot or cold

1 (1-pound) can pink salmon
½ teaspoon salt
¼ teaspoon pepper
2 eggs, beaten well
2 tablespoons lemon juice
2 teaspoons instant onion
1 cup cracker crumbs
1 cup milk

1. Start heating the oven to 350° F. Grease a 9×5×3-inch loaf pan. Place a piece of foil in the pan so it covers

Red Salmon
A lovely color—salmon—is named for sockeye salmon. It's a deep pink with a touch of yellow. In Alaska, the sockeye is called red salmon, but many people near Puget Sound call it blueback salmon. The canned sockeye is delicious—a fork breaks it into large flakes. It's especially good for salads and other dishes that show off its vivid color, even if it costs more than other kinds of salmon.

Pink Salmon
About half the salmon canned in America is pink salmon, the smallest fish in the salmon family. It varies from a light to a deep pink in color and is small-flaked. It's ideal for use in salmon loaves. It costs less than the red salmon.

How to Fix Cracker Crumbs
Place several crackers in a sturdy paper bag or between two large sheets of waxed paper. Roll with a rolling pin to crush. Pour the crumbs into a measuring cup. Roll and pour until you have enough crumbs. You can keep leftover crumbs in a closed jar in the refrigerator.

the pan bottom. Let the ends of the foil extend about 2 inches above the top of the pan ends. Grease the foil with butter or margarine.

2. Put the salmon with the liquid on it in a large bowl. Remove the skin and bones. Flake the salmon with a fork. Add the salt and pepper.

3. Beat the eggs well with a fork or a wire beater and add the lemon juice, instant onion, cracker crumbs and milk. Mix well. Add the egg mixture to the salmon and mix.

4. Spread the salmon mixture in the loaf pan. Bake it on the rack in the center of the oven 1 hour. Remove the loaf from the oven and loosen it around the edges with a knife or spatula. Turn it out of the pan. (The foil keeps the loaf from sticking to the pan.) Cut the loaf into slices for serving. Makes 5 servings.

Tuna Tip for the Cook
Spread crackers in a shallow pan, sprinkle with grated cheese and heat in a 325° F. oven several minutes. Spoon hot Tuna Rarebit over the warmed crackers.

TUNA RAREBIT

Cheese gives fish a delicious flavor and the soup is an easy and quick way to get the cheese flavor—just open a can

1 (11-ounce) can Cheddar cheese soup
1 can condensed tomato soup
½ cup water
1 teaspoon Worcestershire sauce
½ teaspoon dry mustard
2 (6½- or 7-ounce) cans light meat tuna
Toast

Add a Shake or Two of Seasoning Sauces
Good cooks use a little, often a shake or two or 1 teaspoon, bottled seasoning sauces to make their dishes interesting. Among the greats is Worcestershire (pronounced Woos'ter-sheer) that originated in Worcester, England. It's especially good with meats and fish. Use the amount given in the recipes.

1. Stir the cheese and tomato soups in a medium saucepan to mix. Add the water, Worcestershire sauce and dry mustard. Stir until smooth.

2. Stir the tuna into the soup mixture and heat until piping hot. Serve the mixture over toast or baked potatoes. Makes 4 servings.

Country-fresh eggs

EGGS are so easy and so quick to cook. And so very delicious when they are fixed right. That's why it is surprising many cooks make only *fairly* good egg dishes when they could, with no more work, make perfect ones. The main mistake cooks make is using too high heat. Egg whites are a protein, called albumen, and *high heat* makes them tough and leathery. Cooking eggs *too long* also makes them tough.

Some people think brown eggs have orange yolks and white eggs have paler yolks. This is a mistake—don't let the color of eggshells mislead you. They may be lily white, sunny beige or a deeper brown, but the color has nothing to do with the yolk color or the quality, food value or taste of the egg. Hens of different breeds lay eggs of different-color shells. Most egg yolks today are a medium yellow, and the shade of yellow depends on the feed the hens eat, not on the shell.

Eggs are perishable—they lose quality unless they are kept in a cool place—and that means the refrigerator. Store them with the narrow end down to reduce the size of the airspace at the top of the egg—this makes them keep better. It's a good idea to store them covered, in an egg carton or a casserole. If they aren't covered, eggs may pick up odors and lose moisture.

Our recipes tell how to soft- and hard-cook eggs (there's no such thing as a boiled egg because you cook them in water below the boiling point so they'll be tender), fry eggs, poach and scramble eggs and to make omelets and deviled eggs. See the Desserts section for custards and the Sandwiches section for egg sandwiches. Read our recipes for fixing eggs and see if you don't think you can get perfect results.

SOFT-COOKED EGGS

1. Start cooking the eggs as for hard-cooked eggs, but when the water comes to a boil, turn off the heat, cover the saucepan and let the eggs stay in the hot water 2 to 4 minutes, depending on how you like your eggs.

2. Cool the eggs in cold water for a few seconds to

So handy: an egg cup

stop the cooking and to make the eggs easier to handle.

3. Break the center of the egg with a knife and with a teaspoon scoop out the inside into cups or other serving dishes. If you follow the European way and use eggcups, stand an egg, large end up, in an eggcup and let each person cut off the top of the egg and eat the egg from the shell.

HARD-COOKED EGGS

1. Place the eggs in a saucepan and add enough cold water until it is at least 1 inch above the eggs. Cover the saucepan and set it on high heat. Bring the water quickly to a boil.

2. If you are cooking no more than 4 eggs, remove the saucepan from the heat as soon as the water boils. If you are cooking more eggs, leave the saucepan over very low heat for 20 minutes. The water should not boil or simmer.

3. Cool them at once for a few minutes under cold running water or in a pan of cold water.

4. Tap each egg all over to crackle the shells. Then roll each egg between your hands to loosen the shell. Peel off the shell, starting at the large end of the egg. If you dip the egg in cold water a few times during the peeling, the shell will come off more easily.

BAKED EGGS

1. Start heating the oven to 325° F. Grease custard cups or ramekins (pronounced ram'ee-kin, individual baking dishes) with butter or margarine and set them in a shallow pan. Ramekins are not as deep as custard cups.

2. Pour 1 tablespoon light cream into each cup and add an egg. Be careful not to break the yolk.

3. Sprinkle with salt and pepper and dot with a little butter.

4. Place the baking pan on the rack in the center of the oven and bake until the eggs are done the way you like them, about 12 to 18 minutes.

For a change
· *Cheese baked eggs:* Instead of light cream, put a layer of bread crumbs in the bottom of the custard cups or ramekins. Place a slice of process Cheddar cheese on top. Add the eggs, salt and pepper. Scatter a little of the

What's in an Egg?
A lot of good eating and plenty of good nutrition! Also, eggs are one of the most digestible foods we have. They give us excellent protein, iron and some of the B vitamins. The protein and iron (in the yolks) help build your blood—the red cells or hemoglobin that carries oxygen to every cell in the body. Protein also builds and repairs body tissues. And the B vitamins help give you steady nerves and enable the body cells to get pep and energy from food. It's a good idea to eat 4 eggs a week. Eggs are important in low-calorie meals because they provide fine protein.

cheese, grated, on the eggs. Bake at 325° F. until the eggs are done the way you like them.

POACHED EGGS IN A SKILLET

Drain off the water

1. Grease a skillet with butter or margarine and pour in about 2 inches of water (the water should just cover the eggs). Bring the water to the simmering point—do not let it boil.

2. Break each egg into a sauce dish or cup and lower it almost to the water in the skillet. Quickly slip the egg into the water. Add the rest of the eggs at once in the same way.

3. Cover the skillet and *keep the water hot,* but do not let it simmer. Cook the eggs until the whites are firm, from 3 to ·5 minutes.

4. Lift the eggs out of the water. If you have either a slotted spoon or a slotted spatula, use it to lift out the eggs so the water can drip back into the skillet. Hold the spoon or spatula with the egg against the side of the skillet for a few seconds to let more water drain off.

FRIED EGGS SUNNY SIDE UP

Sprinkle the eggs with seasoned salt instead of plain table salt—a quick, easy way to make them different

3 tablespoons butter or melted bacon or other fat
6 eggs
Salt
Pepper

1. Put the butter or bacon fat in a medium skillet and place over medium heat until a little water dropped in the skillet sizzles.

2. Break the eggs, one at a time, into a sauce dish or cup, and lower each egg almost to the top of the butter in the skillet. Slip the egg into the skillet. Turn the heat to low.

3. Cook gently over low heat, spooning some of the hot fat in the skillet over the top of the eggs. This is called basting, and you can use a baster instead of a spoon. If you don't want to baste the eggs, cover the skillet. Enough steam will collect to cook the tops of the eggs. Cook the eggs until they are as firm as you like them, about 3 or 4 minutes.

An Egg Poacher
You can use an egg poacher if you have one. It consists of a shallow pan into which little eggcups fit. Some egg poachers are electric. Pour about 2 inches of water into the bottom of the pan, lightly grease the cups with butter or margarine and break an egg into each cup. Put the lid on the pan and cook the eggs over medium heat (the water makes steam) until they are done the way you like them. Or follow the manufacturer's directions that came with your egg poacher.

When Is the Skillet Ready for Eggs?
Shake a couple of drops of cold water into the heated skillet containing the butter. If the water sizzles (makes a hissing sound), it's time to add the eggs. If the skillet smokes and the butter has turned brown, it's too hot.

4. Remove the eggs with a broad spatula or pancake turner. If the spatula is slotted, the fat drains off more easily. Tilt the spatula, with each egg on it, against the side of the skillet and let the fat drain off for a few seconds.

5. Place the eggs on a warm platter and sprinkle lightly with salt and pepper. Serve at once.

For a change
· *Fried eggs over:* Cook the eggs like Fried Eggs Sunny Side Up until they are as firm as you like them. Then turn each egg over with a broad spatula. Cook the eggs to the doneness you like.

SCRAMBLED EGGS

Remove the skillet from the heat while the eggs look moist and turn them at once from the skillet to stop the cooking

  6 eggs
½ teaspoon salt
⅛ teaspoon pepper
  6 tablespoons light cream or milk
  2 tablespoons butter

1. Break the eggs, one at a time, into a cup to make sure each egg is fresh. Put the eggs in a medium bowl. Add the salt, pepper and cream. Mix well with a fork or a wire hand beater.

2. Heat the butter in a medium skillet (9-inch) until it melts but do not let it brown. Tilt the skillet to coat the sides with butter so the eggs will not stick.

3. Pour the egg mixture into the skillet and cook over low heat. Cook slowly, lifting up the cooked eggs from the bottom with a fork or spatula so the uncooked eggs can flow to the bottom of the skillet. Cook the eggs until they are almost set, but still look shiny and a little underdone.

Stir Scrambled Eggs the Right Way
Don't overstir the eggs . . . avoid constant stirring. Insert a fork or spatula at the edge of the egg mixture in the skillet or double boiler, hold it straight up and gently pull the cooked part of the eggs up toward the center. Do not stir around and around.

4. Remove the eggs from the heat and turn them at once onto a warm platter or into a warm dish. Makes 4 servings.

For a change
· *Cheese scrambled eggs:* After the scrambled eggs are in the serving dish, sprinkle their tops with ¼ cup grated cheese.
· *Eggs with chives:* Sprinkle the tops of the scrambled eggs with snipped chives.

Onion eggs: Or cook 2 teaspoons minced green or dry onions in the eggs.

Double boiler scrambled eggs: Melt the butter in the top of the double boiler over hot water. Tilt the top pan until the butter coats the sides and bottom. Then add the eggs as for Scrambled Eggs and stir them the same way. Cook the eggs slowly over hot, not boiling, water. It's actually easier to make perfect, tender scrambled eggs in the double boiler because you can keep the cooking temperature low.

GOLDEN OMELETS

Omelets are made with the same ingredients as scrambled eggs, but you cook them differently. While a French-Style Omelet cooks, you loosen it around the edge with a spatula and tilt the skillet so that the uncooked part can run underneath. You keep on tilting the skillet and loosening the omelet around the edge until its top is almost dry and it is golden brown on the underside. Occasionally you shake the skillet gently so the omelet will not stick—cooks say you "keep it moving."

With scrambled eggs, you gently push the cooked part of the eggs to the center of the skillet with a fork, heaping them up, but you try to keep an omelet the same thickness —level. When the omelet is cooked, you fold it in half and carefully roll it from the skillet onto a hot platter.

FRENCH-STYLE OMELET

A little practice in flipping one half is all it takes to master the omelet folding—it's an art worth learning

8 eggs
1 tablespoon cold water
1 teaspoon salt
2 tablespoons butter

1. Break the eggs, one at a time, into a cup and pour them into the electric mixer's bowl or a large bowl. Add the water and salt and beat with the mixer or a hand beater just enough to mix.

2. Heat the butter in a large skillet (10-inch) and tilt the skillet until the melted butter coats the inside.

3. Use low heat. When the butter is hot enough so that a drop of water will sizzle in it (makes a hissing sound),

How to Make Yellow Scrambled Eggs
Mix the eggs with a fork or wire hand beater before cooking. If you like streaks of white in your scrambled eggs, do not mix the whites and yolks too well. For a clear golden yellow, avoid using high heat. Use butter, not bacon fat, in the skillet and do not let the butter brown before adding the eggs. Cooking eggs in a light-colored skillet or a double boiler also helps to keep them clear yellow.

Easy . . . try not to break it

Roll in onto a warm platter

How to Keep Yolks Yellow in Hard-Cooked Eggs

The yolks of eggs contain some iron, the white some sulphur. If you cook eggs at too high a temperature or longer than our recipes say or if you cool them in the cooking water instead of cold water, the iron and sulphur may unite, making what the chemist calls ferrous sulfide. It shows up in a greenish coating around the egg yolk. You may get this same coating if you use what farmers call "old" eggs instead of fresh eggs. The green coating is not harmful, but it makes the eggs unattractive.

add the egg mixture. When the eggs set at the edge, loosen them with a spatula and tilt the skillet so that the uncooked egg can flow to the bottom. Shake the skillet *gently* from time to time to keep the omelet from sticking—it should slide around in the skillet. Try to keep the egg mixture the same thickness all the time (not heaped in the center).

4. When the omelet is almost set and the egg no longer flows, turn the heat up a little and quickly brown the bottom of the omelet. It will take 1 minute.

5. Loosen the edge of the omelet with a spatula and fold half the omelet over on the other half, without breaking it in two.

6. Lower the skillet until the top edge touches the rim of a warm platter. Slowly tip the skillet toward the platter until the omelet rolls onto it. Serve at once (with ketchup, if you wish). Makes 4 servings.

For a change

· *Jelly omelet:* Spread jelly on half the omelet just before folding it.

· *Strawberry omelet:* Sugar 1 cup hulled strawberries and heat them a little in a saucepan over low heat or in the double boiler over hot water. Spread the berries on the omelet just before folding it.

· *Bacon Omelet:* When the eggs are set, crumble 6 cooked bacon slices over half the omelet before folding.

· *Cheese omelet:* When the eggs are set, sprinkle ⅓ cup grated process Cheddar cheese over half the omelet before folding.

· *Ham omelet:* Fold ½ cup cooked ham, cut very fine, into the omelet mixture before cooking. Omit salt from the omelet if the ham is salty.

DEVILED EGGS

Their white and yellow color and sharp taste make these eggs welcome at picnics and on the supper platter

12 hard-cooked eggs
 2 teaspoons vinegar
¾ teaspoon salt
⅛ teaspoon pepper
 1 teaspoon prepared mustard
 2 tablespoons melted butter or margarine
 3 tablespoons mayonnaise

1. Cut the cooked eggs in halves, lengthwise or crosswise. Take out the yolks and mash them with a fork until there are no lumps. Or put them through a sieve.

2. Add the vinegar, salt, pepper, mustard, butter and mayonnaise and mix well. Then beat with a fork until the mixture is light and fluffy.

3. With a teaspoon, heap the egg-yolk mixture into the hollow in the whites. With a fork make a crisscross design on the yolks. Place the eggs in the refrigerator to chill. Makes 24 deviled egg halves.

For a change

· You can add other things to deviled eggs. Try whipping 3 or 4 tablespoons of soft cream cheese (at room temperature) into the yolk mixture, or grated cheese, deviled ham or chopped cooked ham, or bits of crisp bacon. Then heap the yolk mixture in the egg whites.

Trim with fork crisscross

RICKRACK EDGES FOR DEVILED EGGS

Remove the shell from the hard-cooked egg. Use a small, pointed knife and start at the middle of the egg. Make a tiny cut at an angle, then cut back at an angle to the center of the egg. You will have one point. Make these cuts all around the center of the egg. Gently pull the egg halves apart and carefully take out the yolks. Mash the scraps of egg white with the yolks and season. Pile the mixture back into the egg halves so that the white scallops show.

Zigzag cut with knife tip

COTTAGE CHEESE DEVILED EGGS

If you have vinegar with dill added, use it. The flavor is interesting and unusual. But cider vinegar is good, too

  6 hard-cooked eggs
½ cup cream-style cottage cheese
  1 tablespoon dill or cider vinegar
¼ teaspoon salt
⅛ teaspoon paprika
¼ teaspoon dry mustard
  3 tablespoons mayonnaise

1. Cut the eggs in lengthwise halves and place the yolks in a shallow dish. Set the egg-white halves aside.

2. Mash the egg yolks with a fork. Add the cottage cheese,

dill or cider vinegar, salt, paprika, mustard and mayonnaise. Mix lightly with a fork.

3. Heap the yolk mixture into the egg-white halves. Refrigerate until serving time. Double all the ingredients to make 24 deviled egg halves.

SCALLOPED DEVILED EGGS

See recipe for Deviled Eggs, page 158

A favorite hot supper dish in many country homes is Scalloped Deviled Eggs. You place the eggs in a baking dish and cover them with a warm white sauce, sprinkle with bread crumbs and grated cheese and then bake them to heat and to melt the cheese.

You can make the sauce either in a double boiler, which is the easiest way to get good results, or in a saucepan, which is faster. The trick is to turn out a perfectly smooth white sauce. One sure way to avoid lumps is to use instant-type flour, which does not form lumps when added to cold milk or other liquids.

What Makes a Smooth White Sauce
In making white sauce by thickening milk with flour, you first melt the butter or other fat and then stir in the flour to make a smooth paste. The butter coats the tiny starch grains in the flour. Then you add the cold milk gradually, stirring all the time. You cook and stir the sauce until it thickens. The heat melts the butter and lets the starch grains escape into the milk. They swell, soften and thicken the sauce. Unless you stir the cooking sauce constantly, some of the starch grains fall to the bottom of the pan and stick to it, forming lumps and sometimes scorching. If the sauce scorches, it has an unpleasant taste. Another help in making a smooth sauce is to melt the butter in a saucepan over low heat and remove the pan from the heat while stirring in the flour to make smooth paste.

¼ cup butter or margarine
¼ cup flour
½ teaspoon salt
¼ teaspoon pepper
2 cups milk
12 deviled egg halves
½ cup dry bread crumbs
½ cup grated or finely cut-up cheese

1. If you make the sauce in the double boiler, melt the butter in the top pan over boiling water. Stir in the flour, salt and pepper and stir until the mixture is smooth and free of lumps. If you use a saucepan, melt the butter over low heat (do not let it brown). Add the flour, salt and pepper and stir until the mixture is smooth.

2. Take the double boiler or the saucepan from the heat and slowly add the milk, stirring well. Place it over low to medium heat and stir all the time until the sauce thickens. Then set it aside.

3. Start heating the oven to 350° F.

4. Place Deviled Eggs in rows in a square or other baking pan. Pour the hot sauce over them. Sprinkle with the bread crumbs and cheese.

5. Bake the eggs until the cheese melts, about 18 to 20 minutes. Makes 6 servings.

Main dishes made with cheese, macaroni products and rice

MANY recipes in this Cookbook call for cheese, but here is a collection of hearty *main dishes*—country lunch and supper favorites—in which it's an important ingredient. There are also recipes for the macaroni products—macaroni, spaghetti and egg noodles—and for rice. Cheese delightfully seasons many of the dishes made with these mild-flavored foods.

There are two big families—natural cheese and process cheese. Natural cheese came first. A way to "preserve" milk, it was made for hundreds of years before home refrigeration was even a dream. People found that many kinds of cheese kept longer than the milk from which cheese is made, and they liked its taste. Process cheese is made from natural cheese, which we'll talk about first.

Natural cheese

Cheese makers add rennet or bacteria or both to milk to curdle it. Then they heat, stir and press to separate the solids, called the curd, from the whey. They form the curd in different shapes, often in blocks or rounds, called wheels, and coat them with wax or wrap with a covering that protects them. If the cheese is to be cured, they give it time to age, the way fruit growers let their fruits ripen. During the curing, changes occur in the taste and texture of the cheese, and when it is at its best, the blocks or wheels are cut in smaller pieces and packaged. You see these packages on the refrigerated shelves in supermarkets.

Pasteurized process cheese

Process cheese is natural cheese that has been shredded and melted. The heating (pasteurizing) stops the curing so that the cheese does not change in flavor or texture. It may be a mixture of more than one natural cheese, such as a fresh Cheddar and an aged Cheddar, or different kinds of cheese, such as Cheddar and Swiss. Sometimes pimientos, fruits, vegetables and meat are added, and the cheese also may be smoked or seasoned with smoke flavoring.

The taste of process cheese depends largely on the natural cheese from which it is made. *It melts easily and without stringing*—reasons why it's a favorite with many cooks.

Always read the label on the package to find out what kind of cheese you have. Here are the important kinds of process cheese products.

Packaged process cheese: The packages vary in size from ¼ to 5 pounds. Among the flavors are Cheddar, pimiento, Swiss, Limburger, Gruyère and brick. (The Gruyère does not have the holes of natural Gruyère and its flavor is somewhat sharper.)

Packaged sliced process cheese: These cheeses are the same as packaged process cheese, but they are sliced before packaging.

Process cheese food: It is made much the same way as process cheese except it contains less cheese and less milk fat. Nonfat dry milk or whey solids and water are added, making cheese foods more moist. Often pimientos, fruits, vegetables and meats are added to them and sometimes they are smoke-flavored. Process cheese foods taste milder than process cheese and they are softer, and spread and melt more easily. You can use cheese foods in any recipe calling for process cheese, but remember that they do not add as much cheese flavor. They are marketed in slices, rolls, links and loaves.

Cheese spreads: They are made much like the process cheese foods but they generally contain more moisture and less milk fat. A chemical, called a stabilizer, is added to keep the ingredients in the spreads from separating. They spread very easily and often are flavored with other foods, such as pimientos, fruits, vegetables and meats. They may have a smoked flavor. Their taste depends on the cheese from which they're made and how it is changed by foods that are added. Among the most popular cheese spreads are pineapple, blue cheese and pimiento. They are packaged in jars and loaves convenient for use in snacks, stuffing celery stalks, deviled eggs, sandwiches, sauces and cooked dishes.

Where to keep cheese

Always keep cheese, natural and process, well covered and in the refrigerator. It's a good idea to leave it in the wrapper or package. Or you can wrap it tightly in aluminum foil or saran. Cured or aged natural cheeses and process cheeses will keep several weeks. Uncured cheeses, such as cottage and cream cheese, are perishable, and they should be used within a few days after you buy them. Cheeses with a strong aroma, like Limburger, are best kept in a tightly covered glass jar. Since these cheeses are fast cured, it's best to use them shortly after you buy them.

The mold that sometimes gets on cheese is not harmful. Just scrape or cut it off. The blue-green threads or veins in some natural cheeses are produced by molds that are added to give the cheeses their fine flavors.

CHEESE-BREAD FONDUE

A perfect supper dish. Serve with buttered asparagus or peas, a green salad, garlic bread, applesauce and cookies

5 slices bread
¼ cup butter or margarine
3 eggs, separated
1 cup milk
¼ teaspoon salt
½ teaspoon prepared mustard
½ pound sharp Cheddar cheese, grated (about 2 cups)
Curried Dried Beef (recipe follows)

What Makes Some Cheese Stringy When Heated Natural cheese that is cured or ripened contains acid that helps give it fine flavor. When you heat the cheese, the acid breaks apart the protein in the cheese and makes it stringy. Process cheese has been heated by the cheesemaker, who adds a substance (emulsifier) that holds the cheese together and helps it melt smoothly.

1. Start heating the oven to 375° F. Lightly grease a 6-cup (1½-quart) casserole with butter or margarine.

2. Trim the crusts from the bread with a knife. Spread the bread slices with the butter, place them on a cutting board and cut them in cubes. Put the bread in the casserole.

3. Beat the egg yolks until foamy. Add the milk, salt, mustard and cheese and stir to mix.

4. Beat the egg whites until stiff and fold them into the egg yolk mixture; pour over the bread.

5. Bake, uncovered, about 35 minutes or until the fondue is puffed and brown. Serve hot with Curried Dried Beef. Makes 6 to 8 servings.

CURRIED DRIED BEEF

You can leave out the curry powder but you'll miss some fine flavors. This dried beef also is good on buttered toast

¼ cup butter or margarine
¼ cup flour
¼ teaspoon curry powder
⅓ cup chopped green onions
1¼ cups milk
1¼ cups light cream
1 (4-ounce) package dried beef

1. Melt the butter in a medium saucepan, stir in the

flour, curry powder and chopped green onions. Cook over medium heat 1 minute, stirring all the time.

2. Gradually stir in the milk and light cream and stir and cook until the sauce thickens.

3. Pull the dried beef into shreds with your fingers and mix it into the sauce. Serve hot in a bowl to spoon over the Cheese-Bread Fondue. Makes 3 cups.

CHEESE MEAT LOAF

A hurry-up main dish—you can fix it in about 30 minutes

  2 (12-ounce) cans luncheon meat
¼ teaspoon ground cloves
  4 teaspoons prepared mustard
16 slices process Cheddar cheese
  1 (1-pound 8-ounce) jar sweetened pie cherries

1. Start heating the oven to 400° F.
2. Cut each can of meat into 9 slices, cutting almost, but not quite, through the bottom of the loaves.
3. Mix the cloves and mustard in a cup and spread the mixture between the slices of meat.
4. Put a slice of cheese into each slit in the meat loaves.
5. Arrange the meat in a baking dish and pour the cherries around it.
6. Bake, uncovered, 15 minutes or until the cheese melts. Slice loaves at right angles to the slits holding the cheese. Makes 8 servings.

Cheese wedges in meat loaf

CHEESE-BACON PIE

A hearty main dish pie that's just right for supper or lunch

   1 (9-inch) unbaked pie shell
 10 slices bacon
1¼ cups chopped onions
   1 tablespoon flour
   2 eggs
  ¾ pound grated Cheddar cheese
   1 cup milk
  ½ teaspoon salt
  ⅛ teaspoon pepper
  ⅛ teaspoon cayenne pepper

1. Start heating the oven to 450° F.

2. Make a (9-inch) pie shell, using Pastry Made with Solid Fat, Pastry Made with Oil or Beginner's Pastry. Put it in the refrigerator.

See pastry recipes, pages 74–78

3. Fry the bacon until crisp. Drain it. Measure 2 tablespoons bacon drippings (melted fat) back into the skillet. Add the onions and cook and stir over low heat until they are clear and soft, but do not let them brown.

See directions for cooking bacon, page 142

4. Remove the skillet from the heat and stir in the flour.

5. Beat the eggs with a hand beater until frothy and add the cheese, milk, salt, pepper, cayenne, onions and bacon, crumbled. Stir this into the bacon-fat mixture in the skillet and mix well.

6. Pour the mixture into the pastry-lined piepan (pie shell) and bake about 25 minutes. Serve hot, cut into 8 wedges.

CHEESE RABBIT

Cook this rabbit over very low heat so it will be creamy. Spoon it hot over buttered toast slices or plain crackers

2 cups shredded process Cheddar cheese
½ cup milk
1 teaspoon dry mustard
1 teaspoon Worcestershire sauce
1 egg

1. Heat the cheese and milk in a medium saucepan over *very low heat*. (If you shred the cheese, you will need a half-pound package.) Stir with a spoon or a wire hand beater until the cheese melts and the mixture is smooth. Add the seasonings and stir to mix.

2. Beat the egg thoroughly and gradually stir it into the cheese mixture. (Some cooks add a few grains of cayenne pepper to the rabbit.) Continue to cook and stir until the rabbit thickens and becomes creamy. Serve at once. Makes 4 servings.

For a change
· *With tomato:* Place a slice of fresh tomato on each piece of hot buttered toast. Spoon on the hot Cheese Rabbit.
· *With tuna:* Place chunks of drained, canned tuna on hot buttered toast and spoon on the hot Cheese Rabbit.

MAIN DISHES MADE WITH MACARONI PRODUCTS

Macaroni, spaghetti and noodles are a big three in main dishes. All of these foods are made with durum wheat, a very hard spring wheat that grows in North Dakota and other north-central states. When you cook these products, notice how clear the water stays—that's because no starch dissolves in it.

Macaroni comes in many shapes. Look at the collection on the shelves in your supermarket. You will see macaroni shells, elbows, wagon wheels, bows and other shapes along with the long tubes. Spaghetti is a solid rod, but it comes in different widths. Noodles contain eggs and are often called egg noodles. They come in ribbon lengths that are fine, medium and wide in width.

Be careful not to cook these favorites too long. If you do, they will be soft and flabby. They are best firm, but tender. To tell when they are done, take a piece of the cooking macaroni from the kettle with a fork. Bite into it. If it is just barely tender and not hard in the center, take the kettle off the heat at once and drain off the cooking water so the macaroni will not keep on cooking.

How to cook macaroni products

1. Bring 3 quarts of water, with 1 tablespoon salt stirred in, to a rapid boil.

2. Gradually add 1 (8-ounce) package of macaroni, spaghetti or egg noodles so the water does not stop boiling. Boil rapidly without covering, stirring occasionally with a long-handled kitchen fork, until just tender —from 12 to 15 minutes. Drain in a colander or other large strainer. To cook larger amounts of macaroni products such as 1 (16-ounce) package, use 4 to 5 quarts of boiling water and 2 tablespoons salt. You'll need a large kettle for this.

An 8-ounce package of macaroni will measure 4 to 5 cups when cooked. The same size package of spaghetti or noodles will make 3 to 4 cups. Eight ounces of these macaroni foods will make from 4 to 5 servings.

SKILLET MACARONI AND CHEESE

You cook this dish from beginning to end in your electric skillet—the cooking takes no longer than 25 minutes

½ cup butter
1 (8-ounce) package elbow macaroni
½ cup chopped onion
1 teaspoon salt
¼ teaspoon pepper
⅛ teaspoon dried orégano
¼ teaspoon dry mustard
2 cups water
1½ tablespoons flour
1 (14½-ounce) can evaporated milk
2 cups sharp Cheddar cheese, shredded (about ½ pound)
1 tablespoon instant minced parsley

1. Turn the electric skillet to 200° F. Melt the butter in the skillet and add the macaroni (uncooked), onion, salt, pepper, orégano and dry mustard.

2. Turn the heat up to 260° F. and cook, stirring occasionally for 5 to 7 minutes or until the onion looks clear (transparent).

3. Add the water and bring to a boil. Cover the macaroni and simmer it at 200° F. for 6 to 12 minutes or until the macaroni is tender. Test for doneness by taking a bite.

4. Sprinkle the flour over the macaroni mixture and stir to mix well. Stir in the evaporated milk and shredded cheese.

5. Simmer the mixture 5 minutes longer at 200° F. or until the cheese completely melts. Stir occasionally while it cooks.

6. Sprinkle it with parsley and serve. Makes 6 servings.

ONION MAC

Make this in the morning and chill in the refrigerator so the flavors will blend by evening—for supper or a picnic

1 (8-ounce) package elbow or shell macaroni, cooked
2 cups dairy sour cream
1 cup cut-up green onions
⅓ cup chopped canned pimientos
1 teaspoon salt

See how to cook macaroni products, page 166

1. Cook and drain the macaroni. Rinse the hot, drained macaroni under the cold water faucet a few minutes to separate the pieces of macaroni. Drain again.

2. Put the macaroni in a medium bowl and add the sour cream, cut-up onions, chopped pimientos and salt. Mix well.

3. Cover and chill 1 hour or longer. Serve from a salad bowl or on lettuce-lined salad plates. Makes 6 servings.

ITALIAN SPAGHETTI

Gain time by cooking the spaghetti while the sauce simmers

¼ pound bacon slices, cut up
¾ cup sliced onions
½ pound ground beef
1 teaspoon salt
⅛ teaspoon pepper
1 clove garlic, minced
1 teaspoon Worcestershire sauce
1 tablespoon sugar
3 (8-ounce) cans tomato sauce
1 (8-ounce) package spaghetti
Grated Parmesan cheese

1. Cook and stir bacon pieces in a large heavy skillet until light brown. Pour off the fat.

2. Add the onions and ground beef and cook and stir with a fork until they are brown. Stir in the salt, pepper, garlic, Worcestershire sauce, sugar and tomato sauce. Cover and simmer 35 minutes.

3. While the sauce simmers, cook the spaghetti as directed on the label. Drain it and place on a warm platter.

4. Pour the sauce over the spaghetti and sprinkle with grated Parmesan cheese. Serve the spaghetti at once. Makes 4 servings, but you can double this recipe to make 8 servings.

How to Get Long Spaghetti in the Kettle
If you want to serve the spaghetti in long strings or rods without breaking it, the way Italians do, take small bundles of it in your hand and put one end in the kettle of boiling salted water. As it softens, coil in more spaghetti. Repeat until you add all the spaghetti you are cooking.

WHERE PIZZA WAS BORN

No one knows for sure where in Italy the first pizza was made, but it is believed that it was in Naples. The folk story is that a cook had scraps of bread dough that he wanted to use so he rolled the dough thin, then topped it with cheese and tomatoes, added seasonings and baked it. His experiment was a success.

HAM AND NOODLES

Allow 15 minutes to fix this dish, 50 minutes to bake it

1½ teaspoons salt
1½ quarts boiling water
 ½ of 1 (8-ounce) package noodles
 1 small green pepper
1½ cups (¾-pound) ground ham
 1 egg, beaten
 2 tablespoons melted butter or margarine
 1 (1-pound) can cream-style corn
1½ cups corn flakes
 ¾ cup diced process cheese (4 ounces)

1. Add the salt to the boiling water and gradually stir in the noodles so the water will not stop boiling. Cook, uncovered, until the noodles are just tender. This will take about 10 minutes. Drain in a colander or sieve.

2. Start heating the oven to 350° F. Grease a 6-cup (1½-quart) casserole.

3. Cut 6 crosswise slices from the narrow end of the washed green pepper and save for a garnish. Throw away pepper seeds and finely chop the rest of the pepper.

4. Mix the ham, beaten egg and melted butter in a large bowl. Fold in the drained noodles, chopped pepper, corn, corn flakes and cheese.

5. Spoon mixture into the casserole. Bake 50 minutes.

6. Remove the casserole from the oven and garnish the top with rings of green pepper. Makes 6 servings.

LASAGNE CASSEROLE

Use lasagne noodles with rippled edges if you can get them

 1 (8-ounce) package broad noodles
 1 tablespoon salad oil
 1 (8-ounce) package heat and serve sausages
 1 (1-pound) can tomatoes
 1 (6-ounce) can tomato paste
 1 tablespoon instant onion
·1 tablespoon mixed Italian herbs
 1 cup drained cottage cheese
 ¼ cup grated Parmesan cheese
 1 (6- or 8-ounce) package Mozzarella cheese, cut into
   ½-inch strips

1. Cook the noodles as directed on the package and drain.

2. Put the noodles back in the saucepan in which they cooked. Add the salad oil and toss so the noodles will not stick.

3. Lightly grease an 8-cup (2-quart) casserole with salad oil. Start heating the oven to 350° F.

4. Dice the sausages and brown them, stirring often, in a medium skillet. Stir in the tomatoes, tomato paste, onion and herbs. Cook over medium heat until the mixture boils; lower heat and simmer, stirring occasionally, for 5 minutes.

5. Spread half the noodles in the casserole and top with layers of half the sausages, cottage cheese, Parmesan cheese, tomato mixture and Mozzarella cheese. Repeat layers. Crisscross a few slices of Mozzarella cheese on top.

6. Bake 30 minutes, until bubbling at the edge and the cheese is browned. Makes 6 servings.

Crisscross cheese on top

MAIN DISHES MADE WITH RICE

There are several kinds of rice on the market. *Brown rice* has an outer coating of bran, while in regular *white rice,* the covering has been removed. *Processed rice,* sometimes called parboiled or converted rice, has been treated to keep some of the minerals the bran contains. And *precooked rice* has been cooked, dried and packaged. You can fix it in a hurry.

Read the cooking directions carefully on the package of rice before using it. And do remember that rice swells in cooking. One cup of regular white rice makes about 3 cups cooked rice, 1 cup processed rice makes about 4 cups cooked rice, 1 cup brown rice makes 4 cups cooked rice and 1⅓ cups precooked rice makes 2⅔ cups cooked rice when fixed by package directions.

Cooks often talk about long-grain rice—it's just what you'd expect. The rice grains are long. It is especially nice to use in making main dishes because it is plump and flaky when cooked. Medium- and short-grained rice types are good choices for making puddings and other creamy dishes. Regular and brown rice is marketed in short-, medium- and long-grain types. Processed rice is packaged long-grain rice and precooked rice is made of long-grain rice.

SPANISH RICE

You can make three different dishes with this easy recipe

1 cup uncooked regular white rice
2 tablespoons salad oil
1 cup cut-up onion
½ cup cut-up green pepper
1 (1-pound) can tomatoes (2 cups)
2 tablespoons vinegar
2 teaspoons sugar
1 teaspoon salt
⅛ teaspoon pepper

1. Cook the rice as directed on the package. You will have about 3 cups cooked rice.

2. While the rice cooks, heat the salad oil in a skillet and add the onion and green pepper. Stir and cook, uncovered, over low heat until the onion turns pale yellow and is tender. This will take about 15 minutes.

3. Add the tomatoes, vinegar, sugar, salt and pepper. Simmer, uncovered, 15 minutes. Add the cooked rice and mix well. Cover and simmer 20 minutes longer. Makes 6 servings.

For a change
· *Spanish rice with cheese:* Start heating the oven to 375° F. Grease a 6-cup (1½-quart) casserole with salad oil. Add the cooked rice to the tomato mixture and put it into the greased casserole. Spread a layer of cut-up sharp process Cheddar cheese pieces over the top. Bake, uncovered, 30 minutes.
· *Chili rice:* You can add 1 teaspoon chili powder with the salt and pepper.

WILD RICE IS A WATER GRASS

Wild rice now rates as a gourmet food—it's very expensive in specialty grocery departments. It grows in northern Minnesota and Wisconsin lakes and is harvested by Indians, who paddle out to it in canoes. This food is not really rice, but it's been called wild rice ever since the first explorers in the then American wilderness saw it and learned from the Indians that it was good to eat. Many Americans have discovered the delicacy and the demand for it is almost greater than the supply.

Leftover Rice? Good!
If you cook more rice than you need, you can store it, covered, in the refrigerator for a week. If you wrap the container of rice with freezer wrapping paper or foil, you can freeze it for use any time up to 6 months. When you want to use it, thaw it, unwrapped, at room temperature. It will take 3 to 4 hours. To reheat cooked rice, cover the bottom of a saucepan with water, add the rice and simmer it over low heat about 10 minutes.

PORCUPINE BALLS

Rice cooks with the meat and the soup makes a tasty sauce

1½ pounds ground beef
½ cup uncooked regular rice
2 tablespoons cut-up onion
1 teaspoon salt
⅛ teaspoon pepper
1 can condensed tomato soup
1 soup can water

1. Mix the beef, rice, onion, salt and pepper in a medium bowl. Shape into 18 balls of the same size.

2. Stir the soup and water together in a deep skillet. Heat to boiling. Lower heat. Add the meat-rice balls, cover the skillet and cook over low heat for 1 hour. No pot watching with this dish! Makes 8 servings.

TEXAS RICE BOWL

A cold rice treat for a hot day—serve on lettuce if you like

1 cup cooked regular long-grain rice (⅓ cup uncooked rice)
1 (1-pound) can kidney beans, drained
2 hard-cooked eggs, cut up
½ cup cut-up sweet pickles
¼ cup chopped onion
¼ cup chopped celery
¼ cup chopped green pepper
½ teaspoon salt
¼ teaspoon pepper
⅓ cup mayonnaise

Cook the rice by package directions. While it is warm, put it in a medium bowl and add all the ingredients. Mix well. Cover and refrigerate several hours. Makes 6 to 8 servings.

Sandwiches—hot and cold

IN Grandmother's day all sandwiches were cold and they usually were tucked into lunch boxes. Today, hot sandwiches also are popular, especially for lunch or supper, and we give you recipes for both kinds.

You can keep out of a rut in sandwich making if you use different kinds of breads. Next time you are in a supermarket look at the many kinds displayed on bakery counters, in refrigerator cases and even in cans on the shelves. You will be surprised how good many of them are and how different they will make sandwiches look and taste.

Tips on making cold sandwiches

1. Use butter or margarine at room temperature. If you are making a lot of sandwiches, beat the butter until creamy so it will spread easily.

2. Take the bread slices, two at a time, from the loaf of bread and arrange them side by side on the kitchen counter. Put the next two slices directly in front of the first two slices, making two rows. Repeat until you have as many slices in one row as you need sandwiches.

3. Spread butter on one row of bread slices. Spread it thin and all the way to the edges of the bread—this will keep the filling from soaking into the bread and making the sandwich soggy. Spread the filling on the other row of bread slices.

4. Close the sandwiches. They will fit together for each sandwich is made of two bread slices that were next to each other in the loaf.

5. If the sandwiches must wait before you serve them, cut each sandwich in half, diagonally if you like. Use a sharp knife to cut them. Then wrap each sandwich in waxed paper, aluminum foil or saran, using the Drugstore Wrap (see page 22). Keep in the refrigerator until time to serve.

Sandwich Families
The two important sandwich families are open-face and closed sandwiches. An open-face sandwich, the popular kind in Denmark and other Scandinavian countries, is made with one slice of bread with the filling on top. It is served with knives and forks. This type of sandwich invites garnishes or decorative touches, like the tomato slices on Egg Salad Sandwiches. Closed sandwiches are the familiar American kind with the filling between two bread slices.

EGG SALAD SANDWICHES

Make open sandwiches and top them with thin tomato slices
—serve with knives and forks

6 hard-cooked eggs, finely chopped
½ cup finely cut-up celery
¼ cup pickle relish, well drained
½ cup mayonnaise
1 teaspoon salt
Bread

Mix all ingredients, except the bread, in a medium bowl. Cover the mixture and refrigerate until ready to make the sandwiches. Egg salad sandwich fillings are perishable so serve them at once after they're made or keep them in the refrigerator. Makes about 2½ cups or enough for 8 to 10 sandwiches.

For a change
· *Onion-egg sandwiches:* Use ⅓ cup of finely chopped green onion instead of the pickle relish.
· *Egg salad boats:* Cut off the tops of long sandwich buns (Coney buns) and scoop out some of the inside to make hollows. (Save these crumbs in a covered jar in the refrigerator to use when a recipe calls for bread crumbs.) Fill the hollows in the buns with the filling for Egg Salad Sandwiches. To make really pretty sandwiches, line the buns with a leaf of garden lettuce before adding the egg mixture.

Egg salad in bread boats

PEANUT BUTTER SANDWICHES

You could fill a whole cookbook with different recipes for peanut butter sandwiches and still have some left over. We asked schoolboys of many ages to name their favorites. Here are the sandwiches they like best.

1. Two slices of white bread put together with peanut butter and a little honey. Butter the sandwich on the outside and brown on both sides in a skillet.

2. Whole wheat or white bread, one slice spread with peanut butter, the other with cherry jam (or jelly), and the two put together.

3. White bread, both slices spread with peanut butter and put together with cooked and crumbled bacon and thin apple slices between.

HAM SALAD SANDWICHES

Cut the lettuce for these sandwiches into ribbons with scissors. You'll find it will be much easier to eat

  2 cups ground cooked ham
½ cup ground sweet pickles or pickle relish, drained
  2 hard-cooked eggs, chopped
½ cup finely chopped celery
½ cup mayonnaise or salad dressing
  1 teaspoon prepared mustard
Bread

Snip for lettuce ribbons

   Put the ham through the food chopper and measure. Put pickles through the food chopper and measure. In a small bowl thoroughly mix the ham and pickle with the chopped eggs, celery, mayonnaise and prepared mustard. Refrigerate the ham salad until needed. Spread it on slices of white or whole wheat bread. Put a lettuce leaf in each sandwich before serving. Makes 2½ cups filling, or enough for about 8 sandwiches.

HAMBURGER BUNWICHES

Process cheese is mild-flavored and melts easily. Use it if you want the cheese to melt completely over the hamburger

1½ pounds ground beef
  1 small onion, chopped very fine
  1 teaspoon salt
¼ teaspoon pepper
½ teaspoon powdered sage
  1 egg, slightly beaten
½ cup milk
  1 cup fresh bread crumbs
  6 hamburger buns, split
  6 slices process or natural Cheddar cheese

   1. Start the broiler heating. Remove the rack.
   2. Mix the ground beef, finely chopped onion, salt, pepper, sage (you can omit if you want to) and the egg, beaten with a fork or a wire beater, milk and fresh bread crumbs, made by crumbling bread with the fingers.
   3. Spread the beef mixture on the bottom halves of the buns. Press the meat well over the edges of the buns to keep the buns from browning too much in cooking.

4. Place the bunwiches on the broiler rack and broil about 5 inches from the heat to the desired doneness, about 10 to 12 minutes. When the hamburger is almost done, put the bun tops, cut side up, under the broiler to toast them. It will take only a minute or two.

5. Place a slice of cheese on top of each meat-topped bun half about a minute before you take the sandwiches from the broiler.

6. Remove the broiler rack from the oven and put the bun tops over the cheese. Makes 6 bunwiches.

SKILLET GRILLED CHEESE SANDWICHES

The buttered sandwiches brown beautifully—they're toast-crisp on the outside and soft inside

2 cups shredded process Cheddar cheese (about ½ pound)
6 tablespoons mayonnaise
2 tablespoons barbecue sauce
12 slices bread
Soft butter

1. Mix the cheese, mayonnaise and barbecue sauce. Spread mixture on 6 slices of the bread. Top with the other 6 bread slices.

2. Butter both sides of the sandwiches and brown them on an electric sandwich grill, in the electric skillet or a heavy skillet over medium heat. Turn and brown on the other side. Serve at once. Makes 6 sandwiches.

HOT TUNA SUPPERWICHES

Tuna from the Ocean Tuna is America's most popular canned sea food. It contains fine body-building protein. Most of it is packed in a vegetable oil—soy, corn or cottonseed oil, which you usually drain off.

It will take about 45 minutes to fix these sandwiches the first time—the next time will be faster

1 (6½- to 7-ounce) can tuna
¼ cup chopped celery
3 tablespoons mayonnaise
2 teaspoons lemon juice
1 teaspoon finely cut-up onion
8 slices bread
2 eggs
½ teaspoon salt
½ cup milk
1 to 2 tablespoons salad or cooking oil

1. Drain the tuna, flake it with a fork and empty it into a medium bowl. Add the celery, mayonnaise, lemon juice and onion. Mix well.

2. Spread the tuna mixture on 4 slices of bread. Top each with a slice of bread. Cut each sandwich in half to make 8 triangles.

3. Beat the eggs with a fork. Add the salt and milk. Stir to mix.

4. Heat the salad oil over medium heat in a large skillet.

5. Dip one side of a sandwich in the egg mixture. Turn it with a wide spatula (a pancake turner with slots is a good tool to use). When the second side of the sandwich is coated with the egg mixture, lift it out with the turner and put it in the hot skillet.

6. Brown the sandwich and turn it over. Brown the second side. Place the sandwich on a hot plate. Brown all the sandwiches in this way. Serve at once with Carrot Curls. Makes 8 sandwiches, enough to serve 4.

CARROT CURLS AND STICKS

Peel a long carrot with a vegetable peeler or slicer. Use the same peeler or slicer to cut the carrot in thin slices. Wind each slice of carrot around the finger. Fasten with toothpicks and drop into a bowl partly filled with ice water. Cover and refrigerate. Remove the toothpicks from the carrot curls and drain them on paper towels. Or cut washed, peeled and chilled carrots in pieces 2 to 3 inches long. Cut pieces into sticks about ⅜ inch thick.

PIZZA HAMBURGERS

The Pizza Sauce makes these hamburgers special. You'll want to keep a jar of it in the refrigerator ready to use

Pizza Sauce:

1 (8-ounce) can tomato sauce
1 teaspoon salt
1 teaspoon dried parsley flakes
1 teaspoon instant onion
¼ teaspoon ground orégano
¼ teaspoon pepper
1 clove garlic, minced

Butterfly Sandwiches
Place a pickle body between sandwich wings. Add carrot curls for antennae.

Patties:

1 pound ground beef
4 to 6 slices Mozzarella cheese
4 to 6 hamburger buns

1. Start the broiler heating.

2. Mix all the ingredients for Pizza Sauce in a small saucepan and simmer 5 minutes.

3. Make 4 to 6 patties with the ground beef. Place them on the broiler pan 3 inches from the heat and broil, turning once. When the second side is almost done, top each patty with a slice of cheese. Broil until the cheese melts. It takes a total of 8 to 12 minutes to broil the hamburgers.

4. Place the hamburgers between split buns and spoon Pizza Sauce on the top of the meat patties. Makes 4 to 6 servings, depending on how thick you like your hamburgers.

HERO SANDWICHES

You can build these layered sandwiches to suit your fancy with the ingredients you have on hand—do use crusty bread

1. Bake 2 loaves of brown-and-serve French bread by package directions. Each loaf is about 14 inches long. When the loaves are cool, split them in half lengthwise.

2. Spread the cut side of the bread with butter, garlic butter or mayonnaise and then with prepared mustard.

3. On the bottom halves of the bread spread slices of baked ham or boiled ham. Then top with thin tomato slices and sprinkle with a little salt. Over the tomato slices arrange slices of bologna or salami (or both). Then top with Swiss or other cheese slices. You can cover the cheese with thin onion slices if you like. Top with lettuce leaves and then with the top halves of the bread. Cut each loaf in two and you have 4 servings.

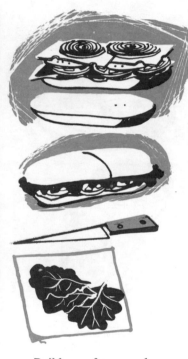

Build one for your hero

For a change

· If you like liver sausage, or Braunschweiger, spread it evenly on the bottom half of the buttered bread and spread the prepared mustard on the cheese. Some people like slices of corned beef in their Hero Sandwiches.

Vegetables—garden goodness

VEGETABLES are the Cinderellas in meals. More cooks abuse them than all other foods put together, but many of them are color-bright and can be the princess of a meal. These garden foods are important to good health, and too many people cook the health right out of them. If you can cook vegetables well, it's usually a sign that you're a good cook all around.

Here are the rules to cook glamorous, tasty vegetables. Let's cook fresh vegetables first and then move on to the frozen and canned vegetables. We give you the basic methods of cooking the three types (fresh, frozen and canned), and then some favorite *Farm Journal* recipes.

Cooking fresh vegetables

Wash all vegetables before cooking. Cook in 1 inch of water in the saucepan unless the directions that follow tell you otherwise, and add ½ teaspoon salt for every pound of vegetables you are going to cook. If you don't know how much the vegetable weighs, add ½ teaspoon salt to every cup of water. To know how much salt to add, measure the water into the saucepan so you'll know how much it takes to make it 1 inch deep.

Bring the water with salt added to a boil. Add the vegetable and bring to a boil again over high heat. Lower the heat, but keep the vegetable boiling gently. If you boil vegetables rapidly, they may lose shape and it's easy to scorch or burn them. The cooking time begins when the vegetables start to boil, and varies with each vegetable, depending on how young it is. We give the *average* cooking time.

To keep the best color in green vegetables, such as broccoli, Brussels sprouts, cabbage, green beans, green lima beans and greens (except spinach), cook them *uncovered* briefly, then cover to complete the cooking. Cooking them uncovered at first permits chemicals that discolor these vegetables to escape in the steam; the cover then holds in the steam, which cooks the vegetable faster. Cook a green vegetable both ways, and see for yourself what the difference is.

Cook vegetables until just tender—never mushy. They should be a little crisp—tender-crisp. They taste better when cooked this way and also keep more of their vitamins and minerals. Test their tenderness by sticking them with a kitchen fork. If there is any liquid left, drain the vegetable before serving. Here are directions for boiling some of the most common vegetables.

Asparagus: Break off the stalks where they snap easily—they snap easily where the tender part ends. Cut off the scales with a paring knife. Wash off any sand—you may need to use a vegetable brush. Then cook the stalks whole, 15 to 20 minutes, or cut up, 10 to 15 minutes. Cook uncovered the first 5 minutes, then cover.

Beans, Green and Wax: Remove strings if there are any. Snap the beans with your fingers into 1-inch pieces. Or cut into thin crosswise slices or lengthwise strips, French-style (see page 184). Cook snapped beans 10 to 25 minutes, crosscut beans 5 to 15 minutes and the strips, 10 to 20 minutes. Green beans will keep more of their color if you boil them 5 minutes before covering.

Beets: Leave beets whole and the roots on. Cut off all but 1 inch of the stems. Cover with cold water and cook young beets 30 minutes to 1 hour, old beets 1 to 2 hours. Drain and cool, slip off the skins with your hands and cut off stems and roots. Or peel the raw beets with a vegetable peeler, shred, dice or cut them into cubes and cook 20 to 30 minutes.

Broccoli: Cut off the large leaves and the ends of the stalks. If the stalks are thick, slit each stalk lengthwise 4 times almost to the blossoms. Cook 10 to 15 minutes. For the best color, cook uncovered 5 minutes and then cover and cook 5 to 10 minutes longer, or until tender.

Brussels Sprouts: Cut off the stems and remove yellow leaves. Soak the sprouts in cold water 15 minutes. Then cook them whole until tender, 10 to 20 minutes. Their color will be brighter if you boil them 5 minutes before covering.

Cabbage: Shred on a medium or coarse grater, but do not use the core. Cook 4 to 10 minutes. Or cut the cabbage in wedges, cutting off most of the core, and cook 10 to 15 minutes. For the best color, let the cabbage boil 1 minute before covering. Shred red cabbage and cook 8 to 12 minutes. Add 1 or 2 tablespoons lemon juice or vinegar to cooking water when the vegetable is tender. This will bring back the red color.

Carrots: Scrape or peel thinly. Leave them whole, cut them into lengthwise halves or quarters or slice them. Cook whole carrots 20 to 40 minutes; the halves, 15 to 25 minutes; quarters, 12 to 20 minutes; slices, 10 to 20 minutes—it depends on how you like carrots, tender-crisp or well done. Add 1 teaspoon sugar with the salt.

Cauliflower: Cut off the outer leaves and any blemishes or spots on the flowerets. Break into flowerets, wash thoroughly and cook 10 to 15 minutes. You can slice the flowerets—then they cook in 7 minutes.

Corn, Fresh Ears: Cover with cold water and cook over high heat. As soon as the water comes to a full boil, the corn is cooked.

Green Lima Beans: Snap or cut the pods open with scissors and push out the beans. Do this just before cooking. Cook them 20 to 25 minutes, the first 5 minutes of boiling uncovered for the best color.

Greens (except Spinach): Discard the ends, coarse stems and wilted leaves. Wash them in lukewarm water 3 times, lifting the leaves out of the water, shaking them, so the sand will fall into the pan. Cook in ¼ inch water (instead of 1 inch) and add ¼ teaspoon salt to every pound of greens. Cook them covered until the leaves wilt, about 1 minute; lift off lid to let steam escape, and stir. Then cook uncovered 5 to 15 minutes.

Okra: Leave the pods whole and do not cut off the stem ends or tips. Or cut them into ½-inch slices. Cook whole pods 7 to 12 minutes and the slices 5 to 7 minutes. To keep the best color, boil okra 5 minutes before covering.

Onions: Cut a thin slice from the stem and the root ends. Then peel off the 2 outer layers. Hold the onion under running cold water while cutting it so the chemicals that escape and bring tears will be kept in the water—out of your eyes. Cook small onions whole 20 to 35 minutes and onions about 2 inches across, cut into ½-inch slices, about 20 minutes. If you slice them thinner, about ¼ inch, they will cook in about 10 minutes.

Parsnips: Peel thinly and cut off the stem and root ends. Cook whole 20 to 40 minutes. Or slice or cut in halves or quarters, cutting out the hard, center core, and cook 10 to 20 minutes.

Peas: Shell by pressing the pods between your thumbs and push the peas into the saucepan. Discard peas with sprouts or those that are discolored. Cook 8 to 20 minutes. The peas will retain more of their green color if you boil them 5 minutes before covering. Add 1 teaspoon sugar with the salt.

Potatoes, Sweet or Yams: Cook in their skins—called jackets—30 to 35 minutes.

Potatoes, White: Peel and remove eyes. Cook whole potatoes 35 to 40 minutes; quartered potatoes, 20 to 25 minutes; and whole new potatoes (small), 20 to 25 minutes.

Spinach: Cut off ends and coarse stems and discard discolored or blemished leaves. Wash in lukewarm water 3 times, like other greens. Cook covered without adding water (enough water clings to the leaves), 6 to 10 minutes. Add ½ teaspoon salt to 1 pound spinach.

Squash, Acorn: Cut in half, remove seeds and strings and cook 20 to 30 minutes, cut side down.

Squash, Butternut: Cut into serving-size pieces and peel off the rind. Cook 12 to 15 minutes.

Squash, Hubbard: Cut into serving-size pieces and peel off the rind. Cook 25 to 35 minutes.

Squash, Summer: Cook young, yellow crookneck squash that have tender skins. Do not peel or remove seeds if squash are small, but do cut off stem and blossom ends. Cook whole or cut up 10 to 20 minutes. Cook young, tender pattypan squash or cymblings like yellow crookneck squash. Directions follow for cooking zucchini, another summer squash.

Turnips: Use firm, heavy turnips; if they are lightweight they may be pithy. Peel thinly and cut into ¼-inch slices or ½-inch cubes. Cook the slices 8 to 12 minutes, the cubes 12 to 20 minutes.

Rutabagas: Peel thinly, cut into 2-inch slices or ½-inch cubes and cook the slices 35 to 40 minutes, the cubes, 20 to 25 minutes.

Zucchini: Cook the small or medium squash and do not peel. Cut off the stem end and any dark spots. Cut into ½-inch slices and cook in ¼ inch boiling water (instead of 1 inch). For the best color, cook zucchini 5 minutes uncovered. Then boil 5 minutes longer.

Cooking frozen vegetables

If you buy frozen vegetables, cook them by the directions on the package. Here are the general rules:

Drop the unthawed vegetable into a saucepan, over high heat, containing a little boiling water. If you break up the block of frozen vegetable with a kitchen fork, it will cook more quickly.

When the water, which stops boiling when you add the frozen vegetable, starts to boil again, turn the heat to low, cover the saucepan and simmer the vegetable just until tender, 4 to 15 minutes. The cooking time varies with many things—the kind of vegetable, the variety, age, size of pieces and the way the vegetable was handled before freezing. Cook it *only until tender*.

Usually, ¼ to ½ cup water is enough to cook a frozen vegetable, but use as little as you can without burning the vegetable.

Heating canned vegetables

You don't need to cook canned vegetables because they are cooked in the canning process. You heat and season them (unless seasonings are added before canning, as with stewed tomatoes and baked beans).

Drain the liquid from canned asparagus, carrots, green and wax beans, green lima beans and peas into a saucepan and cook over high heat until you have half as much liquid as you had before heating. Then add the vegetable and bring to a boil over low heat. Or drain off most of the liquid and store in a covered jar in the refrigerator to use in stews, soups and gravy. It contains vitamins and minerals the body needs. Or follow label directions on the can.

Heat such vegetables as tomatoes, cream-style corn and squash as they come from the can.

Ready to season

Now that the fresh and frozen vegetable is cooked and the canned vegetable is heated, you are ready to season it. Always taste to find out if you need to add more salt. Try seasoned, onion or garlic salt if the vegetable needs more salt.

Buttered Vegetables: Add butter or margarine to the hot vegetable, 1 to 2 tablespoons to 2 cups vegetable. Or use heavy cream instead of the butter or margarine.

Crumbed Vegetables: Melt 3 tablespoons butter in a small skillet and add ½ cup fresh bread crumbs (you can make the crumbs with your fingers). Stir over medium heat to brown lightly. Then add ⅛ teaspoon salt and ½ cup grated cheese. Stir and pour over hot cauliflower, green beans, broccoli or asparagus. Enough for 4 servings.

Minted Peas: Cook a few fresh mint leaves with the peas—4 or 5 leaves are enough.

Greens with Bacon: Add bits of crisp bacon to spinach or other greens before serving.

Sweet-Sour Cabbage: Heat ¼ cup vinegar and 2 tablespoons sugar together, add ¼ cup heavy cream and pour over shredded cabbage or green beans before serving. Enough for 4 servings.

Special Beets: Add ¼ to ½ teaspoon grated orange peel, 1 teaspoon caraway seeds, 1 teaspoon prepared horse-radish or ⅛ teaspoon cloves to 4 servings of hot buttered beets.

Mashed Carrots: Whip cooked carrots with the electric mixer and then season to taste with salt, pepper and butter. Add a dash of nutmeg (less than ⅛ teaspoon) if you like.

GREEN BEANS WITH BACON

Tarragon-flavored vinegar gives these beans an interesting taste but if you don't have it, you can use cider vinegar

  6 slices bacon
  6 tablespoons chopped onion
  2 tablespoons tarragon vinegar
½ teaspoon salt
  3 cups hot cooked green beans

1. Cook the bacon until crisp, but not brittle. Lift it onto paper towels to drain.

See directions for cooking bacon, page 142

See how to cook beans, pages
179–82

How to Cut Green Beans
Place green (or wax)
beans flat on a cutting
board and cut each bean
into *narrow, lengthwise*
strips with a knife. Or
you can pull the beans,
one at a time, through
the cutting slot at the end
of your vegetable peeler.
Beans cut this way are
French-style.

A quick way to cut
beans is to hold a bunch
of several beans on the
cutting board with your
hand and cut through
them *crosswise* to make
slices from ½ to 1 inch
or longer. These are called
crosscut beans.

2. Pour bacon fat from the skillet. Then measure 3 tablespoons of the fat back into the skillet. Add the onions and cook over low heat until the onions are soft, but do not let them brown. Add the vinegar and salt.

3. Place the drained and hot fresh beans, frozen green beans cooked as directed on the label, or heated canned green beans in a serving dish and pour the hot onion-vinegar mixture over them. Crumble the bacon over the top. Makes 5 to 6 servings.

BEETS IN ORANGE SAUCE

Fix this when you start dinner—it needs to stand 30 minutes

½ cup sugar
1 teaspoon salt
1 tablespoon cornstarch
¼ cup lemon juice
¼ cup water
3 cups cooked sliced beets
2 tablespoons butter or margarine
2 oranges, peeled and sliced

1. Mix the sugar, salt and cornstarch. Add the lemon juice and water. Stir to mix. Cook over medium heat until the mixture thickens. Remove from heat.

2. Add the sliced beets and butter. Let stand 30 minutes so the flavors will blend. Just before serving, heat to boiling, and add the orange slices. (Be sure to peel off all the white membrane under the yellow-orange peel before slicing the oranges.) Makes about 4 cups.

BROCCOLI PLATTER

The easy sauce adds a delightful taste to the hot broccoli

2 tablespoons butter or margarine
2 tablespoons minced onion
1 cup dairy sour cream
½ teaspoon poppy seeds
½ teaspoon paprika
¼ teaspoon salt
⅛ teaspoon pepper
2 pounds cooked broccoli
⅓ cup chopped salted peanuts

1. Cook the butter and onion together in a small skillet over medium heat until the onion is soft—do not let it brown. Remove from the heat and stir in the sour cream, poppy seeds, paprika, salt and pepper. Heat in the top of a double boiler over boiling water.

2. Cook the broccoli, lift onto a warm platter and pour on the hot sauce. Sprinkle on the chopped peanuts, or use cashew nuts instead for company. Makes 6 to 8 servings.

GLAZED CARROTS

A new carrot dish with a hint of orange-pineapple flavor

  3 cups thinly sliced peeled carrots
⅓ cup orange juice
  2 to 3 tablespoons sugar
¼ teaspoon cloves (optional)
¼ teaspoon salt
½ (5-ounce) jar pineapple cheese spread

1. Cook carrots in a medium saucepan until tender. This will take 6 to 20 minutes, depending on the age of the carrots. Drain.

2. Mix the orange juice, sugar, cloves, salt and cheese spread. Pour over the carrots and cook over low heat, stirring all the time, until the cheese melts and the mixture thickens. Do not let it boil. Makes 6 servings.

CAULIFLOWER WITH CHEESE

The process cheese spread melts and seasons the cauliflower

  1 medium cauliflower head (4 cups flowerets)
½ teaspoon salt
  1 cup soft process cheese spread
  2 green onions, finely cut
¼ teaspoon garlic salt

1. Remove the leaves from the cauliflower and cut off some of the hard stems. Separate into flowerets, and wash well. Cut off any dark parts with a paring knife. Cook in water to cover, with salt added, over high heat 10 to 15 minutes, or until tender. Drain.

2. Add the cheese, onions and garlic salt. Stir gently until the cheese is melted and mixed well with the cauliflower. Serve it hot. Makes 6 servings.

The Chinese Cut
You can cut beans (carrots, too) the way the Chinese do. Hold the bundle of beans the same as for crosscut beans, but cut them on the *diagonal*. Each piece of bean should be about 1 inch long. Diagonally cut beans cook somewhat faster because a larger cut surface is exposed to the boiling water.

See how to cook carrots, pages 179–82

From Carotene to Vitamin A
Yellow and green vegetables (also yellow fruits) do not contain vitamin A. They contain carotene, which your body changes to vitamin A. Milk contains vitamin A because cows change the carotene from the plants they eat to vitamin A and store some of it in the fat of their milk. This explains why butter, whole milk, cream, cheese and ice cream are good sources of vitamin A and why skim milk is not— most of the cream is removed from skim milk. Vitamin A helps keep the skin healthy—also the linings in the body, inside the nose, for instance. And it also helps your eyes to see in the dark.

See how to cook cauliflower, pages 179–82

COUNTRY-STYLE CABBAGE

You can fix this homey dish in jig-time—that means fast

1 medium head cabbage, shredded
½ cup butter or margarine
½ cup light cream
½ teaspoon salt

1. Shred the cabbage on a broad grater or with a sharp knife. Put it and the butter in a medium saucepan or skillet, cover and cook over medium heat 5 to 6 minutes.

2. Take the cabbage from the heat and add the cream and salt. Return to the heat and cook just until the cream is hot—about 3 minutes. Makes 6 servings.

CORN ON THE COB

Husk the corn just before you cook it. Cook enough ears to serve everyone once. Place the ears in a large kettle and cover them with cold water. Put the lid on the kettle and cook over high heat. As soon as the water comes to a full boil, the corn is cooked. Lift the ears to a warm platter with tongs at once to prevent overcooking. Cover them with a napkin to hold in the heat. Start the next batch of corn cooking the same way. Let it cook while you serve the first cooked ears.

Always serve corn hot with butter or garlic butter and with salt and pepper. For a change, try adding minced green onions to the butter for spreading on corn—or a little chili powder.

SCALLOPED CORN AND TOMATOES

Perfect with ham or pork chops—it's hearty and colorful

1 egg, beaten
1 (12-ounce) can whole-kernel corn, drained
1 (1-pound) can tomatoes
⅓ cup cut-up onions
1 teaspoon sugar
2 teaspoons flour
¾ teaspoon salt
½ teaspoon chili powder
1 cup coarse cracker crumbs
¼ cup melted butter or margarine

1. Start heating the oven to 375° F. Grease a 6-cup (1½-quart) casserole with butter or margarine.

2. Beat the egg in a large bowl. Add the drained corn, tomatoes and onions.

3. Mix the sugar, flour, salt and chili powder together and sprinkle over the vegetables. Add half the cracker crumbs and half the butter. Mix lightly and pour the mixture into the greased casserole. Top with the rest of the cracker crumbs (½ cup) and dribble on the rest of the melted butter (2 tablespoons).

4. Bake the casserole 35 minutes. Makes 6 servings.

ONION-CHEESE BAKE

You can mix this ahead, chill and then bake at mealtime

Dribble butter on top

  4 cups peeled sliced onions
  1 can condensed Cheddar cheese soup
½ cup milk

1. Start heating the oven to 375° F. Grease a 6-cup (1½-quart) casserole lightly with butter, margarine or shortening.

2. Separate the onion slices into rings.

3. Mix the soup and milk in the casserole and stir in the onions, mixing well.

4. Bake uncovered 30 minutes, or until hot and bubbly. If you want to give this dish a fancy look, garnish it just before serving with strips of drained canned pimiento. Makes 8 servings.

BUTTERED PEAS

Cook two or three pods with the shelled peas for extra-fine flavor. Remove them before serving. An elegant garden dish

So handy: a pan drainer

  2 pounds fresh peas (about 2¼ cups shelled)
  1 teaspoon sugar
½ teaspoon salt
  3 small green onions, sliced thin
  2 tablespoons butter or margarine
Pepper

1. Wash pea pods and shell peas.

2. Pour 1 inch water into a medium saucepan. Add sugar

and salt and bring to a boil over high heat. Add the peas and onions. When the water boils again, turn down the heat. Keep the peas boiling gently. Cook them uncovered 5 minutes, then cover and cook until tender, 3 to 15 minutes longer or until tender. You should have little liquid left.

3. Stir in the butter and season with pepper. Makes 4 servings.

KNOW YOUR POTATOES

Some potatoes are especially good for baking, others are just right for boiling and use in salad. Among the good bakers (also good for frying) are long russets, or Idaho bakers. They are oval-shaped and when cooked, they are mealy, dry and fluffy. You can buy them the year around.

Round whites, often called Maine or eastern potatoes, are fine for boiling and for salads. Then there are round reds, which have red skins, that are also good for boiling and salad making. They are available throughout the year. Sometimes they're called Florida new potatoes.

Long white potatoes from California have smooth, thin skins that are light in color. They are long in shape and are fine for boiling. These potatoes come on the market in April and are available through August.

The color of potatoes is due mainly to the variety, but also to the soil and climate. Those grown in the San Luis Valley of Colorado are famed for the high red color of their skins and their high vitamin C content.

FLUFFY MASHED POTATOES

What could taste better than fluffy, light mashed potatoes without a lump served piping hot? If you had a dollar for every bowl of far-from-perfect mashed potatoes served in just one day, you'd be rich. That's because too many cooks do not take the trouble to make them *really* good. It takes only a few minutes more. Mashing perfect potatoes is especially easy if you let the electric mixer do the work. Here's how to do it.

9 medium potatoes, peeled
6 tablespoons butter or margarine
¾ cup hot milk
Salt
Paprika

1. To a large saucepan containing 1 inch boiling water, add ½ teaspoon salt for each cup water. Add the peeled potatoes, cover and cook until they are tender, about 35 to 40 minutes. Drain off the cooking water and place the pan over low heat for a couple of minutes. Shake the pan. This dries out the potatoes and makes them mealy and good.

2. Add the butter or margarine to the milk and heat in a small saucepan over low heat to melt the butter. Do not let the milk come to a boil. Heating the milk makes better mashed potatoes.

Shake dry over heat

3. Mash the hot potatoes with the electric mixer on low speed, or with a potato masher, until *no lumps are left*. Then beat them until fluffy with the electric mixer, potato masher or wooden spoon while gradually adding the lukewarm butter-milk mixture. If you use the electric mixer, gradually increase its speed. Taste the potatoes. Even if they have been cooked in salted water, they usually need a little more salt. Pile the potatoes lightly in a warm serving dish and top them with a little square of butter. Sprinkle them lightly with paprika and serve at once. If mashed potatoes must wait, leave them in the pan after mashing. Cover the pan and set it in another pan of hot water over low heat. Makes 6 servings.

SKILLET SCALLOPED POTATOES

A cool way to scallop potatoes on hot days—no oven heat

5 cups cubed, peeled raw potatoes, about 2½ pounds
3 tablespoons butter
1 cup boiling water
1 (14½-ounce) can evaporated milk
¾ teaspoon salt
⅛ teaspoon pepper
Snipped parsley

1. Cut the peeled potatoes into ½-inch cubes.

2. Melt the butter in a 10-inch skillet. Add the potatoes and cook them 3 or 4 minutes. Stir two or three times while they are cooking.

3. Add the boiling water and evaporated milk. Cook 20 to 30 minutes over low heat. Stir once or twice. Season the potatoes with the salt and pepper.

4. Turn them into a serving dish and sprinkle parsley, snipped finely with scissors, over the top. Allow 45 minutes to fix and cook these potatoes. Makes 6 servings.

Why Potatoes Sometimes Have Green Skins
Farmers, who grow potatoes, take great pains to protect them from bright sunshine in the fields during the digging. And they are even careful to protect their potatoes from electric lights while they are stored because exposure to light often gives potato skins a green color. Sometimes potatoes displayed in supermarkets under electric lights also discolor. It's a good idea to store potatoes in a dark place, for the green skin gives potatoes a bitter taste. Always peel off the green portions before cooking potatoes—it is not good to eat.

Quick! Let the steam out!

BEST-EVER BAKED POTATOES

1. Scrub potatoes of the same size thoroughly with a brush. If you want them to have soft skins when baked, rub them with salad or cooking oil. Bake them on the rack in a hot oven, 450° F., 40 to 50 minutes, or until tender when you stick a kitchen fork into them.

2. When the potatoes are done, remove them from the oven at once. Hold each potato in your hand with a dish towel or pot holder and cut a cross in the top with a paring knife. Press the ends of each potato to push out a little of the soft inner part. This lets the steam escape through the cross and makes the potato mealy. Break up the inside of the potato a little with a fork. Drop a square of butter or a spoonful of dairy sour cream into the opening. You can add snipped chives or green onions to the sour cream. Serve at once to keep the potatoes from becoming soggy.

Potatoes Done?
The baked potato is done if it feels soft when you press it. Protect your hands with a pot holder. Or you can pierce the potato with a kitchen fork to tell if it is tender.

TWICE-BAKED POTATOES

One of the best and easiest ways to use leftover potatoes

6 medium baked potatoes
1½ teaspoons salt
½ teaspoon pepper
1 cup light cream or half and half
¾ cup grated mild soft cheese

1. Start heating the oven to 425° F.

2. Cut the cold baked potatoes in halves lengthwise. Then slit the potatoes twice lengthwise and several times crosswise, but do not cut through the skins. Spread them in a shallow baking pan.

3. Stir the salt and pepper into the cream and pour the cream over the potatoes. Sprinkle the potato tops with the cheese.

4. Bake the potatoes 10 to 15 minutes or until browned. Makes 6 servings.

Cut grooves to hold cream

BROWNED POTATOES

This is the way to fix browned potatoes with a roast

6 medium potatoes
3 tablespoons salad oil
1 teaspoon salt

1. Peel the potatoes and cook them, covered, in a medium saucepan in 1 inch of boiling water, 15 minutes. They will not be tender. Drain.

2. While the potatoes cook, put the salad oil in a 13×9×2-inch baking pan and sprinkle the salt over the oil.

3. Roll the potatoes in the salad oil and salt, coating them thoroughly, and put the pan of potatoes in a slow oven to bake with a beef, lamb or pork roast (325° F.). Bake 30 minutes, turn the potatoes and bake 30 minutes longer. Makes 6 servings.

WHIPPED SWEET POTATOES

These sweet potatoes are fixed like white mashed potatoes with orange juice added instead of milk—good for a change

6 medium sweet potatoes or yams (3 pounds)
6 tablespoons butter or margarine (¾ stick)
3 tablespoons brown sugar
¼ cup orange juice

1. Peel sweet potatoes with a vegetable peeler.

2. Put 1 inch water in a large saucepan, add ½ teaspoon salt and bring to a boil. Add the sweet potatoes and cook, covered, until tender, about 15 minutes. Drain.

3. Shake the saucepan of sweet potatoes over low heat to dry them. This will take 2 or 3 minutes. Then mash them thoroughly with a potato masher.

4. Stir in the butter, sugar and orange juice and beat with a spoon until they are fluffy.

5. Spoon the sweet potatoes into a serving dish and garnish with a few teaspoons butter or chopped parsley. Makes 6 servings.

BAKED ACORN SQUASH

Stir ¼ teaspoon cinnamon in the honey for a faint spicy taste

3 medium acorn squash
6 tablespoons honey
¼ cup butter or margarine

1. Start heating the oven to 375° F.

2. Wash squash and cut in lengthwise halves. Remove the strings and seeds. Place squash cut side down in shallow baking pan. Surround with ½ inch hot water. Bake un-

What Makes Vegetables Taste So Good?
The flavor of vegetables is due to many things— one of them is an acid called glutamic acid. This helps to give young, freshly harvested vegetables their wonderful taste. You can also buy this acid in most supermarkets among the seasonings. It comes in shakers and the seasoning looks like tiny white crystals. It is called monosodium glutamate. It brings out the natural flavors in meats, fish, chicken, gravy, soup, salad and vegetables. Mushrooms contain lots of glutamic acid which explains why they (and cream of mushroom soup) are used in so many dishes to provide flavor. Use monosodium glutamate in these amounts: 1 teaspoon to 1 pound ground beef, or to 1 chicken; ¾ teaspoon for 4 servings of a vegetable and ½ teaspoon for every pound of a roast.

Honey for the Gods
Ancient Greeks believed honey was eaten by their gods. Some of the best Grecian desserts to this day are sweetened with honey gathered from blossoms on the mountain sides.

covered 30 minutes. Pour off water and with a fork and broad spatula, turn the squash halves cut side up.

3. To each half, add 1 tablespoon honey and 2 teaspoons butter or margarine.

4. Bake 15 minutes longer, or until squash is tender. Makes 6 servings.

SKILLET TOMATO SCALLOP

Quick to make—adding the toast last keeps it crunchy

1 (1-pound 12-ounce) can tomatoes
1 tablespoon butter or margarine
1 tablespoon sugar
1 teaspoon salt
⅛ teaspoon pepper
1 teaspoon instant onion
2 slices white bread

1. Put the tomatoes, butter, sugar, salt, pepper and onion into a medium saucepan. Bring the mixture to a boil over high heat. Lower the heat and simmer 5 minutes. Stir once.

2. Toast the bread. Place it on a cutting board and cut it in small cubes.

3. Spoon the tomatoes into a serving dish or into small bowls. Sprinkle toast cubes over the top. Makes 6 servings.

For a change
· Add ¼ teaspoon dried basil instead of the onion.

Picture-pretty salads

EVERY meal needs at least one bright-color dish. The salad is one of the easiest ways to introduce color with such treats as red-ripe tomatoes, shredded carrots, frills of leaf lettuce, rings of green peppers, chunks of unpeeled red apples, sections of oranges and the sunshine of peaches, apricots and pineapple. And *eating* salads is one of the easiest and most delicious ways to get the daily quota of green and yellow vegetables and fruits.

Some salads, like lettuce, are light and others, like tuna, are substantial enough to make the main dish for supper or luncheon.

First, let's consider lettuce and other salad greens that you use in the popular tossed salads and under many vegetable, fruit, fish and other salads. If you will sprinkle a little French-type dressing on these lettuce liners for salads, you'll find most people will eat the leaves as well as the salad itself.

Kinds of salad greens

When you are in a supermarket, look at the many kinds of greens for sale. Here are some of the vegetables you may see and want to try.

Leaf lettuce: It's often called garden lettuce—it grows in loose bunches and in many home gardens. The young leaves are tender and crisp, and some of them have ruffled edges. One of the popular kinds is oak-leaf lettuce—the leaves are shaped like those on oak trees.

Red lettuce: This bunching lettuce grows in California the year round and is shipped to many areas. You will know it by its reddish-bronze leaves, which are very tender.

Bibb lettuce: This delicately flavored, tender salad green grows in small cup-shaped heads—one head is often the right size for a serving. It's sometimes called limestone lettuce because it grows in lime-rich soils. It originated in Kentucky.

Boston lettuce: Another name for this lettuce is butterhead. It grows in soft heads and the inner leaves feel slightly buttery. The green to light yellow leaves have an excellent delicate flavor.

Curly endive or chicory: The floppy heads have feathery leaves that vary from dark to a very pale green. Their flavor is pleasingly bitter.

Escarole: It's a cross between lettuce and chicory and has broad, curly leaves and a yellowish center. It has a slightly bitter taste.

Iceberg lettuce: You probably call it head lettuce. It's the kind that almost every supermarket has throughout the year. The head is firm and it can be shredded, cut in wedges or broken in bite-size pieces. Usually the medium-size heads taste better than very large heads, which may be overgrown and a little bitter.

Romaine: This is Cos lettuce. It has a long head and the long leaves have heavy ribs. Romaine is tender; its flavor is a little sharp.

Mustard greens: The young, tender, deep green leaves often are added to green salads. The leaves are smooth and broad and they are toothed on the edges.

Spinach: This vegetable with arrow-shaped leaves on coarse stems adds a pretty dark green touch to tossed salads. Use only the young, tender leaves and discard the stems—cook the big leaves.

Parsley: You may see two kinds, one with curly leaves and the other with plain leaves. Chopped parsley is a green salad favorite. Often the salad maker snips it into small pieces with scissors.

Water cress: The small, shiny, dark green, round leaves grow on slender stalks. Water cress is fine with other greens in salads and it also is a pretty garnish.

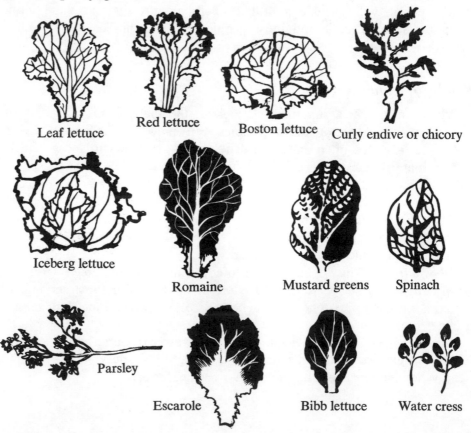

Leaf lettuce

Red lettuce

Boston lettuce

Curly endive or chicory

Iceberg lettuce

Romaine

Mustard greens

Spinach

Parsley

Escarole

Bibb lettuce

Water cress

Storing salad greens

Once the salad greens are in the kitchen, clean and put them in the refrigerator. They then will be ready to use and will keep about a week. This is the way to do it.

Remove all discolored or badly bruised outer leaves, but keep firm heads of lettuce (iceberg) and cabbage heads whole. Save all the green outer leaves possible even if they are somewhat coarse—they contain lots of vitamins and minerals the body needs. You can tuck them in sandwiches or shred them with scissors and add to salads. Now you are ready to wash the greens, which hold their best flavors and food value if kept cold and moist. If you put them away too wet, bacteria may grow in them and cause spoilage. So let them dry before storage.

Cut out the core of *iceberg lettuce* with a small knife or hit the core on the side of the sink and then lift it out. Leave the core in *cabbage*. Wash the lettuce and cabbage heads. Put washed heads of lettuce and cabbage in a colander or on a wire rack to drain. Then store them in large plastic bags in the refrigerator or place them in the refrigerator's crisper.

Wash *leaf lettuce, Boston lettuce, Bibb lettuce, curly endive, escarole, romaine* and *red lettuce,* leaf by leaf. Swish the leaves up and down in lukewarm water—gently. The lukewarm water will not wilt the leaves and it helps remove all the sand. Give them a final rinse in cold water. Then drain them by shaking in a wire salad basket, on paper towels or by rolling in a clean dish towel. Put each kind of the drained leaves in a separate plastic bag and place them in the refrigerator.

Open the bunches of *parsley* and *water cress* (also *fresh mint*), pick over and discard discolored leaves. Wash under running cold water and dry between paper towels, by shaking in a wire salad basket or by rolling in a clean dish towel. Store the parsley and water cress (also fresh mint) separately, stems down, in a jar. Cover and place in the refrigerator.

Wash *spinach* and *mustard greens* through two or three changes of lukewarm water. Lift the leaves up out of the water, shaking them. The sand will fall to the bottom of the pan. Give them another rinse in cold water and then dry them on paper towels, by shaking in a wire salad basket or by rolling in a clean dish towel. When dry, put the leaves in plastic bags and store in the refrigerator.

Preparing greens for salad

Tossed salad: With your fingers, tear the greens into pieces about the size of a half dollar. If you are in a hurry, you can cut them with kitchen scissors.

Lettuce cups: Hold the head of iceberg lettuce under running cold water, cored end up, and gently pull the leaves off. Drain them by shaking in a wire salad basket or on paper towels. Use the leaves to hold fruit, fish, chicken and other salads.

Lettuce wedges: If you want to serve iceberg lettuce in wedges, cut the head with a sharp knife into wedges the size you want, often in four or six. Serve with salad dressing.

Shredded lettuce: Cut the head of iceberg lettuce into halves and then shred each half fine, starting at the cut side, with a sharp knife. Shredded lettuce makes a fine lining for fruit and other salads.

VEGETABLE SALADS

TOSSED GARDEN LETTUCE SALAD

If you grow leaf lettuce in your garden, you're lucky. You can toss wonderful salads with the tender, young leaves and salad dressing. If you have more than one kind of lettuce, use two or three kinds in the same salad.

Cut the lettuce early in the morning while it's still dewy and crisp after a cool night. Wash, dry and put it in a plastic bag or wrap it in saran and store in the refrigerator. Or gather the lettuce just before mealtime and wash, drain and dry. This is how to make the salad.

1. Wash and dry the leaves thoroughly. It's important to dry the lettuce so that the dressing will stick to the leaves and the water will not thin the dressing. Tear the leaves into pieces the size of half dollars.

2. If you like a taste of garlic, peel a garlic clove, cut in half and rub the salad bowl with the cut sides. Then discard the garlic. Or use a garlic press. Put the lettuce in the bowl and sprinkle the dressing on it—no more than 1 tablespoon of dressing to every serving of salad. Most cooks allow about 2 quarts lettuce for 6 generous servings.

3. Toss the salad lightly with 2 forks or a fork and a spoon until you coat the leaves with the dressing. Toss the salad just before you are ready to take it to the table—the leaves wilt quickly after you add the dressing.

TOSSED GREEN SALAD

Make it like Tossed Garden Lettuce Salad, using one, two or more washed, dried and chilled greens, such as iceberg lettuce, young spinach leaves and curly endive or with Boston lettuce, Romaine and chopped parsley. Remember to tear the greens into pieces about the size of half dollars (bite-size) when you put them in the salad bowl.

Jade Trees
Garnish the bowl of Tossed Garden Lettuce or Green Salad, when the salad is served at the table, with small green onions fixed this way: Cut off the onion bulbs and add them, sliced, if you like, to the salad. Then slit the onion tops and upper part of the stem lengthwise in small strips. Put them in ice water to chill, as the tops will curl. They look like little trees.

For a change

To vary Tossed Garden Lettuce Salad and Tossed Green Salad, add one of these before tossing:

· *A vegetable* such as raw or cooked broccoli flowerets, chopped pickled beets, cucumber slices, chopped sweet green peppers, strips of canned water chestnuts, grated carrots, 2 or 3 small green onions, sliced with part of their tops.

· *Leaves of fresh herbs* such as chervil, summer savory, orégano, tarragon, marjoram, thyme or parsley, snipped fine. Or add dill seeds or caraway seeds.

· *A hearty food* such as narrow strips of lunchmeat, cooked chicken or turkey. Or narrow strips of Swiss or Cheddar cheese. Also good: crumbled cooked bacon, circles of frankfurters, tiny cooked shrimp or chopped hard-cooked eggs.

· *A few more suggestions:* Sliced pickles, croutons, circles or wedges of avocado, stuffed green olives or pitted black olives stuffed, if you like, with a cheese spread.

· *Sliced tomatoes:* Add the sliced tomatoes just after you've tossed the salad to keep their juices from thinning the salad dressing. Toss the salad a few times after you add the tomatoes —just enough to distribute them in the salad. It's a good idea to slice the tomatoes European-style or vertically instead of crosswise. They'll lose less juice.

So handy: a salad basket

WILTED LETTUCE

The hot dressing wilts the lettuce slightly—a great country salad in spring when garden lettuce is in season

Slice tomatoes European way

> 2 large bunches leaf lettuce
> 1 teaspoon salt
> 2 teaspoons sugar
> 2 green onions, sliced
> 4 slices bacon
> ¼ cup vinegar
> 2 tablespoons water
> 2 hard-cooked eggs

Cherry Tomatoes
Hollow out cherry tomatoes and fill them with a cheese spread. Arrange one, two or three of these stuffed tomatoes on top of each serving of Tossed Green Salad.

1. Wash the lettuce and tear it in bite-size pieces into a large bowl. Sprinkle on the salt, sugar and green onions. Use some of the green onion tops.

2. Cook the bacon until crisp, but not brittle, in a medium skillet. Drain the bacon on paper towels.

See directions for cooking bacon, page 142

Fantans

Turn firm, ripe tomatoes stem side down on a cutting board. Use peeled or unpeeled tomatoes. Cut down in the tomato, but not quite through, to make 5 slices in each tomato. Pull slices apart gently and stick a thin onion or cucumber slice in each pocket.

Make fork lines on cucumber

Then slice—edges are fancy

3. Add the vinegar and water to the bacon drippings in the skillet. Heat the mixture to the boiling point. Pour the hot dressing over the lettuce and toss until all the lettuce is partly wilted.

4. Sprinkle the salad with the bacon, crumbled, and eggs, chopped or sliced, and serve at once. Makes 4 servings.

SUMMER SALAD BOWL

Serve with fried chicken and corn on the cob for a feast

5 large ripe firm tomatoes
2 cucumbers
1 green pepper
1 large sweet onion
Salt
Pepper
¼ cup French dressing

1. Use chilled vegetables. Wash and slice, but do not peel, the tomatoes. (Tomato slices and quarters hold their shape better if not peeled.) Wash and peel the cucumbers, run a fork up and down on them to make lines, and slice. Wash and cut the green pepper and the peeled onion into slices to make rings. Discard pepper seeds.

2. Spread the vegetables out in a salad bowl. If you are not going to serve the salad at once, cover the bowl (you can use a piece of aluminum foil) and put it in the refrigerator.

3. When you are ready to serve the salad, sprinkle it with salt and pepper and drizzle the French dressing over the top. Mix lightly. Pass cottage cheese to spoon over the salad if you wish. Makes 6 to 8 servings.

SUN-GLOW CARROT SALAD

This colorful salad is one of the all-time favorites

2 cups grated carrots
½ cup light or dark raisins
⅓ cup mayonnaise
¼ cup salted peanuts
Lettuce

1. Peel the carrots with a vegetable peeler (potato peeler) and grate on a coarse grater.

2. Add the raisins, mayonnaise and salted peanuts, saving a few peanuts to garnish salads. Stir to mix thoroughly.

3. Line 4 or 5 salad plates with lettuce leaves and divide the carrot mixture among them. Sprinkle the rest of the salted peanuts over the salads.

For a change

· *Carrot-pineapple salad:* Omit salted peanuts from Sun-Glow Carrot Salad and add 1 (13-ounce) can pineapple tidbits, drained. Thin the mayonnaise with a little juice drained from the pineapple and toss with carrots, pineapple and raisins. Makes 4 to 5 servings.

CABBAGE SALADS

Coleslaw is a great country salad. There are many recipes for it—we give you a good one. Green cabbage is a favorite salad vegetable because it is a pretty, bright green and has a mild, sweet taste. It's the kind you get in the spring at supermarkets and in early summer from your gardens. The late and winter cabbages are silvery green and the heads generally are firmer.

Red or purple cabbage has many friends. Its heads are firm and its flavor is somewhat stronger than other cabbages. Slaws made with two parts shredded green cabbage and one part red cabbage are attractive—make them when you want a change.

You'll also see Savoy or curly cabbage in markets and some home gardens. It has loose, flattened heads and the leaves are crinkled and dark green with heavy veins. It tastes like green cabbage. Then there is Chinese or celery cabbage, which really isn't cabbage at all. It belongs to the mustard family and tastes something like both cabbage and celery. It grows in long, oval heads somewhat like celery and the leaves are a pale green to white. You chop instead of shred it for salads. It gives green salads an interesting taste and texture you'll want to try.

To shred cabbage, cut the washed, chilled head in half and place one half at a time on the cutting board. Shred it fine, starting at the cut side, with a knife with a long, sharp blade. Or shred it on a grater. If you spread a sheet of waxed paper under the grater to catch the cabbage shreds, your cleaning job will be easy. All you have to do is gather up the paper, empty the cabbage into a bowl. (You may need to do this several times.) Then discard the paper.

How Much Will It Take? If you want to fix 4 servings of green salad, a good general rule to follow is: Buy 1 medium-size head of lettuce, 1 pound of loose greens or 1 (1½-pound) head of cabbage.

Shred cabbage on grater

Shred cabbage with a knife

COLESLAW

Make the dressing when you start to get a meal so it will have time to chill—toss with vegetables just before serving

½ cup mayonnaise
¼ teaspoon salt
⅛ teaspoon paprika
1 teaspoon sugar
1 tablespoon vinegar
1 tablespoon light cream
4 cups shredded cabbage
1 tablespoon minced onion
⅓ cup diced celery
⅓ cup grated carrot or chopped green pepper

1. Mix the mayonnaise, salt, paprika, sugar, vinegar and light cream in a small bowl. You will have about ½ cup of dressing. Cover and chill in the refrigerator.

2. Just before mealtime, put the cabbage, onion, celery and carrot or green pepper in the salad bowl. Add the chilled dressing. Toss to mix. Makes 4 servings.

FRUIT SALADS

You can combine many kinds of fruit in a salad so use your imagination. Be sure to have the fruits cold and in large enough pieces that everyone will know what they are. If you mix the dressing with the fruits, toss the salad gently so it will not get mushy. You may prefer to pass the salad dressing or to garnish the salad with a spoonful of it.

Drain the fruits thoroughly and place them on plates lined with crisp, dry lettuce or other greens. Or serve the salad in lettuce cups. When the weather is warm, salads taste more delicious when served on plates that have been chilled in the refrigerator. Here are a few good fruit salads.

Cubes of different kinds of melon, such as cantaloupe and watermelon or honeydew

Cooked or canned prunes, pitted and stuffed with cottage cheese, garnished with cut-up or sliced oranges

Canned pineapple slices spread with cream cheese, garnished with fresh strawberries or cut-up pitted dates

Canned or fresh pear or peach halves, their centers filled with cottage cheese in which chopped celery and a little mayonnaise are mixed

Canned apricot halves surrounded by banana slices

Canned pear halves with canned light cherries
Cantaloupe cubes and seedless green grapes
Diced apples and bananas with red or green grapes
Cut-up oranges, seedless green grapes and banana slices

APPLE-PEAR SALAD

Black walnuts are excellent in this and other apple salads

 1 cup diced, peeled fresh pears
 1 cup diced, unpeeled red apples
 2 tablespoons lemon juice
1½ teaspoons sugar
 1 cup thin-sliced celery
 ⅛ teaspoon salt
 ½ cup salad dressing
 ¾ cup broken walnuts or pecans
Lettuce

 1. Toss the pears, apples, lemon juice, sugar, celery, salt and salad dressing together in a medium bowl.

 2. Add the nuts and serve on lettuce. Makes 4 servings.

For a change
 • *Coconut pear-apple salad:* Use ¾ cup flaked coconut instead of the nuts.
 • *Apple salad:* Omit the pears and use 2 cups unpeeled, diced apples. Use black walnuts for the nuts and add ½ cup raisins.
 • *Apple-banana salad:* Omit the pears and use 1 cup each of apples and cut-up, peeled bananas.
 • *Apple-grape salad:* Omit the pears and use 2 cups red grapes, cut in halves and seeds removed, or 1 cup seedless green grapes.

PEANUT-BANANA SALAD

Make this salad for boys if you're eager to please them

4 large firm bananas
Peanut butter, crunchy or smooth
Lettuce
Mayonnaise

 1. Peel and cut each banana in half, crosswise. Then cut each piece of banana in half, lengthwise.

So handy: a ½ teaspoon measuring spoon with a round bowl to scoop out the core from pears.

Why Fruits Darken
Some peeled fresh fruits, such as bananas, apples and peaches, turn dark when allowed to stand before serving. They contain chemicals called enzymes that combine with the oxygen in the air and discolor the fruits. When you dip the fruits in lemon juice, mixed with a little water, or in orange or grapefruit juice, you coat the fruits with the citrus juice and keep the oxygen and enzymes apart for a time. The acid in the citrus juice also slows down the enzymes. You can substitute ascorbic acid mixture—the same product used in freezing many fruits—for the lemon or citrus juice.

Cut banana in quarters

Peanut butter between

Then slice in rounds

2. Spread the cut side of half of the banana pieces with peanut butter. Put the other banana halves on top and gently press together. The bananas will look like half bananas, only there will be a strip of peanut butter showing along the sides.

3. Cut the bananas again into crosswise slices and place them on lettuce. Serve with mayonnaise, if desired. Makes 6 servings.

SUMMER FRUIT SALAD

Fix this and toasted ham sandwiches for lunch on a hot day

¼ watermelon, cut lengthwise
1 medium cantaloupe
Snowy Cottage Cheese
Lettuce
4 fresh peaches

How Fruits Ripen
Several changes take place when fruits ripen, but one of the important changes is that the starch is turned to sugar by enzymes in the fruit. This makes fruits less tart, because sugar is sweeter than starch. If you put fruit in the refrigerator or other cool place, you slow down the work of the enzymes. But if the enzymes work too long, the fruit spoils. When you heat fruit, either in cooking or canning, you destroy the enzymes and the fruit does not get sweeter.

1. Cut the watermelon into slices ½ inch thick and peel off the rind. Cut the red part of the melon into 18 wedges. Put in a bowl, cover and put in the refrigerator.

2. Cut the cantaloupe in half, then in quarters. Peel off rind and cut the yellow part of the melon into cubes. Put in a bowl, cover and put in the refrigerator.

3. Make the Snowy Cottage Cheese (recipe follows) in a medium bowl, cover and put in the refrigerator.

4. At mealtime, arrange lettuce leaves on 6 salad plates. Heap a mound of Snowy Cottage Cheese in the center of each plate and surround with the watermelon, cantaloupe and fresh peaches, peeled and sliced. You can garnish with berries, if you have them. Serve at once.

SNOWY COTTAGE CHEESE

It's white as snow and really refreshes in sultry weather

½ cup heavy cream
2 tablespoons sugar
1 pint carton cream-style cottage cheese
½ teaspoon grated lemon peel

Red Stem Ends
Sometimes you see a reddish discoloration on the stem end of iceberg lettuce. Don't let it trouble you. It's nature's way of sealing the cut made when the head was picked and trimmed.

Beat cream with sugar added in a medium bowl until light and fluffy. (Use a hand or electric beater.) Fold in the cottage cheese and lemon peel. Cover and chill. Makes 6 servings.

TUNA SALAD

Old standby with a new twist—crunchy potato chips

¼ cup mayonnaise
2 tablespoons diced sweet pickles
1 tablespoon pickle juice
1 (6½- to 7-ounce) can tuna
½ cup diced celery
½ cup cooked fresh or frozen peas or canned peas
Salad greens
1 cup crushed potato chips

1. Toss the mayonnaise, pickles, pickle juice, tuna, flaked with a fork, celery and peas together in a medium bowl. Cover and chill if you are not ready to serve the salad.

2. Just before serving, arrange lettuce or other salad greens on 4 salad plates. Toss the coarsely crushed potato chips into the salad and evenly divide the salad among the salad plates. (If you prefer, you can use coarsely crushed corn chips instead of potato chips.) By adding the potato chips at the last minute, they will be crisp. Makes 4 servings.

POTATO SALAD

Some good cooks sprinkle grated pimiento cheese on this

4 cups diced cooked potatoes
1 cup sliced celery
3 hard-cooked eggs, cut up
½ cup finely cut onion or sliced green onions
¼ cup sliced radishes
1 cup mayonnaise
1 tablespoon vinegar
1 teaspoon prepared mustard
1½ to 2 teaspoons salt
⅛ teaspoon pepper
Lettuce

Mix all the ingredients in a bowl. Cover and refrigerate several hours so flavors can blend. Serve on crisp lettuce. Makes 6 servings.

Red Cups
Peel firm tomatoes or leave their skins on. Cut a thin slice from the top (stem end). Scoop out part of the center. Turn tomato upside down in a shallow pan, like a piepan, and chill. Serve filled with tuna, chicken or other salad or with seasoned cottage cheese.

Tomato Blossoms
Peel firm, ripe tomatoes and dribble a little French or Italian salad dressing over them to season. Cover and chill. When ready to serve, put each tomato stem end down on a cutting board and cut into 6 wedges or petals. Gently pull down every other wedge to make zigzag petals. Spoon tuna or chicken salad, shredded lettuce mixed with French dressing, cottage cheese or other salad into the tomato blossoms and then top the filling in the tomatoes with a spoonful of mayonnaise or dairy sour cream.

How to Fix Onion Rings
Peel a large sweet onion.
Cut off stem and root
ends. Then cut in slices
¼ inch thick. Separate
each slice of onion in
rings with your fingers.

What you can add

· If you have a cucumber, add ½ cup of it, diced and peeled, to Potato Salad. Some good salad makers like to stir ¾ teaspoon celery seeds into their potato salad. Others add ½ cup chopped dill pickle instead of the cucumber. You will enjoy varying the flavor these ways.

For a change

· *Macaroni and cheese salad:* You can use the recipe for Potato Salad to make a wonderful macaroni salad. Use 4 cups cooked elbow or shell macaroni (one 8-ounce package before cooking) instead of the diced potatoes. Add another tablespoon of vinegar and 1 cup finely cut-up process Cheddar cheese. Be sure to rinse the hot macaroni with cold water after cooking and draining to separate the "elbows" or "shells." Then drain again thoroughly in a sieve or colander.

MOLDED SALADS

Molded salads are picture-pretty. You make them ahead and chill them until firm. Many good cooks find it's easier to get a meal if they fix the salad a few hours early, put it in the refrigerator and forget about it until time to unmold and serve.

There are two kinds of gelatin, the base for molded salads—flavored and unflavored. The flavored gelatin comes in packages and contains gelatin, sugar, fruit or vegetable flavoring and food color. Unflavored gelatin comes in little envelopes and is all gelatin. The cook adds sugar, if the recipe calls for it, and sometimes she also adds food color. Follow the label or the recipe suggestions with both kinds.

To make a molded salad, you first dissolve flavored gelatin in a liquid, usually in boiling hot water or fruit or vegetable juice. Then you chill it until it thickens slightly—it should be as thick as unbeaten egg whites. Next you add the fruits, vegetables, nuts, marshmallows or whatever food the recipe calls for. If you let the gelatin *set* before adding these foods, it's impossible to fold them into the mixture, but if you do not let it *thicken,* the gelatin mixture will not hold the foods in place: Some of the foods, like fresh apple, pear or peach slices, strawberries cut in half, raspberries, grapefruit sections, broken nut meats and marshmallows, float to the top. Other foods, such as canned apricots, peaches, pears and light cherries, whole strawberries, prunes, grapes and fresh orange sections, sink to the bottom of the salad. The food should be distributed evenly throughout the gelatin mixture.

After you add the foods to the slightly thickened gelatin, you chill the mixture until it becomes firm, or set. Allow 2 to 3 hours, several hours or overnight for gelatin salad to set.

Time it takes for gelatin to set

If you haven't time to let the gelatin salad set properly, make some other kind of salad. One of the best points of molded salads, in addition to their beauty and fine taste, is that you can make them hours or a day ahead and skip that last-minute rush before a meal.

Some good cooks, who don't want to give up gelatin salads even though they are hurried, have tricks to fast-fix them. But remember that the time it takes for a gelatin mixture to thicken until it is as thick as unbeaten egg whites and then to become firm after the fruits, vegetables, etc., have been added depends on many things that vary from kitchen to kitchen. The temperature of the refrigerator is one thing. The amount of the mixture and its depth in the bowl are other influences. And the size and shape of the mold has something to do with how quickly a salad sets. It takes longer for big than for small molds and more time for deep than for shallow molds. Here are ways some cooks speed up these salads.

Suppose the recipe calls for 2 cups water or other liquid. Dissolve the flavored gelatin in half the liquid (1 cup). Have this liquid boiling hot, but never cook gelatin. That makes it tough. Then stir in the other half of the liquid (1 cup). Have this liquid cold. Then put the mixture in the refrigerator to thicken. When it is as thick as unbeaten egg whites, fold in fruits or other food. Pour into molds and refrigerate until firm (about 2 hours) or until you are ready to serve it.

Or use the ice-cube method. Pour half the liquid (1 cup), heated to the boiling point, over the gelatin and stir until all the gelatin dissolves. Then add ½ tray ice cubes (7 to 10 cubes) to the gelatin mixture. Stir all the time until the mixture is as thick as unbeaten egg whites. It will take about 3 minutes. Remove any unmelted ice. Fold the fruits, vegetables, nuts, marshmallows or the foods you are molding into the gelatin mixture, pour it into molds and place in the refrigerator. The salad will be set in about an hour, but you can leave the salad in the refrigerator several hours or overnight.

How to unmold gelatin salads

Cut around the edge of the salad with a small pointed knife, but first dip the knife's blade in warm water. Gently press against the side of the salad in one place to let in air—this breaks the vacuum so the gelatin can slip out.

If you want to serve the salad on a plate, wet the plate with cold water. This makes it easy to move the salad to the proper place on the plate, usually in the center. Place the plate on top of the mold and turn the plate and mold upside down. Shake the mold gently to loosen the salad and then lift off the mold. If the salad sticks, dip the mold quickly in warm water, using care not to let the water touch the salad. Then place the wet plate on top of it again, invert the plate and mold together, shake the mold gently and lift it off.

Arrange lettuce, water cress or other greens on the plate around the salad—you can shred or tear the lettuce into small pieces. If you want to place a lettuce leaf under the salad, carefully lift the salad up with a broad spatula and tuck the lettuce under it.

Dip mold in warm water

What Makes Gelatin Set? Gelatin is a protein that can absorb lots of water or other liquid, such as fruit or tomato juice. It is important to have the right measure of water or other liquid, though. If you add too little, the salad will be tough and stiff. If you add too much, the gelatin cannot absorb all of it—the salad will not set. When you put the salad in the refrigerator, the cold congeals (or sets) it—makes it jellylike. At this point cooks say: The gelatin is set.

LIGHTNING SALAD

This is a streamlined recipe. The frozen grapefruit chills the hot gelatin quickly—it sets in half an hour or less

1 (3-ounce) package lime-flavor gelatin
1½ cups boiling water
1 (13½-ounce) can frozen grapefruit sections
Lettuce
Mayonnaise

1. Pour the gelatin into an 8-inch square pan. Add the hot water and stir until the gelatin dissolves.

2. Add the unthawed grapefruit sections and stir until the sections separate. Chill in the refrigerator until set, or 20 to 30 minutes.

3. Cut in servings. Place on lettuce arranged on a plate or in lettuce cups. Guests or family will eat the lettuce, too, if you pour a little French salad dressing on it before adding the gelatin salad. Garnish salads with mayonnaise. Makes 6 servings.

AUTUMN-RED SALAD

This salad is a wonderful color—makes meals look festive

1 pound fresh or frozen cranberries
2 medium red apples, cores removed
¾ cup sugar
1 (3-ounce) package strawberry-flavor gelatin
1 cup boiling water

1. Put the cranberries and cored apples through the food chopper using the coarse blade. Add the sugar and stir until it dissolves.

2. Put the gelatin in a medium bowl and add the boiling water. Stir until the gelatin dissolves. Chill in the refrigerator until the gelatin mixture is as thick as unbeaten egg whites.

3. Fold in the cranberry mixture. Pour the salad into 1 (4-cup or 1-quart) mold or into 6 to 8 individual molds. Chill until set, about 3 hours or overnight.

4. To serve, turn the gelatin from the mold or molds and garnish the plates with lettuce. Pass the salad dressing. For a holiday look, garnish each serving with 1 or 2 orange sections or slices. Makes 6 to 8 servings.

JELLIED TOMATO SALAD

An easy recipe to double if you want larger servings

1 envelope unflavored gelatin
1 teaspoon sugar
2 cups tomato juice
¼ teaspoon salt
¼ teaspoon celery salt
1 tablespoon onion, finely chopped
2 tablespoons lemon juice
Lettuce
Mayonnaise

1. Stir the gelatin and sugar together in a small saucepan to mix thoroughly. Slowly add 1 cup of the tomato juice and stir well to soften the gelatin.

2. Set over medium heat, stirring all the time, just until the gelatin dissolves. *Do not let the mixture come to a boil.*

3. Remove from the heat and stir in the rest of the tomato juice, salt, celery salt, onion and lemon juice.

4. Pour the mixture into 6 individual molds.

5. Place in the refrigerator until firm and time to serve. It usually takes about 1½ hours for the tomato salad to set, but you can leave it in the refrigerator longer.

6. To serve, run a spatula around the edge of the molds and turn the salads out on 6 plates lined with lettuce leaves. Garnish tops of salad with spoonfuls of mayonnaise. Makes 6 servings.

Fresh Pineapple Behavior
Fresh and frozen pineapple and pineapple juice contain an enzyme that prevents gelatin from setting. If you want to use either the fresh or frozen fruit or juice in gelatin salads, first heat it to the boiling point. That destroys the enzyme. You can use either canned pineapple or pineapple juice because the enzyme is destroyed by the heat necessary in canning.

See how to unmold gelatin salads, page 205

How to Dissolve Unflavored Gelatin
If a recipe calls for more than 1 tablespoon sugar to 1 envelope unflavored gelatin, mix the gelatin and sugar, add the hot liquid and stir to dissolve the gelatin. The sugar separates the gelatin granules which then dissolve quickly in hot water. Since flavored gelatins contain enough sugar already, you always add the hot liquid directly and stir to dissolve the gelatin. When a recipe calls for 1 tablespoon sugar (or no sugar) to 1 envelope unflavored gelatin, first soften the gelatin in a little cold water before adding the hot water. Gelatin, a protein, becomes very tough if hot water is added to it without first softening it in cold water or separating the granules with sugar.

Fancy molds: pretty salads!

See how to unmold gelatin
salads, page 205

ORANGE SHERBET SALAD

You can serve this salad for the dessert—it's a salad-dessert

2 (3-ounce) packages of orange-flavor gelatin
1 cup boiling water
1 pint orange sherbet
1 (11-ounce) can mandarin oranges, not drained
1 cup heavy cream, whipped
Lettuce

1. Pour the orange-flavor gelatin into a medium bowl and add the boiling water. Stir mixture to dissolve the gelatin. Add the sherbet and mix well.

2. Cool the mixture in the refrigerator until it is as thick as unbeaten egg whites. Add the mandarin oranges including juice and then fold in the whipped cream.

3. Pour the gelatin mixture into a 6-cup (1½-quart) mold. Chill until set. It will take at least 3 hours, and it's safer to allow more time. Or chill the salad overnight.

4. Unmold or spoon the salad onto lettuce-lined plates. Makes 8 servings. To make 4 servings, cut the ingredients in half.

SALAD DRESSINGS

Salad dressings have much to do with how good salads taste. So give them some thought. By using different kinds, you can change the taste of salads made with the same ingredients—tossed green salads, for instance.

Look over the many kinds of salad dressings in bottles and jars on the shelves in your supermarket. Many of them are really good, but do shake the bottled dressings before you add them to the salad. And don't miss the packaged salad dressing mixes that you can use to season oil and vinegar, French-type, salad dressing. Use them and you'll have no seasonings to measure. And their flavors are interesting. Some of the most popular packaged salad dressing mixes are garlic, Parmesan cheese, Italian, blue cheese, cheese garlic and creamy French.

You'll find a selection of salad oils in most markets. The most commonly used ones are corn, cottonseed, olive, soybean, peanut and safflower oils. The labels on the oils tell what kind they are.

Vinegars are made with many things—fruit juices, malt, beer and wine—and they come plain or seasoned with herbs, such as tarragon, garlic and dill. Lemon and lime juices often take the place of vinegar in salad dressings, especially in dressings for fruits. Then you will want to add honey or sugar to sweeten slightly.

Mayonnaise-type salad dressings are old standbys. They're made by beating together the oil, vinegar and egg yolk. The egg holds the oil and vinegar together—keeps them from separating. Here are a few good changes to make with the plain dressing. Stir into ½ cup mayonnaise—

Cheese: 1 cup grated process cheese, 1 tablespoon vinegar, ½ garlic clove, minced or put through a garlic press, ¼ teaspoon salt.

Cucumber: ½ cup drained minced cucumber and ¼ to ½ teaspoon dried dill.

Onion: 1 tablespoon minced onion, 6 drops lemon juice and ¼ teaspoon salt.

Mustard: ½ teaspoon dry mustard (good with fish salads).

Blue Cheese (or Roquefort): ¼ cup crumbled cheese and ½ cup French dressing.

Parsley or Chives: 1 tablespoon snipped parsley or chives.

SIMPLE FRENCH DRESSING

Shake this dressing to mix thoroughly—real good on lettuce

1½ cups salad oil
½ cup cider or wine vinegar
1 teaspoon salt
⅛ teaspoon pepper
½ teaspoon sugar

1. Pour the oil into a pint bottle with a tight-fitting lid. Use a funnel if you have one, to avoid spills.

2. Pour in the vinegar. Add the salt, pepper and sugar. Refrigerate.

3. Just before serving the dressing, shake the bottle to mix the oil and vinegar. Makes 1 pint.

For a change
· Add *one* of these seasonings to Simple French Dressing: 1 teaspoon paprika, 2 teaspoons sugar, ½ teaspoon dry mustard or ½ teaspoon curry powder. You can also use lemon juice instead of vinegar, but add ¼ to ⅓ cup sugar if you do.

Slick Trick
Use three parts salad oil to one part vinegar when making French salad dressing. Pour the vinegar into the salad bottle first. With red nail polish, mark the vinegar level on the bottle. Then add the oil and mark its top level. You will not need to measure the vinegar and oil in a cup the next time you make French dressing. Shake the dressing each time before you use it, because the oil and vinegar separate.

Mix in a measuring cup

COUNTRY CREAM DRESSING

This is an excellent dressing for leaf lettuce from the garden

½ cup light cream
2 tablespoons sugar
1 tablespoon vinegar

Mix the cream, sugar and vinegar in a measuring cup with a spoon. Pour it over the lettuce leaves—just enough to coat the leaves when you toss the salad. Makes ¾ cup.

For a change
· *Horse-radish cream dressing:* For a dressing with a "bite," stir 2 teaspoons prepared horse-radish into Country Cream Dressing.

RUSSIAN SALAD DRESSING

Dress up wedges of head lettuce with this colorful dressing

½ cup mayonnaise
½ cup French salad dressing
1 medium green pepper, minced
2 tablespoons chili sauce
1 tablespoon minced onion

With a spoon, mix all the ingredients together in a small bowl. Makes about 1½ cups.

THOUSAND ISLAND SALAD DRESSING

This dressing makes lettuce salad exciting and taste good

½ cup mayonnaise
1 tablespoon chili sauce
2 teaspoons minced onion
1 hard-cooked egg, chopped
1 tablespoon minced green pepper
2 tablespoons snipped parsley

Mix all the ingredients in a small bowl. Makes about 1¼ cups.

Snacks—little fourth meal

SNACKS are happy-time food—for you and your friends who come over to visit you or stop in after school. Your company usually enjoys helping you fix snacks, too. Eating them really helps company to have a good time and makes them want to come back again.

Snacks are part of the fun of getting home from school, skating, skiing, football and basketball games. Some snacks are party refreshments—things like fruit drinks, dips and chips, ice cream sodas and cookies.

Snacks also are pickups for busy people in midafternoon and mid-morning between regular meals. Often someone in the family takes them to workers in the field or yard so they'll stop what they're doing for a few minutes and relax.

So snacks really are a small fourth meal, always extra-tasty. This Cookbook has many recipes for foods that are perfect for snacking—cookies and sandwiches, for instance (look in the Index for the Cookies and Sandwiches sections). Here we give you a collection of other good snacks you'll want to make.

DRINKS—FOR MEALS, FOR SNACKS

Let's start with drinks, sweet and tart and milk specials. Drinks made with milk and with fruit and tomato juices are a delicious way to help get your day's quota of minerals and vitamins necessary for pep and clear skin.

SOUTH SEA SNOWSTORM

Thread a few canned pineapple cubes or strawberries on colored drinking straws and insert in glasses—pretty

1 quart vanilla ice cream
3 cups canned pineapple juice, chilled
1 (8-ounce) bottle carbonated water
Fruited drinking straws

Thirst Quencher
Pour equal measures of ginger ale and orange or pineapple juice in glasses filled with ice cubes. Or mix apple and cranberry juices, half and half, and add as much ginger ale as you have mixed fruit juice.

What Makes the Fizz
You've noticed how small bubbles rise in the glass when you pour out ginger ale or other carbonated beverages. These bubbles are carbon dioxide gas, the same kind of gas made by yeast, baking soda and baking powder in breads and cakes. In carbonated drinks gas is added when they are bottled, and airtight caps hold it in the bottles. When you remove the caps, the gas bubbles form and start to escape. They make that fizz you hear.

1. Place the ice cream in a large bowl and let it soften enough so that you can beat it with the electric mixer or a hand beater.

2. Slowly add the pineapple juice while you beat the ice cream.

3. Stir in the carbonated water and pour it into a pitcher. The drinks will be colder if you chill the carbonated water before using. Pour into tall glasses. Insert drinking straws. Makes 6 servings.

HOOTENANNY RASPBERRY FRAPPÉ

A wonderful drink to serve a crowd. You can have it in the freezer ready to add quickly to the glasses at serving time

3½ cups water
1½ cups sugar
1 (6-ounce) can frozen orange juice concentrate
1 (8½-ounce) can crushed pineapple
2 (10-ounce) packages frozen raspberries
Ginger ale or carbonated water

1. Mix the water and sugar in a large saucepan; stir and cook until the sugar dissolves. Remove it from the heat and add the undiluted frozen orange juice concentrate and undrained canned pineapple and raspberries.

2. Pour the mixture into a covered pan or container and put it in the freezer. Freeze 2 to 4 hours to form a firm slush or until firm.

3. When ready to serve, crush and scoop some of the raspberry mixture into glasses and fill glasses with chilled ginger ale or carbonated water. If you do not use all the frappé, cover it and put back in the freezer to use later. Makes 20 servings.

How to Make Sugar Syrup
Stir 1 cup sugar into 2 cups water and heat and stir until all the sugar is dissolved. Cool, cover and store in the refrigerator. Use to sweeten iced drinks the way you like them. There will be no unmelted sugar layer in the bottom of your glass.

LEMON-GRAPE PUNCH

With grape juice in the refrigerator and lemonade in the freezer, you're ready to stir up this drink in a hurry

4 cups grape juice (1 quart)
1 (6-ounce) can frozen lemonade concentrate

1. Pour the grape juice into a covered container and place it in the refrigerator to chill well.

2. Make the lemonade by directions on the can, but use only half as much water as directions call for (2 brimful cans). Pour the lemonade into a pan and set it in the freezer.

3. When it is time to serve the punch, crush the frozen lemonade with a fork and divide it up into 7 or 8 glasses. Pour the cold grape juice over it and serve immediately.

CHOCOLATE SODA

A favorite of chocolate lovers the year round, it refreshes and fills the hollow spot in your stomach—try it

3 tablespoons chocolate syrup (canned)
1 tablespoon light cream
2 scoops chocolate ice cream
1 scoop vanilla ice cream
Carbonated water

1. Measure the chocolate syrup into a tall glass (10-ounce). Add the light cream, the chocolate and vanilla ice creams.

2. Pour carbonated water in to fill the glass. Stir lightly and add more carbonated water very slowly until foam rises to the top of the glass. Serve at once with straws. Makes 1 soda.

To Decorate Chocolate Soda
Run 2 straws through a striped hard peppermint-candy circle with a hole in the center. Place in the soda with candy well above the top of the glass.

For 6 Sodas
To make 6 glasses of Chocolate Soda you will need 1 (1-pound) can chocolate syrup, ½ cup light cream, 3 pints chocolate ice cream and 1 quart vanilla ice cream and 2 (1-quart) bottles carbonated water.

SPARKLING PUNCH

Mix and pour over ice in punch bowl for a party—it bubbles

1 (6-ounce) can frozen orange juice concentrate
¼ cup fresh, frozen or canned lemon juice
¼ cup light corn syrup
1 quart ginger ale

1. Add the water to the orange juice as directed on the can. Stir in the lemon juice and corn syrup. Pour the mixture into a pitcher.

2. Slowly pour in the ginger ale. Serve at once in ice-filled glasses. Makes 2 quarts.

POTATO CHIP HISTORY

Saratoga chips is what your grandmother called potato chips. That's because the thinly sliced potatoes were first fried by a hotel cook in Saratoga Springs, New York.

MAPLE MILK SHAKE

Voted the best of all milk shakes by our taste testers

Dairy Drink or Milk
Chocolate dairy drink is made by dairies from skim milk or part skim milk with chocolate added. Chocolate milk is made with whole milk and is a little richer. You can tell the difference by reading the list of contents on the label.

2 cups milk
¼ cup maple-blended syrup
1 pint vanilla ice cream

1. Mix the milk and maple syrup in the electric blender.
2. Add the ice cream to the milk mixture by spoonfuls or slices.
3. Blend a few minutes until smooth. Makes 4 cups (1 quart).

FRENCH CHOCOLATE

This is a sophisticated drink for the young hostess, seated at one end of the table, to pour from a pitcher or pot

½ pint heavy cream
6 cups chocolate dairy drink
Grated nutmeg

See how to whip cream, page 19

1. Whip the cream until it is stiff. Do not sweeten it.
2. Pour the chocolate drink into a large saucepan and heat it over medium heat until small bubbles show around edge of saucepan. Do not let it simmer or come to a boil.
3. To serve, put 1 heaping tablespoon unsweetened whipped cream into a cup, pour the hot chocolate drink from a pitcher or a teapot almost to fill the cup. Shake a touch of grated nutmeg on top (ground nutmeg may be used). Use a salt shaker to hold the nutmeg. Makes 8 to 10 cups.

SPICED TOMATO JUICE

See recipe for Cheese Buds, page 217

Serve piping hot with Cheese Buds or crackers

1 (46-ounce) can tomato juice
6 tablespoons brown sugar
6 whole cloves
2 (2½-inch) cinnamon sticks
½ lemon, sliced

Put all the ingredients in a medium saucepan. Bring to a boil. Turn the heat down and simmer the juice 15 minutes. Remove the juice from the heat and strain it through a sieve into a pitcher. Serve hot. Makes about 5½ cups.

Dips and chips are lots of fun for a gang. People like to help themselves to these refreshments, and you can serve them so attractively. About the best way is to heap the dip in a pretty bowl and set it in the center of a large plate or platter. Arrange some of the "dippers" around the bowl on the plate or platter, the other in bowls and on plates grouped around the dip.

Among the favorite "dippers" are carrot sticks, celery stalks, strips of unpeeled red apples, radishes, potato chips, corn chips, pretzels and many kinds of crackers. Here are 2 favorite *Farm Journal* dips.

COTTAGE CHEESE DIP

Whip 1 (3-ounce) package cream cheese into the cottage cheese for a richer dip when you're having a special party

2 cups cream-style cottage cheese
½ package instant onion soup mix
Carrot and celery sticks

1. Mix the cottage cheese and onion soup mix until smooth—use a blender, the electric mixer or a spoon. Heap it in a bowl. Set the bowl on a large plate and around it lay carrot and celery sticks for dipping. Makes 2 cups.

MEXICAN BEAN DIP

Hot in two ways—you heat it on the stove and season it with chili powder—good with corn chips or crackers

2 (1-pound) cans kidney beans
¼ cup salad oil
1 cup grated Cheddar cheese
½ teaspoon salt
1 teaspoon chili powder

1. Drain the beans in a sieve and save the juice.

2. Put the beans through a food mill or mash them with a potato masher. Add about ⅓ cup bean juice.

3. Heat the salad oil in a large skillet and add the beans. Add the cheese, salt and chili powder and stir and cook over low heat until the cheese melts. If the mixture gets very thick, add a little more of the bean juice.

4. Serve hot in a bowl with corn chips for dunking in the dip. Makes about 2 cups.

Choose colorful "dippers"

See Carrot Curls and Sticks, page 177

Chill Cream Cheese
It is important to keep cream cheese dips in the refrigerator until you are ready to use them. The cold slows down the growth of bacteria that might spoil the taste of the cheese.

MEAT AND CHEESE TREATS

PRONTO PIZZA

See directions for kneading, pages 106–7

You can make marvelous pizzas from a packaged roll mix (follow directions on the label) or from a packaged pizza mix. Here's a "from scratch" pizza that's easy to make

- 1 package active dry yeast
- ¾ cup warm water (not hot, 105° to 115°F.)
- 2½ cups packaged biscuit mix
- 1 pound Italian sausage or pork sausage
- 2 (4-ounce) packages grated Mozzarella cheese (2 cups)
- 2 (8-ounce) cans pizza sauce
- 1 teaspoon dried orégano
- ⅓ cup Parmesan cheese

1. Grease 2 baking sheets or pizza pans.

2. Sprinkle the yeast over the warm water in a medium bowl. Stir until it dissolves. Add the biscuit mix and beat hard until well mixed.

3. Turn the dough onto a board lightly floured *with a little biscuit mix* from the package. Knead it 20 times. Divide the dough in half.

4. Place half the dough on a greased baking sheet (use a pizza pan if you have one) and press it down in a circle or rectangle until it almost covers the baking sheet. Make a little rim around the edge. Set aside while you make the sausage filling.

5. Start heating the oven to 425°F.

6. Place the sausage in a medium skillet and cook over medium heat until it browns. (If the sausage is in a casing, remove it before cooking.) Spoon off the fat.

7. Sprinkle half the Mozzarella cheese over the pizza crust.

8. Spread a can of pizza sauce over the cheese. Use a little less sauce if you like. Top with half the sausage.

9. Sprinkle with half the orégano and Parmesan cheese.

10. Bake the pizza on the rack in the center of the oven 15 minutes.

11. While it bakes, fix the second pizza and bake it while you serve the first one. Cut each pizza into 12 slices.

Pizza Pans

Pizza pans are round and shallow. The rims usually are only an inch or a little less high. The pans come in different sizes, and some of them are made of foil that you use once or twice and then throw away.

Or you can bake pizzas on a greased baking sheet. Place the circle of dough on the baking sheet and pat it out to the size you want. Pinch up the edges to make a small rim. You may find it easier to make the rim if you first make short snips in the edges with the scissors, about 1 inch apart, and then pinch up edges to make a rim. Or you can bake pizzas in piepans. Shallow pans are the best.

For a change

· *Hamburger pizza:* Use 1 pound of ground beef instead of the Italian sausage. Cook like the sausage and drain.

· *Pork sausage pizza:* Use 1 pound of pork sausage instead of the Italian sausage. Cook and drain.

· *Mushroom pizza:* Use 2 (3- or 4-ounce) cans mushrooms or 2 (2-ounce) cans chopped mushrooms instead of the Italian sausage. Drain mushrooms, but do not cook them.

· *Salami pizza:* Use 1½ cups cut-up salami instead of the Italian sausage. Do not cook the salami.

So handy: a pizza cutter

CHEESE BUDS

You can freeze these dainties to bring out and serve with tomato or fruit juice when you don't want something sweet

½ pound sharp Cheddar cheese, shredded
½ pound butter
2 cups sifted flour
¼ teaspoon red pepper
1 egg white, slightly beaten
Pecan halves

1. Start heating the oven to 425° F.

2. Beat the cheese and butter with the electric mixer to mix, or with a spoon.

3. Sift the flour and red pepper onto a sheet of waxed paper. Gradually work the flour into the cheese-butter mixture with a spoon.

4. Roll the dough on a cloth-covered board with a rolling pin until it is ½ inch thick. Cut in 1-inch circles with a cookie cutter. Brush tops of circles with the slightly beaten egg white and place a pecan half in the center of each circle.

5. Lift cutouts onto an ungreased baking sheet with a wide spatula and place the baking sheet on the rack in the center of the oven. Bake 10 to 15 minutes. Makes 96 buds.

What Herb Made Pizza Famous?
Orégano is the herb seasoning that gives pizza some of its good taste. It is a member of the mint family, and *orégano* in Spanish means marjoram, which is another herb. The two herbs have flavors somewhat alike. Orégano is marvelous in Mexican and Italian dishes, especially those made with tomatoes. Try it, or marjoram, sprinkled on red tomato slices. You won't need salad dressing —good for calorie watchers.

TREATS FOR NIBBLERS

Apple snack: *Cut a red apple in quarters and spread one side of each quarter with a soft cheese spread.*

Bologna roll-ups: *Spread thin slices of bologna with cream cheese seasoned with a little grated onion and prepared mustard. Roll up tight and refrigerate.*

LET'S POP SOME CORN

Popcorn is an all-American snack. It was discovered by Europeans with America. The ancient American Indians learned that some kinds of their corn popped when heated. Our popcorn is much better than what they had, however—the flakes are larger and the hulls are thinner and not so coarse.

Popcorn kernels are hard like other dent or flint corns, which also will pop a little. Some hard, flinty-grain sorghums also will pop. And the Indians in the Southwest still pop and eat pigweed seeds.

Sometimes popcorn is too dry to pop well. There's not enough steam formed, when the corn is heated, to force the starch grains to swell and burst. The amount of moisture is right if the kernels start to pop about 1 minute after you add them to the kettle and if they are popped in another minute. When it's too dry, the flakes will have a smoother look and there will be many unpopped kernels.

Fill a quart jar about ¾ full of popcorn and add 1 tablespoon water. Cover the jar and shake a few times. Shake several times during the next 10 minutes, or until all the water is gone. Cover tightly and let stand 3 or 4 days. Then the corn will pop.

When popcorn is too moist, the popped flakes will have a rough surface and many kernels will swell up, but not pop inside out. They are crisp like puffed wheat. Just leave the popcorn sit out, uncovered, on the kitchen counter. It dries out quickly, often in a few hours. If the weather is humid, it may take a day or two.

Fats for Corn Popping
Salad oil is easy to use, but vegetable shortening also is fine. Don't use butter or margarine because they burn at a low temperature and spoil the taste.

You can pop corn without adding fat, but popping it in a little salad oil or shortening is a good idea because the fat carries the heat evenly through the kernels in the kettle. The popping is more even.

BOB'S POPCORN

On cold days few snacks equal bowls of popped corn and red apples, polished, with hot cocoa or glasses of cider

  3 tablespoons salad oil
½ teaspoon salt
½ cup popcorn

1. Put the salad oil and salt in a heavy 4-quart kettle. Set it over medium heat for about 3 minutes.

2. Add the popcorn, cover the kettle and shake over medium heat until the popping stops.

3. Turn the popped corn into a large bowl. Remove all the unpopped kernels. Makes about 2 quarts.

BUTTERED POPPED CORN

Season the hot popped corn with salt to taste and pour on melted butter. Stir to mix. Serve at once.

QUICK CARAMEL POPCORN

Candy and popped corn make this snack special. It's easy to make but do watch the caramels while they're melting

5 cups popped corn
½ pound candy caramels (28)
2 tablespoons hot water

1. Put the popped corn in a medium or 2-quart bowl.

2. Place the candy caramels and the 2 tablespoons hot water in the top of the double boiler. Stir over hot, not boiling, water until the candy melts and makes a smooth sauce. Or melt them in a medium saucepan over low heat, stirring so they won't burn.

3. Pour the syrup over the popped corn. Mix gently with a spoon.

4. Drop spoonfuls of the caramel-coated corn onto waxed paper to make individual servings. Makes about 24 pieces.

When to Pop
Put two or three kernels in the kettle with the heated fat. If they spin around like a top, the temperature is right for popping corn.

Millions of Explosions
The starch grains in popcorn are hard. The moisture in the kernels expands when heated, forming steam that presses on the starch grains and forces them to expand and burst. So when you pop corn, millions of tiny explosions take place in the kernels in the kettle.

CANDIES TO MAKE—AND EAT

How to tell when candy is cooked

You can make many wonderful candies without using a candy thermometer, but with some candies, like Boy Friend Fudge, the only accurate way to know when they're ready to come off the heat is to use a candy thermometer.

Put the thermometer into the *boiling* candy, but do not let the bulb touch the bottom of the saucepan. Watch the silvery mercury climb in the thermometer. Read the temperature with your eyes level with the top of the mercury column. Here are the temperatures for the different stages at which different kinds of candy are done.

Soft ball——234° to 240°
Firm ball——240° to 248°
Hard ball——250° to 266°
Soft crack——270° to 290°
Hard crack——300° to 310°

If you do not have a candy thermometer, you can make the tests in cold water. Here's how to do it:

1. Almost fill a small bowl with cold, not ice, water.
2. Take the saucepan off the heat while you make the test.
3. Drop ½ teaspoon of hot candy into the cold water. If it stays together when it touches the water, instead of scattering or disappearing, it is ready to test.

Soft ball: At this stage you can gather up the candy with your finger tips and make a soft ball that flattens out some, but does not run between the fingers when you lift it out of the water.

Firm ball: The ball you pick up does not flatten when you lift it from the water and it is firm.

Hard ball: The ball you pick up is hard and holds its shape when you lift it from the water, but when you press it, it flattens a little.

Soft crack: The candy dropped into the cold water separates into threads that are hard but not brittle.

Hard crack: The candy dropped in the cold water separates into threads that are hard and brittle.

Sugar Crystals

Good fudge is creamy and velvety. The sugar crystals are so small you can't see or feel them. Under a microscope they look so:

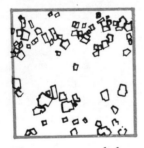

The corn syrup helps keep the sugar crystals small. When fudge is sugary or grainy, the sugar crystals are larger.

BOY FRIEND FUDGE

Smoothest fudge you'll ever make or let melt in your mouth

    3 cups sugar
  ¼ teaspoon salt
  ½ cup sifted unsweetened cocoa or 3 squares
       unsweetened chocolate, cut up
    1 cup milk
    2 tablespoons light corn syrup
    3 tablespoons butter
    1 teaspoon vanilla
    1 cup coarsely broken nuts

1. Lightly grease 8- or 9-inch square pan with butter.

2. Put the sugar, salt, cocoa or cut-up chocolate, milk and corn syrup in a large (3-quart) heavy saucepan. Cook the mixture over medium heat, stirring all the time until the sugar dissolves.

3. Then cook and stir only a few times until the mixture reaches soft-ball stage (234° F. on a candy thermometer).

4. Remove it from the heat, add butter and vanilla, but do not stir while it is hot. Let it cool until the bottom of the pan feels lukewarm to the palm of your hand. (The thermometer in the candy will be 110° F.) You can

hurry the cooling by setting the pan of candy in a larger pan of cold water, or in the sink holding cold water.

5. Beat cooled fudge steadily, but not fast. (If your brother, mother or sister is around, get help in beating the candy and give your arm a rest. It's quite a job.)

6. When it loses its shiny look, thickens some, better test it. If a little fudge dropped from the spoon holds its shape, it's ready. Add the nuts at once.

7. Pour fudge quickly into the buttered pan but don't scrape the sides of the pan in which you cooked it. The scrapings often contain large sugar crystals that make fudge grainy.

8. Cover the fudge and refrigerate it until it's firm. This will take about 2 hours. Then cut the fudge into 1-inch squares with a sharp knife.

For a change
· *Peanut butter fudge:* Use ¼ cup peanut butter instead of 3 tablespoons of butter. Add it after the fudge mixture is lukewarm—before you beat it.

ROCKY ROAD FUDGE

If you've never made candy, try this yummy kind first

4 (4½-ounce) milk chocolate bars
3 cups miniature marshmallows
¾ cup broken walnuts

1. Break the chocolate in pieces and melt them in the top of the double boiler over hot, not boiling, water.

2. While the chocolate pieces melt, grease an 8×8×2-inch pan with butter.

3. Remove the melted chocolate from the heat and beat it with a spoon until smooth. Then stir in the marshmallows and nuts. The candy will look lumpy.

4. Spread the candy in the buttered pan and chill it until it is firm. Cut it into 16 squares.

So handy: a candy thermometer
Put the thermometer into the boiling candy, but do not let the bulb touch the bottom of the saucepan. Read the temperature with your eyes level with the top of the mercury column.

If Your Fudge Fails
Don't cry if your fudge ends up sticky. Just pour the candy back into the saucepan and add ¼ cup milk. Start over again— cook, cool, beat and chill it just as before. It usually will be all right. If it still doesn't harden, use it on vanilla ice cream for a fudge sundae. If your candy gets too hard before you pour it into the pan, work it with your hands until you can pat it into the pan. Cut it into squares at once.

HOW OLD ARE CANDY BARS?

They were first made in the United States, soon after 1900. They were made to sell at baseball games—handy to hold and eat.

DISCOVERED—ICE CREAM CONES

Ice cream cones were invented in St. Louis in 1904 when a stand, selling ice cream to visitors at the World's Fair, ran out of serving dishes. The next-door neighbor, selling waffles to hungry Fair crowds, offered to bake waffles that could be folded to hold ice cream. It worked, and from this beginning ice cream cones developed.

Easy Fudge
Rocky Road Fudge is a snap to fix. When it's in the pan, the chocolate looks like a road and the nuts and marshmallows look like little rocks. Break the nuts coarsely with your fingers. You can use hickory, butternut, pecan, almond or filbert nuts instead of walnuts.

FONDANT PATTIES

These pretty pink and white party candies need no cooking. And if you want to make them a few days before the party, they will keep well in the refrigerator or freezer

½ cup soft butter or margarine
⅓ cup light corn syrup
½ teaspoon salt
 1 (1-pound) package powdered sugar
 2 drops red food color
¼ teaspoon peppermint extract
½ teaspoon vanilla

1. Beat the butter, corn syrup and salt in a large bowl with a wooden spoon to mix well.

2. Gradually add the powdered sugar and beat until it is mixed in.

3. Turn the mixture onto a wooden board and work it with your hands until the mixture is smooth. It's a good idea to knead it like you knead bread.

4. Divide the candy in half. Make a little hole in the top of each half. Drop the red food color and peppermint extract into the hole in one half (the exact amount depends on how pink you want the candy and how much you like the peppermint taste). Add the vanilla to the other half. Work or knead with your hands to mix in the food color and extracts.

5. Roll out (with a rolling pin) the white fondant between sheets of waxed paper until it is ⅛ inch thick. Lift off the top sheet of waxed paper and cut fondant into 1½-inch circles with a cutter. (If you do not have a small cutter, you can use a bottle top or the inside of a doughnut cutter.) Spread candy patties on a baking sheet or in a shallow pan and put them in the refrigerator or freezer. Then roll out and cut the pink patties and store them like

the white ones. If you prefer, you can skip the rolling and cutting and shape the patties with your hands. They will not be as even in shape, as thin or as smooth, but they taste equally good.

CANDIED NUTS

These candy-coated nuts are so good—perfect for nibbling

½ cup brown sugar, packed firmly
¼ cup white sugar
⅓ cup light cream or milk
¼ teaspoon salt
½ teaspoon vanilla
1½ cups walnut or pecan halves

1. Mix the brown sugar, white sugar, cream and salt in a heavy, medium saucepan. (If you have dairy sour cream in the refrigerator, you can use it instead of the light cream or milk.) Cook the mixture over low heat, stirring all the time, until the sugar dissolves. Then cook over medium heat to 236° F. on the candy thermometer or to the soft-ball stage. Remove the syrup from the heat.

2. Add the vanilla and nuts and stir until the mixture starts to coat the nuts. Turn it out at once onto waxed paper or a greased baking sheet. Separate the nuts with 2 forks. Work fast. Cool and serve like candy. Makes 2 cups.

PARTY ICE CREAM CONES

It takes time to fix these party cones but you can get them ready and store in the refrigerator until time to fill

Spread chocolate inside

1 (12-ounce) package semisweet chocolate pieces
12 ice cream cones
Colored candy sprinkles or chopped nuts

1. Put the chocolate pieces in the top of the double boiler, set over hot, not boiling, water. Stir and heat until the chocolate is melted and smooth. Remove the double boiler from the heat but leave the chocolate over the hot water.

2. With a small spoon spread some of the chocolate inside the cones to coat them. Then dip each cone into the

Dip rim in chocolate, too

melted chocolate and turn it around to make a border on the inside and outside of the cone.

3. Sprinkle the multicolored candies or nuts on the outside chocolate border on the cones. Keep them in the refrigerator until ready to fill with ice cream. Makes 12 chocolate-coated cones.

HALLOWEEN CANDIED APPLES

These apples are coated the easy way—with caramels

Chopped walnuts
1 pound vanilla caramels (about 56)
3 tablespoons hot water
⅛ teaspoon salt
6 medium apples
6 wooden skewers

Tilt pan to coat apples

Twirl to spread sauce

Cool on waxed paper

1. Put the chopped walnuts in a shallow pan or in a piepan.

2. Melt the caramels, with the hot water and salt added, in the double boiler over boiling water. Stir them frequently to make a smooth sauce.

3. While the caramels melt, wash and dry the apples and remove the stems and "blossoms." Stick a wooden skewer in the blossom end of each apple.

4. Remove the sauce from the heat. Hold the apples, one at a time, by the skewer and dip them into the melted caramel sauce. Tilt the double-boiler top so you can coat the entire apple with the sauce. If the sauce is a little too thick, stir in a few drops of water.

5. Remove the apple from the sauce and twirl it round and round so the sauce will spread smoothly over the apple.

6. Quickly roll the top half of the apple in the chopped nuts to coat.

7. Place the apple, skewer side up, on a buttered baking sheet or on a baking sheet covered with waxed paper and refrigerate until time to serve. Makes 6 candied apples.

Cooking over coals

FAIR, pleasantly warm weather makes outdoor cooks get on the telephone and invite company for a cookout. Food never tastes better than when you cook it under the skies. And the chef can have as much fun as the guests if he or she plans the meal so that only one or two foods need to cook on the grill. You can fix the vegetables, salad and dessert in the house before the cookout and bring them from the refrigerator at serving time.

Don't try to hurry outdoor cooking—start early enough—give it the time it needs so the food will be up to par. Set out a pitcher of tomato juice and something to nibble on—crackers, a dip and chips, a plate of carrot sticks, celery, radishes and pickles. Then no one will get impatient to eat the hot food before it's ready.

Before you start the cooking, the coals must be ready. Also have asbestos-lined or heavily padded mitts so you won't burn your hands. Here's what to do first.

Get out the charcoal

You can use either of two kinds of charcoal—lumps of different sizes or briquets made of ground charcoal pressed into blocks. Briquets burn longer and make a more even heat that is easier to control.

1. Pile the charcoal in a heap on the center of the firebox of the grill. Use about 2 or 3 pounds.

2. Pour about ½ cup of lighter fluid on the charcoal and let it stand a few minutes before lighting it. Play it smart and safe: *never* use kerosene to start the fire. And *never* add more of the lighter fluid after you light the charcoal.

3. Light the charcoal with safety matches and let it burn until ⅔ of the pieces of charcoal are covered with a gray ash in the daytime—at night it will glow red. This will take at least 20 minutes from the time you light the fire—maybe longer. Spread the coals evenly in the grill with tongs. Put some extra briquets around the edges of the live coals to warm so they will be ready to add if you need more heat.

When to start cooking

Use your hand for a thermometer. Hold it just above where you will place the food. The number of seconds you can hold your hand there in comfort tells you the temperature. Start counting this way at normal

speed: one thousand one, one thousand two, one thousand three and up to one thousand six. If you can count to one thousand five or six, you have slow coals (low heat). If you can count only to one thousand three or four, you have medium coals (medium heat). And if you can count only to one thousand one or two, you have hot coals (high heat). The kind of food you're cooking determines the heat (high, medium or low).

How to change the heat

There are three things to do if the food is cooking too fast or too slow.

1. Change the heat by lowering or raising the distance between the cooking food and the coals. Many grills are made for quick and easy adjustment. The closer the food is to the coals, the faster it cooks.

2. If the heat is too hot, take out some of the coals or push them to one side with tongs. If it is not hot enough, you can add some of the coals that have been warming around the edges.

3. Use a water sprinkler, like a clothes sprinkler, to dampen the fire and cool it down a little if it is too hot. Use this same sprinkler to add water to the flames that flare up when the fat of the meat drops on the hot coals. See that the water touches the lower part of the flare-up (flame).

GRILLED MEATS

Among the best foods to cook over coals are meats and poultry. Many outdoor cooks grill only meat or chicken and serve the other foods cold. There's one thing to remember about meats—use only tender meats such as steaks and chops. Cooking directly over coals is cooking in dry heat and it will not make tough meats tender.

Among the best beef steaks for grilling are tenderloin, sirloin, porterhouse, T-bone, rib and club steaks. Try to use high-quality beef from young animals. These steaks have bright red, lean meat that is marbled with fat—you can see tiny pieces of the suet (fat) throughout the lean meat. The bone looks red and porous.

Hamburgers are great barbecue favorites. Always make the patties at least ¾ inch thick so they will be juicy. Patties less than ¾ inch thick dry out in cooking. Let's start with hamburgers.

GRILLED HAMBURGERS

1. Use 1 pound of ground beef to make 4 patties. Shape the meat lightly. Either grease the grill lightly or brush the meat patties on both sides with salad oil or melted margarine. Use a pastry brush.

2. Cook the hamburgers on the grill 3 or 4 inches from the hot coals (one thousand one or two) for 5 minutes. Turn and cook 3 minutes longer or until they are done the way you like them. Season with salt and serve.

So handy: an electric charcoal lighter

GRILLED STUFFED HAMBURGERS

1. Use 1 pound ground beef for 3 servings. Divide the meat in six equal parts and place on a sheet of waxed paper. Cover with another sheet of waxed paper and press the meat into thin, large patties (about 8 inches).

2. Remove the top sheet of waxed paper and spread half the meat patties with grated cheese, finely chopped onion or drained pickle relish, or all three. Put the other meat patties on top and press the edges with your fingers to seal them. Brush lightly with salad oil or melted butter or grease the grill. Use a pastry brush.

3. Cook 3 to 4 inches from hot coals (one thousand one or two), 5 minutes on one side. Turn the patties and cook them about 3 minutes longer or until the meat is done the way you like it.

GRILLED CHICKEN PIECES

1. Brush a cut-up (2- to 3-pound) broiler-fryer chicken with Refrigerator Barbecue Sauce to cover them so they will be juicy when cooked. You can use bottled Italian salad dressing or a commercial barbecue sauce if you do not want to make your own.

See recipe for Refrigerator Barbecue Sauce, page 232

2. Place the chicken pieces on the grill 6 to 8 inches

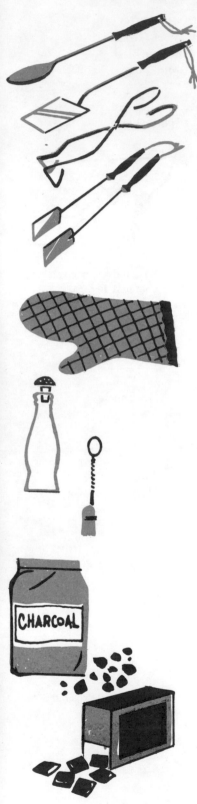

What the outdoor chef needs

from the slow coals (one thousand five or six). Turn them every 5 minutes with tongs. And brush them with the barbecue sauce every time you turn them.

3. Cook the chicken until it is tender, 30 to 50 minutes. The time depends on the size of the pieces. The bony wings cook in less time than the thick breasts or legs.

4. Season the chicken pieces with salt and serve. Makes 4 servings.

GRILLED BEEF STEAK

1. Use steaks 1 to 2 inches thick. One large steak that you can cut in serving pieces after cooking is better than several smaller steaks. You may want to soak the steak half an hour before grilling it in this barbecue sauce: Mix 1 cup salad oil with ⅓ cup vinegar, 1 teaspoon salt and 2 or 3 crushed garlic cloves.

2. Trim off some of the outside fat. Do this and you'll have less fat to drop on the hot coals and cause flare-ups. Slash the fat every 2 inches around the edges so it will stay flat while cooking. Do not cut into the meat but cut through the fat and thin connective tissue next to the meat.

3. Rub some of the fat cut from the steak on the grill to grease it. Cook the steak on the grill 3 to 5 inches from the hot coals (one thousand one or two).

4. Turn the steak a few times as it cooks, but not constantly. Too much turning makes the meat dry.

5. The time of cooking depends on how you like your steak. It takes about 10 to 15 minutes for a steak, 2 inches thick, to cook rare and 15 to 20 minutes for it to cook to the medium-well-done stage. If the steak is 1 inch thick, it needs to grill 5 to 10 minutes for a rare steak, 10 to 15 minutes for a medium-to-well-done steak.

6. Spread the grilled steak with butter and season with salt. And if you like, spread a blue cheese spread thinly on top of the steak or sprinkle on crumbled blue cheese.

GRILLED PORK CHOPS

1. Use center-cut loin chops about 1 or 1½ inches thick. Try to select chops that show little bits of fat in the lean meat—chefs call it marbleized meat.

2. Slash the fat every inch along the outside of the chops so they will not curl while cooking. Do not cut into the meat.

3. Cook the chops about 5 to 8 inches from slow coals (one thousand five or six) until well done, turning once. It will take about 30 to 45 minutes. Season the chops with salt and serve. Brush chops with a barbecue sauce before and during cooking if you like.

Slash fat edges of steak

GRILLED HAM SLICES

1. Use a fully cooked ham slice cut 1 inch thick. It will take less time to cook than fresh pork.

2. Cut the fat around the edges every 2 inches so the ham will lie flat while cooking. Do not cut into the meat.

3. Brush the ham on both sides with a barbecue sauce.

4. Place the ham on a lightly greased grill 4 to 6 inches from slow coals (one thousand five or six).

5. Cook the ham slice 5 minutes or until the underside of it is browned. Turn the ham, brush it with barbecue sauce and cook 5 minutes longer. When serving the ham, you can spoon some of the heated barbecue sauce over it.

See barbecue sauces, pages 231–32

BEEF QUAILS

1. Cut frankfurters in lengthwise halves, but not quite through.

2. Spoon a little ketchup, prepared mustard or Red Sauce into the pockets in the franks. Then add thin strips of cheese. Process Cheddar cheese is a good choice.

See recipe for Red Sauce, page 231

3. Wrap a slice of bacon around each frank, covering as much of it as you can with the bacon and fastening each end of the bacon with a toothpick.

4. Grill over medium coals (one thousand three or four) 6 inches above the coals, turning several times, until the bacon is crisp (about 5 minutes). Serve hot in long buns.

GRILLED FRANKFURTERS

Wrap frankfurters in aluminum foil and cook them over medium coals (one thousand three or four) like Beef Quails. It takes about 10 minutes to brown them. Or lay the frankfurters without wrapping crosswise on the rack about 6 inches above the coals. Turn them with tongs while they cook to brown them evenly. For a snappy flavor, baste them with a barbecue sauce while they are

Frankfurters or Wieners? Frankfurters were first made in Frankfurt, Germany. That's how they got their name. Wieners are a similar sausage, although sometimes they are a little smaller. They were first made in Vienna. You can use sausages labeled frankfurters or wieners in our recipes.

See recipe for Red Sauce,
page 231

cooking. It's a good idea also to dip the frankfurters in the sauce before laying them on the rack. Red Sauce is really good on frankfurters. Or grill frankfurters on pointed green sticks over coals—let everybody cook his own.

GRILLED TURKEY PIECES

See recipe for Grilled
Chicken Pieces, page 227

Buy thighs, drumsticks or turkey rolls or steaks. Cook them like Grilled Chicken Pieces over slow coals (one thousand five or six). They will take a little longer to cook —about 90 minutes. The time depends on the thickness of the pieces.

CAMP-STYLE PORK SUPPER

1. Brown 1-inch pork chops on both sides over slow coals (one thousand five or six). Place each chop in the center of a 20-inch length of heavy-duty aluminum foil.

2. Top with slices of apples, sliced onion and sliced, peeled sweet potatoes or white potatoes and season with salt.

See how to make the
Drugstore Wrap, page 22

3. Wrap the foil tightly around the pork chops and apples and potatoes. Use the Drugstore Wrap. The tight fold is necessary to keep the juices in the packages.

4. Place the packages sealed side down on the grill about 2 inches from the slow coals (one thousand five or six). Cook 1 hour, turning a few times. Fold back the sides of the foil packages and serve.

CAMP-STYLE BEEF SUPPER

1. Place seasoned ground beef patties (⅓ pound to each patty) just off center of a 9×12-inch piece of heavy-duty aluminum foil or two layers of household foil.

2. Cover each patty with enough thinly sliced onions, carrots and peeled potatoes for 1 serving. Season them with salt and pepper. Fold the foil tightly around the food, using the Drugstore Wrap.

See how to make the
Drugstore Wrap, page 22

3. Place the packages, sealed side down, 3 or 4 inches from hot coals (one thousand one or two). Turn the packages in 10 minutes. Cook 15 to 20 minutes longer or until the vegetables are tender. To test, unwrap one package (use hot pads to protect your hands) and try the vegetables with a kitchen fork.

4. Fold back the sides of the foil and serve 1 package to each person. Pass the ketchup.

BARBECUE SAUCES

We give you recipes for three excellent sauces. You cook Red Sauce in the kitchen before the cookout. It's fast-cooking and stores well for reheating just before serving. Peppy Barbecue Sauce really isn't cooked—you just heat it to help mix the ingredients. Refrigerator Barbecue Sauce is mixed in the kitchen and taken to the cookout.

RED SAUCE

Fix this sauce in the kitchen and keep it on hand to use

    1 cup finely chopped onion
    ½ cup salad oil
    1½ cups ketchup
    ½ cup water
    ½ cup lemon juice
    ¼ cup sugar
    ¼ cup Worcestershire sauce
    2½ teaspoons salt
    ½ teaspoon pepper
    3 drops Tabasco sauce

1. Put the onion and salad oil in a medium skillet and cook and stir over medium heat until the onion is soft and yellow (not browned). Add all the other ingredients and stir to mix.

2. Simmer the mixture, but do not boil, over low heat for 15 minutes. Cool and then store in a covered container in the refrigerator or place in freezer container and freeze until ready to use. Heat and serve over hamburgers. Makes about 1 quart.

Soy Sauce Is Oriental
Soy sauce lives up to its name. It is made from soybeans, a bean that was native to the Orient. Soy sauce is widely used in China, Japan and other Asiatic countries to season foods. It has a salty taste. Now the soybean is an important farm crop in many states.

PEPPY BARBECUE SAUCE

Heat this sauce over coals—perfect on ham and good on pork

    ¼ cup prepared mustard
    ¼ cup pineapple juice
    ½ teaspoon prepared horse-radish
    ⅛ teaspoon salt

Hickory Flavor
Some meats are delicious flavored with hickory smoke. If you have an open grill without a smoke cooker, put a handful of dry hickory chips on a sheet of aluminum foil and make a neat package. With a kitchen fork make two holes in the top of the package. Then drop the package on the hot coals. Soon smoke will puff out and season the meat cooking on the grill. The chips do not flare up in flames because the foil keeps the oxygen of the air away from them.

1. Mix all the ingredients in a small saucepan and heat over slow coals, but do not let it come to a boil.

2. Brush sliced ham on both sides with this mixture before grilling and brush it on the ham again when you turn it. Also good brushed on pork chops while on the grill. Makes ½ cup.

REFRIGERATOR BARBECUE SAUCE

Make this sauce, cover and store it in the refrigerator. Brush it on chicken, pork chops or ham cooking over coals

½ cup brown sugar
1 cup chili sauce
½ cup vinegar
½ cup pineapple juice
½ cup salad oil
2 teaspoons prepared mustard
2 teaspoons Worcestershire sauce

1. Mix all the ingredients in a medium bowl and stir until the brown sugar dissolves.

2. Pour the sauce into a covered container and store it in the refrigerator until ready to use. Shake well before using. Makes 1 pint.

VEGETABLES FOR COOKOUTS

Sweet corn, tomatoes, potatoes and baked beans are top choices for outdoor meals. You can use canned baked beans. Just heat the beans in the can on the rack over coals, but open the can first, so steam can escape.

ROASTED SWEET CORN IN FOIL

1. Husk the corn and place each ear on a piece of aluminum foil large enough to wrap around the ear loosely with a 1-inch overlap.

2. Spread the corn with soft butter and sprinkle it lightly with salt. Wrap it loosely in the foil and twist the ends to seal, but do not seal the seam.

3. Cook the corn ears over hot coals. Turn the ears several times so they will roast evenly. Roast them 15 to 20 minutes, or until the corn is tender. Unwrap one ear and test for doneness by sticking kernels with a kitchen fork.

ROASTED SWEET CORN

1. Strip back the husks and remove the silk from ears of sweet corn. Cut off the stem ends and cover the corn with cold water. Let it soak 5 minutes. Remove the corn from the water and put the husks back in shape so they cover the corn completely. Tie the ends shut with strips of the outer husk.

2. About 30 minutes before you want to serve the corn, place the wet ears on the rack over hot coals. Let them cook 15 to 25 minutes. Turn the corn frequently. When it is done, the husks will be dry and brown.

3. If you are not ready to serve the rest of the meal, drop the hot ears into two or three paper bags, one bag inside the other. Close the bags. The corn will stay hot 30 minutes.

Roast sweet corn in foil

GRILLED TOMATOES

1. Cut washed, ripe, firm tomatoes in half, but do not peel. Brush the cut sides with bottled Italian or French salad dressing. Sprinkle each tomato half with a little salt and pepper and ¼ teaspoon sugar or ⅛ (or less) teaspoon dried basil.

2. Place the tomato halves, cut side up, on a sheet of greased heavy-duty aluminum foil.

3. Place them on the grill over hot coals just long enough to heat the tomatoes, about 10 minutes. Do not turn. Remove the tomatoes from the foil with a wide spatula.

FOIL COOKED PEAS

Place 1 (10-ounce) package frozen peas on a large sheet of heavy-duty aluminum foil. Sprinkle them with a little salt and dot them with 2 tablespoons of butter. Bring the foil up over the peas and fold and seal all three edges, using Drugstore Wrap to make a tight package. Cook the

See how to make the Drugstore Wrap, page 22

package of peas 3 or 4 inches from the hot coals 15 to 20 minutes. Makes 3 servings.

POTATOES ROASTED IN FOIL

1. Scrub medium potatoes, dry them on paper towels and brush with salad oil. Wrap each potato in a piece of *heavy-duty* foil to cover completely. Overlap the ends.

2. Bake the potatoes 45 to 60 minutes on the grill over hot coals, turning several times so the cooking will be even. Or bake the potatoes directly on the coals (be sure to turn them several times).

3. Test for doneness—use a heavy pot holder or an abestos-lined mitt, and press the potato. If it feels soft, cut through the foil with a kitchen fork two times to make a cross. Press a little of the hot potato up in the opening. Add a pat of butter and pass the salt shaker with the hot spuds.

FRENCH FRIES

3 (10-ounce) packages frozen French-fried potatoes
3 tablespoons butter

1. Take the potatoes from the packages and place them on 3 sheets of heavy-duty aluminum foil.

2. Dot each mound of potatoes with 1 tablespoon butter. Add salt and pepper to taste.

See how to make the Drugstore Wrap, page 22

3. Wrap the potatoes loosely in 3 foil packages, using the Drugstore Wrap.

4. Cook the packages of potatoes on the rack over hot coals 15 to 20 minutes, turning the packages 3 or 4 times. Makes 6 servings.

For a change
· If you have an old-fashioned wire corn popper, put the partly thawed frozen French fries into it. Shake over coals until the potatoes are hot. Sprinkle them with salt and serve.

"Come and get it!" meals

A MENU is the pattern a cook uses to make good meals. It's like the pattern you use to cut out a dress from a piece of fabric. Instead of patterns for sleeves, collars, blouses and skirts, which the seamstress uses, the parts of the menu pattern are recipes for main dishes, vegetables, salads, relishes, breads and desserts. The cook uses them to plan meals. And that's what a menu is—a meal plan.

1. Be an artist and mix colors. Have at least one color-bright food on the table and on every plate, such as beets, tomatoes, carrots, broccoli and lettuce—along with pale foods, such as mashed potatoes, creamed chicken or tuna and macaroni. Differences in color give foods eye appeal and make everybody want to eat.

2. Select some mild-flavored or bland foods and some with zip or tartness—cranberry sauce or salad with chicken or turkey, chili con carne with banana salad, and corn chowder or potato soup with tomato salad or wilted lettuce.

3. Serve some soft foods with chewy and crisp foods. Variety in texture makes a meal interesting. Here are some examples—you will think of others:

Soft	*Chewy*	*Crisp*
Mashed potatoes	Fried chicken	Celery
Macaroni and cheese	Pot roast	Carrot sticks
Spaghetti with tomato sauce	Steaks	Green salads
Creamed tuna	Pork chops	Crackers
Baked beans	Ham	Toast
Puddings		

4. Select foods of different sizes and shapes, such as baked potatoes and long carrot strips or broccoli spears, French-fried potatoes and small round beets.

5. Have both hot and cold foods in a meal and serve the hot dishes really hot, the cold ones really cold. Even in warm weather, have one

hot dish in a meal, and in winter, one cold food, such as chilled tomato or fruit juice, gelatin salad or ice cream.

6. Plan meals that are nutritious. Get acquainted with the big four food groups—the kinds of food you need to eat every day.

What you need to eat every day

When choosing foods to eat or for a menu, select them from these four groups. Then add other favorites.

1. *Milk and milk products:* 4 or more glasses or servings every day of whole, skim, dry or evaporated milk, buttermilk, cheese, cottage cheese or ice cream.

2. *Vegetables and fruits:* 4 servings every day. One of these should be rich in vitamin C—citrus fruits, cantaloupes, tomatoes, green peppers and broccoli, for example.

Every other day use a food rich in vitamin A.

a. Dark green vegetables—broccoli, spinach, turnip greens, asparagus.

b. Darker yellow vegetables—sweet potatoes, carrots and squash. Or yellow fruits like apricots and peaches.

3. *Meat or other protein-rich foods:* 2 servings every day of lean meat, fish, poultry or eggs. Also use protein foods like cereals, nuts, dried peas, dried beans and others.

4. *Whole-grain and enriched bread and cereals:* 4 servings or more.

Ready to select recipes

1. Look through the pages of this Cookbook, or check the Index to find out what appeals to you.

2. Select the star for your meal—usually the meat or other main dish. Then choose the vegetables, salads or relishes, bread and dessert that are good go-alongs.

3. Select dishes that are not too difficult to make in the time you have for cooking. A hurried cook rarely is happy. That's a shame, for cooking is really interesting.

4. Check to see if you have the necessary ingredients or have time to get them.

5. If you want to make one dish that is rather difficult, have the others easy and quick.

6. Select dishes that do not all need last-minute attention—meat loaves and casseroles, molded salads, chilled puddings. Then you will avoid that nervous rush trying to mash potatoes, pan-fry meat, make gravy and bake biscuits, all just before mealtime.

7. Avoid having the same food more than once in a meal. If you

start off with tomato juice, you wouldn't put tomatoes in the salad or serve spaghetti with tomato sauce for the main dish.

8. End the meal with a sweet dessert—a surprise to make everybody happy.

Ready to cook

1. Decide what you are going to start cooking first. Put it on the heat.

2. While the food cooks, get the salad or relish ready and set the table. Then when it's almost time to serve the meal, pour the water or milk in the glasses, and put the salad or relishes, bread and butter on the table.

3. Now finish up the last-minute cooking.

4. Then tell everybody it's time to eat, and smile to show you're proud of the meal.

Setting the table

Table cover: Be sure the cloth is clean. Spread it smoothly and evenly on the table. Or use place mats of cloth or the easy-to-wipe-off kind.

Centerpiece: It can be flowers from the garden or woods, washed and polished apples or other fresh fruit, a bouquet of leaves, a growing plant—whatever you have that gives the table an inviting look.

Place setting: If possible, allow 18 to 20 inches for each place. Put the dinner plate in the center of the place setting about 1 inch from the edge of the table or place mat. Arrange the knives, spoons and forks in the order in which they will be used, from the outside toward the plate. Place the knives and spoons on the right side, the forks on the left side of the plate and about 1 inch from the plate and 1 inch from the edge of the table or place mat. Turn the cutting edge of the knives toward the plate.

Napkins: Fold the napkins in oblongs and place them on the plates unless you are having soup. Then place the napkins to the left of the forks, the bottom edge in line with the bottom of the forks.

Food: Place the meat or other main dish directly in front of the host who will serve it. Be sure the table is protected from the heat. Place the carving knife to the right of the platter and the fork to the left. (If a casserole dish is being served, place the serving spoon to the right of the casserole.) Place the vegetables around the platter and the serving spoons near them.

Place the salads to the left of the forks and the bread and butter plates, if used, above the tip of the forks, with the butter spreader across the top third of the plate. Place the water (or milk) glasses above the tip of the knives and if tomato or fruit juice is served with the main course, place the glasses for it at the right of the water glasses.

Clearing the table: Remove all the food first. Then remove the dinner plates with the right hand and salad plates with the left hand from each place. If bread and butter plates have been used, remove two of them at a time. Remove salt and pepper shakers and all flat silver that will not be used with the dessert. Refill water glasses.

Desserts: Prepare the desserts in the kitchen and carry them to the table. Place each serving in the center of each place about 1 inch from the edge of the table or place mat.

MEALS YOU CAN GET

You'll enjoy getting a whole meal more if you have first made each of the dishes, one at a time, as part of regular family meals. Then you'll know better what to do and what to expect of each dish when you fix all of them for a meal. You'll also have a good idea how long each dish takes—the time varies with the cook. Our timing will serve only as a guide—you may work faster or slower. And certainly, all cooks fix a meal quicker and easier the second time.

Look up in this Cookbook the recipes that you want to use. Make a list of the ingredients you'll need, and then check to see if you have everything. You may have to delay the cooking until after the next grocery shopping, but you'll have the list ready for foods to buy.

You'll want to plan your own menus with recipes in this Cookbook. Here are a few suggested meals and simple refreshments when company comes. *Recipes for all the dishes marked with an * are in this Cookbook.*

SPRING DINNER

Tuna Rarebit on Crackers*
Buttered Peas or Asparagus
Sun-Glow Carrot Salad*
Hurry-up Cherry Cobbler*

1. Allow 1½ hours to get this dinner the first time. Start the oven heating to 400° F.
2. Fix the cobbler and put it in the oven to bake.
3. Make the salad in a bowl and put in refrigerator.
4. Fix the rarebit and the peas or asparagus.

5. Set the table and pour the water or milk. Arrange the salad on plates and take it to the table.

6. Carry the rarebit and peas or asparagus to the table. Dinner is ready.

7. Take the cobbler from the oven and set it on a wire rack to cool, if you have not done this earlier.

8. Clear the table, refill the glasses with water or milk and serve the cobbler.

SUMMER DINNER

Cold Cuts   Sliced Cheese
Corn on the Cob*
Sliced Tomatoes
Assorted Breads
Summer Fruit Salad*
Snowy Cottage Cheese*

1. Allow 1 hour to get this meal.
2. Fix the cottage cheese and put it in the refrigerator.
3. Set the table.
4. Arrange the meats and cheese on a platter.
5. Husk and cook the corn.
6. Make the salad. It answers for salad and dessert.
7. Put the cold cuts and cheese, butter and breads, salads and cottage cheese on the table. Pour the water or milk.
8. Take the corn to the table. Dinner is ready.

AUTUMN DINNER

Oven-Fried Chicken*
Green Beans with Bacon*
Hot Rolls
Orange Sherbet Salad*
Chocolate-Nut Drops*

1. Allow 1½ hours to get this dinner, but make the salad a day or several hours ahead so it will have time to chill. Also bake the cookies ahead, or make No-Bake Chocolate Cookies.

2. Start heating the oven to 375° F

3. Fix the chicken and put it in the oven.

4. Set the table.

5. Put the rolls in a paper bag and sprinkle with a little water. Put it in the oven about 10 minutes before the chicken is done.

6. Fix the beans (frozen or canned).

7. Unmold the salad and place it on the table or serve it on individual salad plates. Put the butter or margarine on the table. Pour the water or milk.

8. Take the chicken, green beans and hot rolls to the table. Dinner is ready.

9. Clear the table and refill water or milk glasses. Serve the cookies and if you like, canned pears or peaches.

WINTER DINNER

Baked Pork Chops*
Sweet Potatoes
Tossed Green Salad*
Maple Sundae

1. If you are a fast worker, you can get this dinner in 1 hour. You'd better allow 1½ hours the first time you get it.

2. Start the oven heating to 350° F.

3. Wash and drain the lettuce or other salad greens.

4. Fix the pork chops and put them in the oven to bake.

5. Set the table.

6. Put 1 cup light brown sugar, ½ cup orange juice and ¼ cup water in a skillet and boil 5 minutes. Add 6 to 8 cooked or canned sweet potatoes and simmer, turning often, until potatoes are shiny. This will take about 20 minutes.

7. Pour the water or milk. Toss the salad and take it to the table.

8. Take the pork chops and sweet potatoes to the table. Dinner is ready.

9. Clear the table and refill water or milk glasses. Scoop the ice cream into serving dishes and pour over each serving a little maple or maple-blended syrup. Sprinkle on chopped nuts if you like. If you have cookies, serve a plate of them with the dessert.

SPRING SUPPER

*Italian Spaghetti**
*Tossed Green Salad**
Crusty Rolls
Canned Applesauce à la mode
Cookies

1. Bake the cookies several hours or the day before you start to fix supper. Or make one of the No-Bake Cookies. Then allow 1 hour to get this meal. You will not be rushed.

2. Make the spaghetti sauce.

3. Wash the salad greens, shake the water off the leaves and put them in a salad basket or on paper towels to drain. If you are making the salad dressing, this is the time to get it ready.

4. Put the spaghetti on to cook.

5. Set the table and pour the water or milk.

6. Put a platter in the oven to warm for 3 minutes.

7. Drain the spaghetti, put it on the warm platter, pour on the hot sauce and take it to the table. Reheat the sauce if necessary. It should be bubbling hot.

8. Toss the salad greens and salad dressing together and take to the table.

9. Serve the rolls. Supper is ready.

10. Take the cookies to the table after you've cleared away the dishes and leftover food. Refill glasses with water or milk. Top the applesauce, after it's in the serving dishes, with scoops of vanilla or butter-pecan ice cream.

SUMMER SUPPER

*Barbecued Hamburgers**
*Potato Salad**
Cheese Toasted Buns
Sliced Tomatoes
Melon

1. Allow about 1 hour to get this supper, but make the potato salad and barbecue sauce ahead, cool and refrigerate.

2. About an hour before you plan to serve supper, brown the hamburger patties, pour the barbecue sauce over them and let them simmer about 45 minutes.

3. While the hamburgers cook, set the table, slice the tomatoes and put them on the serving plate. Refrigerate them. Then fix the buns. Spread split bun halves with butter, sprinkle on grated or shredded cheese and spread them on a baking sheet.

4. Fill the glasses with water or milk and put the potato salad and tomatoes on the table.

5. Run the buns under the broiler just long enough to melt the cheese a little. This will take less than 5 minutes, but watch them and don't let them burn.

6. Take the buns and the hamburgers to the table.

7. Supper is ready.

8. Clear the table and refill glasses with water or milk. Serve the melon.

AUTUMN SUPPER

*Sausage-Corn Bake**
Pickles
*Sliced Tomato Salad**
Toasted Raisin Bread
ABC Chocolate Pudding

1. Allow 1½ hours to get this supper the first time. Start heating the oven to 350° F.

2. Fix the sausage and corn and put it in the oven to bake. It takes about an hour to make and bake this casserole.

3. Peel the tomatoes and put them in the refrigerator.

4. Make the dessert with regular or instant pudding mix, following directions on the package. Pour into custard cups or other serving dishes. Make everyone's dessert his own by printing his name on the top with letters from ready-to-eat alphabet cereal.

5. Make the salad.

6. Set the table, pour the water or milk and put the salad, pickles, bread and electric toaster on the table.

7. Take the Sausage-Corn Bake to the table.

8. Supper is ready.

9. Toast the bread at the table so it will be hot. To keep

the frosting on the bread and out of the toaster, insert a toothpick through the slice about ½ inch from the top to hold the frosted part out of the toaster.

10. Clear the table, refill glasses with water or milk and serve the dessert.

WINTER SUPPER

*Waffles** *Honey Butter**
*Pan-Broiled Ham**
*Lightning Salad**
Hot Chocolate

1. Allow 45 minutes to an hour to get this meal. Make the salad and Honey Butter. You can serve table syrup and butter or margarine with your waffles instead of Honey Butter.

2. Set the table. Set the waffle iron by your place.

3. Mix the waffle batter.

4. Start the ham cooking.

5. Make the hot chocolate with an instant mix and pour it into a pitcher for serving at the table.

6. Arrange the salads on plates and take them to the table.

7. Start the waffle iron heating. When it signals the right temperature, bake the first waffle.

8. While the waffle bakes, take the ham, Honey Butter and hot chocolate to the table.

9. Split the first waffle in half or quarter it. Supper is ready. Continue baking waffles until everyone has his fill.

GOOD BREAKFASTS

Breakfast is the day's most important meal. When you skip breakfast or eat too little, you cannot think or work as fast or as well as you otherwise would. Just think how long it is between the evening meal until noon the next day. Breakfast takes you through the morning in good shape by giving the body the energy it needs. You get less tired.

People who eat breakfast are not so hungry at noon and often are not so hungry at dinnertime. They usually eat less lunch and rarely gain as much weight as those who eat two meals a day. If you are a weight watcher, eat less toast and fewer pancakes, but drink skim milk. Also cut down on the desserts at lunch and dinner or supper. A neat definition of breakfast: good health insurance.

COLD WEATHER BREAKFAST

Grapefruit Halves
or
Tomato Juice
Baked Eggs* *Sausage Patties*
Buttered Toast
Honey *Apple Butter*
Milk *Coffee*

1. Allow 30 minutes to get this breakfast. Start heating the oven to 325° F.

2. Shape the bulk pork sausage in patties ½ inch thick. Put them in a skillet and cook them over low heat about 15 minutes or until they are brown on the outside and gray with no trace of pink inside. Turn them occasionally while they cook. Spoon off the fat that collects.

3. Get the eggs ready and put them in the oven.

4. Make the coffee and pour the milk.

5. Cut the grapefruit in half or pour the tomato juice.

6. Set the table and put on the grapefruit or tomato juice, bread for toasting, butter, honey and apple butter.

7. Serve the eggs in the custard cups, the sausage on a warm platter. Make the toast and pour the coffee at the table.

WARM WEATHER BREAKFAST

Orange Juice
Ready-to-Serve Cereal *Milk*
Cheese Scrambled Eggs*
Hot Rolls *Strawberry Jam*
Milk *Coffee*

1. Allow 30 minutes to get this breakfast, but you may get it in less time. Start heating the oven to 400° F.

2. Get the eggs ready to cook, but leave them in the mixing bowl.

3. Set the table.

4. Make the coffee.

5. Pour the orange juice and place it, the cereal, the pitcher of milk and strawberry jam on the table. Fill the glasses with milk.

6. Put the rolls in a paper bag and sprinkle them with water. (Or wrap them in foil.) Close the bag and put it in the heated oven. It will take 10 minutes for the rolls to heat.

7. Scramble the eggs and bring them to the table on a warm platter or in a warm bowl. Serve the heated rolls and pour the coffee.

REFRESHMENTS FOR COMPANY

One reason many people like to cook is that they give their friends and families pleasure. Food is something you can fix and share. While good cooks appreciate compliments on what they make, they also get real enjoyment from the fun people have eating what they make.

Most girls and boys start to cook by making refreshments for friends who come to visit them. And often they let their guests help get the food ready—it's part of the entertainment and usually is more fun than playing games. Home kitchens are friendly places that make everybody who pitches in to help fix food, or who watches with interest what's cooking, feel at ease.

Keep the food simple—a two-piece menu is fine. It's usually something to eat and something to drink. But, every bite and sip must *taste* really good. And if the refreshments *look* good, too, they're bound to please.

When you decide on what to make, read the recipes you're going to use and check the ingredients you'll need—you want to be sure you have them. Then consider if the food is the kind your friends can help fix or if you should get it ready before company comes. You'll find it easier to bake a cake and have it cool and ready to frost before guests arrive. And you'll want to have the chili con carne bubbling hot in the kettle—your company can help dish it into bowls or arrange crackers on a plate. But if you're having popcorn and candy, let your friends help make them. You'll turn what might be work into play.

Keep a few extra things on hand to make food fun—colorful drinking straws for sipping cold drinks and fancy paper napkins. Paper plates can be decorative and they don't have to be washed after the guests go home. Paper doilies of different sizes to line plates also make food attractive.

We give you examples of refreshments you will enjoy having your friends help you fix and also for food to get ready before your guests arrive. You'll want to make out your own menus, using recipes in this Cookbook. Remember that you'll find a recipe for every dish marked with an *. The quickest way to locate recipes is to look in the Index. Let's start with menus your friends can help you fix.

South Sea Snowstorm*
Skillet Grilled Cheese Sandwiches*

Brownies à la mode*
Colas

Candy Bar Cookies*
Hot Cocoa

Hero Sandwiches*
Chocolate Milk

Hamburger Goo*
Maple Milk Shake*

Here are refreshments to make before company arrives.

Quick Cocoa Cupcakes*
Milk

Hot Tomato Soup
Egg Salad Sandwiches*
Candied Nuts*

Cottage Cheese Dip*
Carrot and Celery Sticks
No-Bake Chocolate Cookies*

Hootenanny Raspberry Frappé*
Fudge Brownies*

Index

LET'S START TO COOK is a cookbook for beginners—all beginners. Inquisitive teen-agers, intrigued both by the science of cooking and the fun of playing hostess. Girls and boys, measuring and stirring simple recipes under Mother's guidance. Novice cooks who need to teach them-selves everything at once about the kitchen arts.

There are many basic cookbooks, but this one is unique. Here you'll find direc-tions so complete there's nothing to guess at—each step to perfect results is fully ex-plained. And in the margin are extra notes —"science why's" that give reasons for doing what directions say—and more than 250 how-to drawings that illustrate recipe steps and techniques such as rolling pie crust, separating eggs, turning an omelet, even kneading bread.

The beginner who starts with this book will never give it up. The recipes will be her stand-bys even when she's a home-maker, for the foods are family favorites, recipes to relish as well as learn by. There's good variety—among the book's 16 sec-tions are recipes for cookies, cakes, pies,

(continued on back flap)

(continued from front flap)

meats and main dishes; salads, sand-wiches, snacks, cooking over coals and vegetables. The meal planning section not only suggests menus, it tells the beginning cook, step by step, what to do and when to do it so that everything's ready at once.

The curious beginner will learn why poorly mixed biscuits have spots, what makes pastry tender, how yeast works, why custards weep. And she'll find very useful the special sections on measuring, on utensils, tools and cooking techniques and on the cook's vocabulary.

All recipes and directions are completely up-to-date, specifying modern food prod-ucts and cooking appliances. Experienced cooks as well as beginners will find much that's new to them in LET'S START TO COOK.

ABOUT THE AUTHOR—"Most good cooks are made at home, when they're growing up," says **Nell B. Nichols,** author of LET'S START TO COOK, the fifth cook-book she's edited for *Farm Journal* maga-zine. Her own first lessons—patting bis-cuit dough, flouring chicken pieces—were as her mother's helper in a Kansas ranch kitchen. Her life-long love of cooking and writing about it became doubly satisfying when her daughter also became a food professional. Now Mrs. Nichols helps four eager grandchildren discover how much fun it is to cook.

ABOUT THE ARTIST—**Kay Lovelace Smith** studied at the Art Institute of Chi-cago and has traveled extensively in this country and abroad, painting *and* col-lecting recipes. An amateur chef, she has designed and illustrated many cookbooks. Mrs. Smith lives in Chicago with her hus-band and young daughter.

PLANNING MEALS

The Six Rules for Goodness

1. Be an artist and mix colors. Have at least one color-bright food like beets, tomatoes, carrots, broccoli and lettuce along with pale foods like mashed potatoes and creamed chicken. Differences in color give eye appeal.

2. Select some mild-flavored or bland foods and some with zip or tartness, like cranberry sauce or salad with chicken.

3. Serve some soft foods with chewy and crisp foods. Variety in texture makes a meal interesting.

4. Select foods of different sizes and shapes, like baked potatoes with carrot strips or broccoli spears with small round beets.

5. Have both hot and cold foods in a meal and serve the hot dishes really hot, the cold ones really cold.

6. Plan meals that are nutritious. Look at the chart on the facing page for the kinds of foods you need to eat every day.